OVER

THE

TOP

OVER
THE
TOP

The First Lone Yachtsman to Sail
Vertically Around the World

ADRIAN FLANAGAN

**ADLARD
COLES**

LONDON · OXFORD · NEW YORK · NEW DELHI · SYDNEY

ADLARD COLES
Bloomsbury Publishing Plc
50 Bedford Square, London, WC1B 3DP, UK

BLOOMSBURY, ADLARD COLES and the Adlard Coles logo are
trademarks of Bloomsbury Publishing Plc

Original edition published by Orion Publishing 2008
First Bloomsbury edition with new content 2018

A catalogue record for this book is available from the British Library

Library of Congress Cataloguing-in-Publication data has been applied for

ISBN: PB: 978-1-4729-4431-3; ePub: 978-1-4729-4430-6;
ePDF: 978-1-4729-4429-0

2 4 6 8 10 9 7 5 3 1

Typeset in 9.75 pt Haarlemmer MT by
Deanta Global Publishing Services, Chennai, India
Printed and bound in Great Britain by CPI Group (UK) Ltd, Croydon CR0 4YY

To find out more about our authors and books visit www.bloomsbury.com.
and sign up for our newsletters

For Louise, Benjamin and Gabriel
and
in memory of Christian, Tracey and Alexandre Foures

'You will pass through storms and heavy rains and at times you may suffer defeat. The essence of a creative life, however, is not to give up in the face of defeat, but to follow the rainbow that exists within your heart.'

– Daisaku Ikeda

CONTENTS

PART II: OVER THE TOP

PART III: HOMEWARD BOUND

APPENDICES

ROUTE OF THE ALPHA GLOBAL EXPEDITION

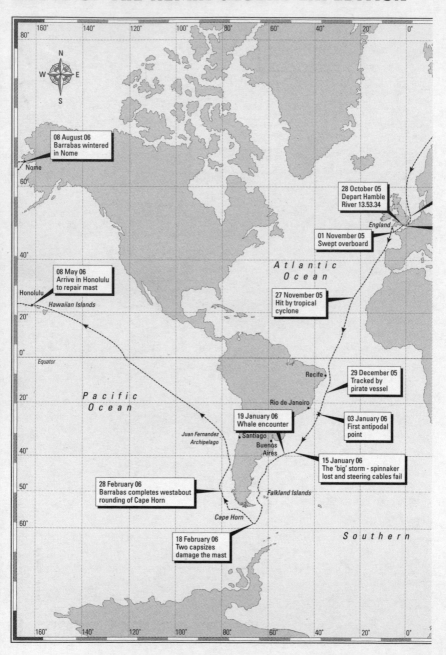

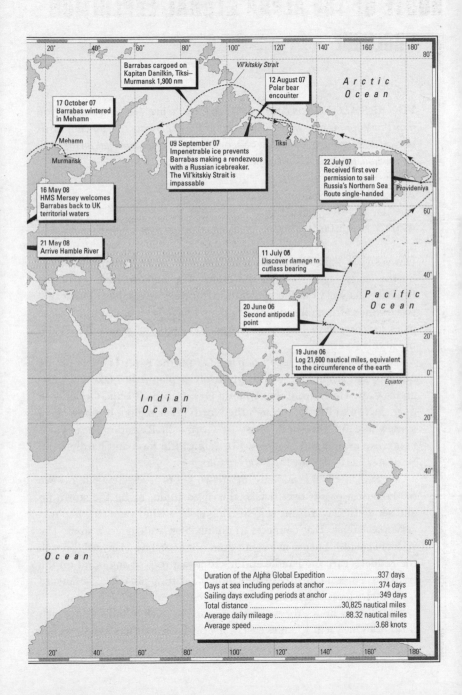

ROUTE OF THE ALPHA GLOBAL EXPEDITION

20° 40° 60° 80° 100° 120° 140° 160° 180° 80°

Vil'kitskiy Strait

Barrabas cargoed on
Kapitan Danilkin, Tiksi–
Murmansk 1,900 nm

12 August 07
Polar bear
encounter

*Arctic
Ocean*

17 October 07
Barrabas wintered
in Mehamn

Mehamn

Murmansk

09 September 07
Impenetrable ice prevents
Barrabas making a rendezvous
with a Russian icebreaker.
The Vil'kitskiy Strait is
impassable

Tiksi

22 July 07
Received first ever
permission to sail
Russia's Northern Sea
Route single-handed

Provideniya

16 May 08
HMS Mersey welcomes
Barrabas back to UK
territorial waters

60°

21 May 08
Arrive Hamble River

11 July 06
Discover damage to
cutlass bearing

40°

*Pacific
Ocean*

20 June 06
Second antipodal
point

*Indian
Ocean*

19 June 06
Log 21,600 nautical miles, equivalent
to the circumference of the earth

20°

0°

Equator

20°

40°

60°

Ocean

20° 40° 60° 80° 100° 120° 140° 160° 180°

Duration of the Alpha Global Expedition ....937 days
Days at sea including periods at anchor ....374 days
Sailing days excluding periods at anchor ....349 days
Total distance ....30,825 nautical miles
Average daily mileage ....88.32 nautical miles
Average speed ....3.68 knots

PROLOGUE

YOU ARE ALONE. You have only seconds left to live. Not long enough, you may think, for the massive database of your life experience to reassemble itself into an order of merit. Time slows. Seconds stretch, hammered flat on the anvil of oblivion, reaching towards infinity.

Alpha Global Expedition, Day 5
Tuesday 1st November 2005
49.09.5° North, 06.50.3° West – Western Approaches, English Channel

Dawn's grey light seeping in from the east makes little impression. Storms have raged through the night. The narrow confines of the English Channel heap the seas into marauding waves. Near hurricane-force winds screech through the rigging. I have been bashing into these gales for three days. Bad weather was predicted, but not to this extent, not at this severity.

It's been five days since I departed from the River Hamble on my quest to sail around the world. My route is planned to take me west-about Cape Horn, from the Atlantic Ocean to the Pacific Ocean then over the top of Russia, through the North Polar region. For now, I am somewhere off the south coast of Cornwall. Relentless headwinds neutralise meaningful progress. I've eaten little food and hardly slept. Seawater has fouled my freshwater tanks.

At 8am, the wind suddenly dies to 16 knots, a respite while the eye of the storm passes over. I take the opportunity to rig the storm jib and set up the Hydrovane self-steering gear: a wind vane attached to a servomechanism that connects to an auxiliary rudder via a shaft. The rudder is made of dense nylon but does not float. I tie a lanyard through the rudder's carrying handle and make it fast to a strong point on the transom, a precaution in case the rudder's securing pin fails. The lanyard is a 2-metre loop. I let it fall into the water and trail behind the boat.

Within five hours, the weather has gone berserk. Wind speeds reach 50 knots. One yacht 15 miles east of my position activates its emergency beacon and an air-sea rescue helicopter flies out to pick up the crew. I listen to the frantic radio exchanges. It is the first of three 'mayday' calls I hear that morning.

The boat takes a wave bow on, riding high, her nose pointing skywards. She comes off the wave with a tremendous crash. A loud cracking sound ricochets from below and I think my yacht has split herself open. I duck down the companionway steps. I use both hands to prevent myself from pitching forward or being flung backward or hurled sideways. In the dim light below decks, I feel immediate relief. There is no water rushing in, drowning my boat. I go to the fore cabin. Eleven fuel cans weighing a combined 220kg have smashed through the storage cage. The stench of spilt diesel percolates the cabin. I rush back to the cockpit, gybe the boat, backing the sails against the rigging and then lash the wheel hard over in the opposite direction so that the sails and rudder are working against each other. This manoeuvre – heaving-to – stops the boat in the pounding seas.

I set about sorting out the mess. My first priority is to stow the fuel. I lash two cans alongside the ones already in the aft deck fuel cages, one either side. I make space for three more in the lazarette. There is space for the remaining six cans in the cockpit, forward of the wheel, which makes getting to and from the cabin awkward in the difficult conditions.

The necessity of maintaining a radar watch in the busy shipping lanes has confined me below decks for most of the time since dawn. I am safer below, and dry. In the early afternoon, I come on deck. My mission is simple and quick: to alter course 15°, which means adjusting the self-steering vane. The control line is a continuous loop running from a cog on the Hydrovane to a small block clipped to the guardrail on the starboard side level with the cockpit. I plan to be on deck for 10 seconds, no more, sufficient to eyeball my horizons for shipping and tug on the self-steering control line. I am dressed in two T-shirts and a pair of longjohns as base layers, an all-in-one fleece-lined mid-layer, heavy-duty oilskins and sea boots. I am not wearing a lifejacket or a safety line.

For the moment, the large cuddy – a tubular steel framework clad in sheets of tough transparent polycarbonate – protects me from the elements. I clamber over the six fuel cans in the cockpit, scanning the forward horizon. A turbulent, cold, grey sea stretches away, lost in mist. I look sternwards. All clear. Now the adjustment. I step onto the starboard side deck. With my left hand, I reach towards the control line, bending at the waist, facing backwards. In that instant, a wave hits the boat on the port side, heeling her over at an acute angle. The starboard toe rail dips below the surface. Water rushes over my left boot.

I never see the wave that sweeps over the bow. Perhaps the seas have lifted the yacht and then she digs her bows into the water. Maybe a second wave has hit the boat on the starboard side in the confused cross chop. I will never know exactly what happened. There is no noise of water charging up behind me, or perhaps the wind has torn away the warning sound. My fingers never make it to the control line.

The impact when it comes is immensely powerful; a vice-like grip against the back of my left leg and the exposed part of my upper body leaning out past the protection of the cuddy. The water knocks me over and picks me up, my body flat, parallel to the deck and four feet above it then sweeps me over the guardrail. My arms flail, trying to propel me back on board, trying to grab a handhold. Through the foaming maelstrom of water, I see parts of the deck, the main block and the cockpit winches flit away to the right. Then I see the bare steel of the hull and through the green lens of sea the blue nameplate of the boat, white lettering spelling out B A R R A B A S. The water releases its hold and I plunge into the sea, completely submerged. When I break the surface, the nameplate is directly above my face. I am completely separated from the boat.

This is what goes through my mind:

- Death is a certainty. Okay, this is it, aged 45.
- I see my French friends, Christian and Tracey Foures and their 10-year-old son, Alexandre, all killed the previous year in the 2004 Boxing Day Tsunami.
- The angelic faces of my two boys, Benjamin and Gabriel, smile at me.
- The startling green eyes of Louise, my ex-wife and expedition manager, twinkle with love or sympathy – I'm not sure which, perhaps both.
- Drowning is too unbearable to contemplate. I will strip down to my base layer and let hypothermia claim my consciousness before the sea takes me down.

Despite the frigid water, I feel warm and irrationally calm. I surmise afterwards that in this moment of extreme danger, adrenalin flooding my system has shut down core functions and diverted blood to the muscles of my arms and legs, bringing warmth. My vision sharpens to the acuity of an eagle. Maybe the calm that I feel is part of this primeval fight/flight response or perhaps it is the simple realisation that the game of life is up. Maybe I even feel some measure of relief. I cannot be certain.

These thoughts and sensations come unbidden, fused like wax crayons suddenly exposed to intense heat, their colours mingling in a kaleidoscope of finality.

PART I

BEYOND THE HORIZON

CHAPTER 1

THE SEED

LATE ON AN APRIL AFTERNOON IN 1976, I peered through the small oval of Plexiglas as the great 747 swooped over tower blocks bristling with bamboo poles strung with laundry clustered near Hong Kong's Kai Tak International Airport. Traffic streamed through the shadowed canyons between the high-rises. Ships cluttered the harbour: British frigates, container carriers huddling around Kowloon's main terminal, tankers moving regally to and from the refinery. Past the harbour, Hong Kong Island rose from the green velvet of the South China Sea, its side peppered with the white confetti of buildings.

As soon as the aircraft came to a stop, I was out of my seat and brushing past the passengers sitting next to me. I dropped the overhead locker, grabbed my hand luggage and strode to the rear door. Through the small window, I could see the stairway truck approach the aircraft. A flight attendant threw some levers. After 24 hours in the air from London with stops in Rome, Bahrain, Bombay, Rangoon and Bangkok, the door swung open. The smell of the Orient – salt and seaweed, avgas and diesel fumes, jasmine, camphor wood and charcoal all mixed, cooked and carried on the humid air – rushed at me.

Inside the terminal building hundreds of jostling Chinese shouted and waved at travel-weary friends. Strip-lighting bathed the crowds in a bright, bluish hue. I spotted my parents among a group of other *gweilos* at the far end of the arrivals area. My father's career – working for Exxon Oil – had already taken the family to postings in East Africa, Japan and Thailand and now here to Hong Kong. The contrast to northern England's pastoral, rolling farmlands, where I went to boarding school, was stark. This was another world and my brief forays into it during school holidays were always adventures.

The squadron of butterflies released in the pit of my belly at that first whiff of promise continued to flutter and tingle as we drove from the airport along the bustling streets. Hordes thronged the sidewalks. Traffic ebbed and flowed in a night awash with multicoloured neon. We drove through the cross-harbour tunnel to Hong Kong Island and climbed the steep, twisting roads towards the residential belt of apartment buildings that ranged along the mid-levels.

We lived in a new block called Cliffview Mansions, on the 18th floor. From the glass-wrapped balcony, the breathtaking view of Hong Kong's downtown district and the harbour rolled away to Lion Rock on the mainland, rising like a great monolithic guardian. Past Lion Rock, the border with communist China lay hidden in the folds of the dark hills.

I opened a sliding window and leaned out against the balustrade. Despite the jetlag and my tiredness, I had, even then, a sense that something was about to change.

Some days later, alone in the apartment and bored with revision for my upcoming 'O' level examinations, I padded into my father's study. Ordered rows of books covered one wall. I scanned the titles and authors' names. At school that term, I had devoured the fiction of A. J. Cronin: *The Keys to the Kingdom*, *The Spanish Gardener*, *The Judas Tree* and *The Citadel*. I had recently read James Clavell's novels: *Shōgun*, *Tai Pan* and *King Rat*. Leon Uris, whose book *Mila 18* I remember still, was a favourite author of mine. I was looking for a novel, perhaps another Leon Uris.

The previous weekend, we had taken the company boat to Lantau Island. A 40-foot cruiser and ostensibly a cross-harbour working boat, the *Esso Victoria* and her three crew were available to Exxon's executives for recreational use. I loved swimming in protected bays, exploring coves and hidden beaches, making landfall in the dinghy and walking among the rocks or along grassy tracks to remote temples. It was with my recent experience of the sea that my eye lingered on the spine of a book depicting a stormy seascape. The author's name, Francis Chichester, was vaguely familiar and the book's title, *Gipsy Moth Circles the World,* promised adventure and escape. I took the book down, glancing at the cover picture: a grey and brooding sky, an avalanche of high waves and isolated among them a sailing boat carrying a small triangle of canvas at its bow. A solitary figure was just visible. The scene, this tiny figure dwarfed in the immensity of the ocean, captivated me. I studied that picture for a long time and then opened the book at a photographic section.

The first photograph showed a ketch-rigged yacht heeled over under full sail. A peculiar sensation fizzed through my body. I felt as if I were there, on the boat, sensing her movement though the water, the wind brushing my skin, the sun's warmth on my back, the tang of salt air in my throat.

The pictures of Chichester himself held the most fascination for me – washing on deck, making a sail adjustment, taking a sun sight, stitching a sail, bandaging his injured right elbow. These showed a man occupying his own, unique world, away from the push and pull of other people and circumstance, the ultimate expression of his own force of will.

I turned the pages to the beginning of the first chapter, entitled 'The Dream', and started to read. Quite soon the seed of my own dream split from its pod and took root in the fertile soil of my adolescent imagination.

Each day at 5.15pm, I would walk from the apartment along Conduit Road and then take a narrow pathway cut into the hillside towards the Ladies' Recreation Club, a sports club set high above the energetic heart of Hong Kong, with floodlit tennis courts, indoor and outdoor pools, squash courts, bars and restaurants. My father usually arrived at the club from his office at around 5.30pm and together we would go to the indoor pool and spend an hour lapping up and down. But on this particular day, I was oblivious to time, interrupting my reading only to switch on the desk lamp as afternoon wore through to evening.

We had dinner, lamb chops, at eight o'clock.

'Where were you?' my father said when I sat down at the table.

'Reading.'

He must have assumed I meant studying.

'I borrowed one of your books,' I said, wanting to share my discovery. Bowls of peas and mash passed back and forth. '*Gipsy Moth Circles the World*, Francis Chichester's book.' The conversation moved on to golf and my father's workday. How could my parents not be interested in this? My father must have read the book, why else was it in his study? I wasn't hungry. I excused myself from the table eager to return to Chichester's world and continue my travels in this new universe of the lone voyager.

I consumed every word, down to the itemised lists of stores *Gipsy Moth IV* had carried outbound from the UK to Sydney, then homebound to Plymouth. As dawn cracked the eastern sky, I felt exhausted and elated. Chichester's story was not simply one of sailing. The dreaming, the planning and the preparation as much as the execution brought the whole voyage into the realm of high adventure: challenge, discovery, exploration, the path to self-knowledge and self-realisation. To sail, powered by nature's engine, to be in the wilderness of the oceans, to be engaged in an endeavour that would strain every sinew, challenge every concept, expose every weakness, call on every asset and demand total commitment was to me simply irresistible, the fullest definition of adventure I could imagine. Perhaps it was my naivety or my adolescence, but it seemed to me entirely reasonable and necessary to find a way to measure myself completely. I stood at my bedroom window looking over the harbour in the burgeoning light of a new day. In that private moment I determined that one day, I too would sail single-handed around the world.

To consolidate the promise I had made to myself, I gathered together all my pocket money, HKG$200 (approximately £12.50). I wanted a watch, something to symbolically mark time. I coveted a Rolex Cosmograph but my naivety was such that as I scoured the jewellery shops downtown my heart plunged when I saw the prices – HKG$4,500. Eventually, in the jewellery shop in the foyer of the Hong Kong Hilton, I spotted a chronograph in the corner of a cluttered display cabinet. I asked to see the watch, a pre-owned Heuer Autavia 7763C circa 1968. It was big, chunky, solid, beautiful and, importantly, affordable. The serial number engraved on the side of the case between the 12 o'clock strap lugs was 113-258. My school number was 258. It seemed like a sign and my heart beat faster as I peeled off banknotes.

Three decades would pass before I finally stepped aboard my own yacht in pursuit of that dream.

* * *

Back at school among the cool, green hills of Lancashire's farmlands, my mind was a jumble of crammed facts and figures – chemical formulae, mathematical equations, Latin and French vocabulary – in preparation for the exams. Behind all that jagged knowledge, my newly formed dream of sailing around the world played like soft music. I shared a room with three other boys. One of them, Roger, listened as I spoke about my aspiration late into the night.

'Where's it coming from, this thing with the sea?'

I shrugged in the darkness. 'Don't know. It's just there.'

I could *feel* the reasons, but words failed me when I tried explaining them. Perhaps there was some biological predisposition to adventure. My father was born in Bangalore in 1931. At 15, he was dispatched to boarding school in England and did not see his parents again until he was twenty-three. He went to London University to study chemical engineering but bunked out halfway through, took a ship to Kenya and found a job with Standard Vacuum Oil, later to become part of Exxon Mobil. It was certainly a maverick action.

I was born in Nairobi several years later on 1st October 1960. I learned to swim before I could walk. My father had a thick green towelling dressing gown. He would take the belt, tie it round my bulging tummy and 'walk' me round the edge of a pond in the garden, suspending me in the water.

As he climbed the greasy pole of corporate life, my father's job took him to far-flung places. He abhorred the weather in England. I think his choices were an unconscious attempt to reclaim a fractured childhood and re-immerse himself in the colonial lifestyle he had known as a boy.

In 1965, we sailed on a P&O ship to Hong Kong. I remember the voyage, the thrill of being at sea and the excitement of arrival in a mysterious place. After three years, we upped and moved to Japan, by sea again, this time on a Dutch ship, the *Boissevain*. After living in Yokohama for three years, we moved on to Bangkok, to a large colonial house surrounded by high walls and green expanses of lawn in Soi Yen Akart, in the heart of the city. I loved the heat, the promise held in a tropical dawn, the Buddhist temples, the gentle countenance of the people. But mostly, I loved the sea. Exxon owned a beach house on the coast at Pattaya, on the Gulf of Siam, two hours' drive from the city. At 10 years of age, I had started going to boarding school in England. To my young eyes, the contrast with the life in Africa and the Far East I had known until then, was stunning. I enjoyed boarding, the independence of it, but was always buoyed by the prospect of returning to Bangkok and our weekend trips to Pattaya.

After a second, longer stint in Hong Kong, my parents retired to South Africa while I went to medical school in London for two years followed by a brief sojourn in the military before rejoining my studies and emerging eventually as an osteopath. I moved to private practice in Yorkshire, but the idea of crunching people's spines for a living quickly palled. I returned to London. Before long, I had started my own business in food distribution, married Louise and fathered two children. Despite the accumulating responsibilities of family and business life, my aspiration to sail around the world never waned, but it seemed, as so often happens, life had ambushed my dream.

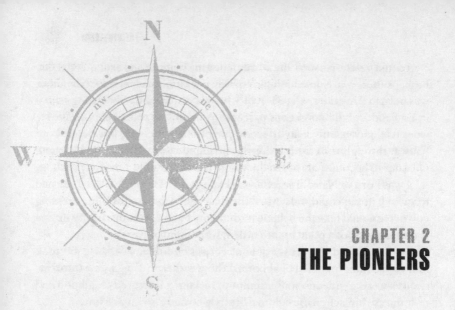

CHAPTER 2

THE PIONEERS

'WHAT'RE YOU DOING?' Louise said, taking a seat in front of my desk.

My laptop was open. I gave a defensive half-shrug. 'Nothing much.' I had been daydreaming: Thailand, 1971. I was 11 years old – my first sailing experience. We had gone down to Pattaya for the weekend. From somewhere, my father had acquired a Sailfish – a flat, plywood hull nine feet long, painted bright red with a square foot well and a slit in the centre to take the daggerboard. A slim mast supported a single sail, and the rudder and short tiller hung from sprockets at the stern.

The small craft did not look seaworthy and I felt myself torn between apprehension and the thrill of taking the boat out on the water. My father had never shown any interest in sailing and I wasn't certain that he knew much about it. Nonetheless, I helped drag the Sailfish across the soft sand.

I looked back towards the beach house, one of four situated on a small bay optimistically called Palm Beach. The Sailfish floated off the bottom and I clambered aboard. A tiny electric buzz prickled my skin. While my father held onto the stern, he explained the basics of sailing and then we were off. At the first practice tack, the Sailfish flipped over and I spilled into the sea. We both swam round to the underside of the upturned hull, stood on the daggerboard and righted the boat. This happened several more times. As we got further from the beach, past the embrace of the bay, my edginess grew. Although I was a competent swimmer, the impenetrable indigo of deep water colluded with my imagination to conjure monsters from the deep. I must have said something because my father lashed me to the mast for safety, confident now in his ability to keep the boat upright. At the next tack, the Sailfish flipped again, trapping me. Panic fizzed along my sinews and my lungs began to heave involuntarily for breath in the soundlessness of underwater. Just in time, the Sailfish righted itself. After that, we sailed the small craft more successfully and eventually found our way back to the beach. By this time, I was cold and afraid. I did not venture out again, preferring to play in the turquoise translucence of the shallows.

The next day, reports reached us that local prawn fishermen had caught a 20-foot great white shark just a little further up the coast.

Louise stood up, reaching across the desk towards a pack of cigarettes. I closed the Word document I'd been working on, a new diary. I'd just written the first entry:

Friday 28th November 2003
Today I have made a decision – to sail a solo circumnavigation west around Cape Horn and through the Russian Arctic. I'm 43. It's 'now or never'. I have cash to part-finance the voyage and with my impending separation from Louise, a mind now urging me on.

I have two young sons. To them alone, I am responsible. Such an undertaking, with the inherent dangers of injury or even death, defines the most reckless action a parent could consider. Equally, I have only one lesson to teach my boys: above all else, they must be true to themselves… it will be only a short time in the totality of their lives…

My choice of route, a westwards 'vertical' circumnavigation, had never previously been attempted. No sailing boat, Russian or otherwise, had ever been into the Russian Arctic singlehanded. Only a handful of singlehanded sailors had successfully rounded Cape Horn westabout against prevailing winds and currents. The challenges were immense but if I was going to circumnavigate alone, there seemed little point in merely mimicking what many others had already achieved by following a lateral route. I would need to find a special boat, one with the strength to get me round Cape Horn and handle pack ice. I would probably need permission from the Russian government to enter their territorial waters. What difficulties might that throw up? And I needed to prepare myself mentally, spiritually and physically for situations that I could not even begin to imagine.

The purpose that had loitered so restlessly over the years, suppressed and shaped by time and circumstance, had finally asserted itself. The realisation that at last I had made the commitment left me feeling altered. The phantasmal apparition of a dream, beautiful and labyrinthine but no more tangible than wind-blown smoke, was suddenly real.

It was too early to tell Louise. The setting wasn't right. Our house was too full of the memories of a marriage that had foundered, not calamitously or abruptly, but which had ebbed insidiously towards the rocky shores of discontent.

Louise left to pick up the children from school. I sat for a long time listening to the quiet hum of the house. Beyond the windows, the lawn spread away towards wooded slopes. A watery sun spilt weak light onto the grass. I went out and wandered among the trees, remembering the summers here, a wide hammock slung between two sturdy trunks, playing with the boys, the air ringing with birdsong and the magical peels of children's laughter, the gentle rustling of the leaf canopy rising high above. Now, in late November, the place was denuded. An Arctic wind blew in from the north. The sunlight dwindled and died. Lights came on in the house, casting cosy oblongs of warmth in the darkness. I sat among the fallen leaves watching the figures of my wife and sons moving behind the windows, listening to the muted clanking of pots and pans, the sounds of children, shouted instructions and mild reprimands that carried no teeth. I savoured this moment of comfortable domesticity, a situation I had grown accustomed to but which, like the diminishing view from a speeding train, would soon be lost to me. The course of all our lives would change. My journey had begun.

* * *

From the time I stumbled on *Gipsy Moth Circles The World*, I scoured libraries and bookshops for any literature by pioneering solo circumnavigators and discovered a world of adventure and daring peopled with eccentric misfits, wanderers and romantics, a tapestry woven with tales of bravery, bravado, competitiveness, fear and wonder. One story in particular stayed with me, the extraordinary voyage of Frenchman Marcel Bardiaux. Born in Clermont-Ferrand in the Auvergne region of France on 2nd April 1910, Bardiaux was a sickly child. The death of his father days before the end of the First World War could only have damaged his psychological well-being. Bardiaux, his mother and younger sister moved to Paris. At 14, he ran away to Le Havre and tried to join a ship but the police returned him to his mother. Working as a joiner, plumber and puppet-maker, Bardiaux found time to make a canoe, which he paddled on the Seine. By the age of 19, he had become the French and European kayak champion. He served his military conscription in the navy and, as a reservist at the outbreak of war, was interned in Germany. He escaped, evading his captors by hiding in a river using a metal breathing tube.

Back in Paris, Bardiaux came across the plans for a Bermudian sloop designed by Henri Dervin, 30 foot in length, 8'10" feet wide and displacing four tons. In 1943, he started construction of his yacht in a workshop at Nogent-sur-Marne, cutting and forming the ribs for the boat with lumber scrounged from dumps and assembling them into frames on paper patterns. The wartime scarcity of materials extended the build period to six years. Finally, on 29th July 1949, with the help of friends, he hauled *Les Quartres Vents* through the cobbled streets of Perreux on two truck axles and launched her. After months of fitting out, Bardiaux sailed from Paris on Sunday morning, 1st January 1950, on a voyage that would cover 68,000 nautical miles westwards around Cape Horn, take eight years to complete and make more than 500 port calls en route.

In 1960, Marcel Bardiaux began construction of a second yacht. *Les Quartres Vents* had been a *wet* boat. This time, Bardiaux wanted a boat that would be strong and dry. He decided to build her of stainless steel. The build took eight years. He named her *Inox* (the French word for stainless steel). Over the next 30 years, Bardiaux sailed 400,000 nautical miles on *Inox*. She ran aground on the northeastern coast of Canada in 1996. Bardiaux spent a year repairing the damage. *Inox* returned to France in 1997. Bardiaux died on board his boat in February 2000, in the harbour at Redon. He was 89 years old.

When I first read Bardiaux's story, my pulse quickened. Even more than his amazing circumnavigation, the idea of a stainless steel yacht seemed fantastic. Could I find such a boat? It seemed unlikely, even impossible.

Nineteen men had sailed solo circumnavigations before Francis Chichester set out from Plymouth, England, on 27th August 1966. When he returned to Plymouth on the afternoon of 28th May 1967 having stopped only once – in Sydney – the challenge became obvious. Could one man, alone, sail around the earth without stopping?

Contenders began emerging before Chichester had even made it home. One was Robin Knox-Johnston, a 28-year-old merchant seaman, on leave before joining his new ship *Kenya* as first officer. He had his own boat,

Suhaili, a 32-foot canoe-stern craft based on a Norwegian lifeboat to a 1924 design by American William Atkin and built of Indian teak.

With interest gathering in the non-stop round-the-world challenge, the *Sunday Times* newspaper stepped in as race sponsor, offering a Golden Globe trophy for the first to finish and, because competitors would set sail on varying dates, a £5,000 cash prize for the quickest finisher on elapsed time in what quickly became dubbed The Golden Globe Race. Of the nine starters, Knox-Johnston was the only one to finish, scooping both the trophy and the cash.

* * *

I first met Sir Robin Knox-Johnston at the London Boat Show in January 1999. His company, Clipper Ventures, organised a round-the-world race sailed in identical 67-foot sloop-rigged monohulls. I joined up for the 2000 race, sailing the trans-Atlantic leg from the United Kingdom to Havana via Vilamoura on the south coast of Portugal. It was an opportunity to get blue-water experience without finding, preparing and equipping a boat myself.

Knox-Johnston struck me as gruff and acerbic. I had learnt from my reading over the years that the great adventurers of rock and water shared several common characteristics, notably a bent towards introversion and a self-effacing demeanour. Outwardly, these behaviours masked a deeply rooted stubbornness, a utilitarian approach to problem solving, an over-reaching determination to achieve a goal once set and a desire for solitude that might strike most people as unusual, if not odd. The manifestation of this complex ran a high risk of misinterpretation.

Rather than engage Sir Robin in protracted conversation, I chose instead to observe and learn.

Louise and Benji, who was not yet two, flew out to Vilamoura to meet the boat. We had finished last in the fleet of eight. Morale on board was low. At the re-victualling stage, shore crews piled boat provisions on the dockside, similar piles for each boat. We found that our pile had been raided and our cheese taken by another crew. Louise decided to take the matter up with Sir Robin.

'It's not my problem,' Sir Robin said.

'You can't allow *Liverpool* to go to sea without cheese!'

'*Liverpool*'s crew is responsible for their provisions and it's up to them to get their act together.'

Louise blanched. 'That's unacceptable! You're not seriously suggesting that my husband and the rest of *Liverpool*'s crew sail across the Atlantic Ocean without any cheese, are you?'

Sir Robin was at a loss for words, visibly taken aback.

'You're in charge here, Sir Robin, and you need to sort this out.'

Sir Robin slowly shook his head, arms crossed. '*Liverpool*'s crew will have to deal with it.'

With that, Sir Robin ambled off and I joined Louise on the dockside. I felt a confusing mix of embarrassment and pride at Louise. Didn't she know who he was, what he had done?

'Are you nuts?' I said to her.

'You're not going to sea without cheese. Come with me.'

Louise marched into town. She found a delicatessen and bought a huge block of Cheddar weighing several kilos. I lugged it back to the boat. Everyone on board cheered. When she spotted Sir Robin, she went over. 'Here,' she said presenting the bill. 'You have to pay this.'

Sir Robin looked at the bill, then at Louise. He seemed to gauge her then nodded sagely. He handed the bill back. 'Send it to the office. They'll settle up with you.'

So we went to sea with our cheese (and Sir Robin reimbursed Louise).

* * *

During the second phase of the Atlantic crossing, Vilamoura to Havana, we passed through one truly horrific storm. The anemometer showed wind speeds exceeding 100mph as we joined with the storm, passing between two enormous pillars of black cloud that seemed to touch the surface of the sea and spiral upwards to the heavens. The sea became a maddened confusion of broken water. I was on watch at the helm. After six hours, sailing directly through the eye signalled by a ring of blue sky far above, I came off watch shaking with exhaustion and fear.

The Atlantic crossing had taken six weeks, slowed by several periods of calms that lasted for days. Twice squalls overtook the boat with winds accelerating from 10 knots to 50 knots in a matter of seconds, shredding spinnakers both times.

Perhaps the most valuable knowledge I gained was not to do with sailing but with myself. I did not enjoy long-haul sailing with other people. Being in a confined space under a degree of pressure starts to peel away the rind of conformity. Soon, psychological debris litters every nook and cranny. I tranquilised myself by finding some quiet part of the deck, sitting so that I could not see anyone else and pressing my hands over my ears to block their noise. In that cocoon, I imagined myself alone, in a place where I governed myself, where my survival depended on my own abilities, a place where the only laws were nature's laws, a place of immense power and humbling beauty, of tranquillity and isolation.

Whenever I practised, my spirits soared.

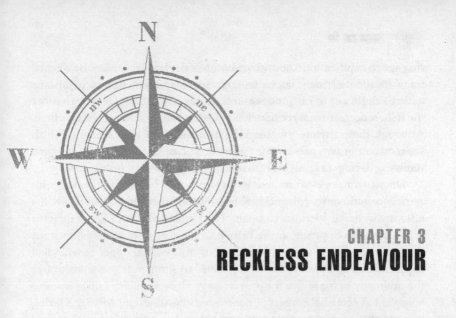

CHAPTER 3
RECKLESS ENDEAVOUR

EVERYTHING BECAME A JUMBLE in my mind: getting the boys settled in their new home with Louise when we sold the house, starting Benji at a new school and added to that, I had to think about finding somewhere to live – should I buy or rent?

As for the proposed voyage, who would manage the shore-side operation? I would need someone to manage a website, handle the media (if the media took an interest in what I was doing), get spare parts out to distant ports if I had to stop for repairs and take care of all kinds of problems I hadn't yet thought of. I began work to consolidate the project on paper while trawling the internet for boats. Scarcity of money and time precluded a new-build boat, but there were good boats about and I eventually came across one lying in Gibraltar, a French-designed Trireme 38. The price was above my budget. The broker suggested an opening offer, but it was too early to commit money. I wanted to see the specifications and then I'd think about getting over to Gibraltar to look at the boat.

* * *

It was time to tell Louise.

We first met in London in April 1996. I was running my own company, Supermarket Direct, an early foray into the grocery home shopping market that was to explode with the dotcom boom of the late 1990s. Louise worked for a local magazine. She visited our south London offices to discuss advertising ideas. On 11th June, we went on our first date and on 18th October the following year we were married in Oxfordshire. It was a difficult time. Although the company was working in association with a major British supermarket group, persuading shoppers to change their buying habits to remote ordering was proving difficult. The company was losing money.

Deceit from one of my fellow directors in a boardroom awash with arrogance and avarice led quickly to hostility and recrimination. Six months after my wedding, I left the company I had built and took a job as director of business development at the British College of Osteopathic Medicine, from where I had graduated in 1988, but my residual anger at what had happened at Supermarket Direct continued to simmer. It was shortly after this unhappy episode that I dislocated my right shoulder and went into hospital for remedial surgery. I contracted the superbug MRSA. During two months of convalescence at home, I began writing a novel, *Cobra*. I also thought about gaining blue-water experience and it was then that I investigated Sir Robin Knox-Johnston's Clipper Ventures.

My ambition of sailing a circumnavigation was not new to Louise – much of our conversation during dinner on that first date centred on the plans each of us had. At the time, she had listened. Over a year later, she confessed that she had dismissed what I'd said as a fantasy that would be dissolved quickly by marriage and children. Soon after my recovery from the MRSA infection, Louise gave birth to Benjamin.

* * *

The Fox and Hounds was a cosy pub set high in the Chiltern Hills.

'What's the occasion?' Louise asked, sipping at a glass of wine.

'Several things – getting divorced.' The words came out wrong, sounding glib. My mind was elsewhere.

Louise clinked her glass against mine. She knew what I meant – a toast to getting divorced without rancour.

'And?' she questioned, setting her glass down.

'And what?'

'Several things, you said.'

'I'm going to do it – the circumnavigation. I don't have a boat yet, but I've found some possibles. I may fly out to Gibraltar to have a look at one.'

Louise laid down her knife and fork. She looked at me for a long moment. 'You're crazy!'

'Maybe. But I'm going to do it anyway.'

'You're absolutely out of your bloody mind!'

'How's your food?'

'What about me, the children, have you thought about that?'

'I've thought about all of that, yes.'

'It's completely bloody selfish and irresponsible.'

I nodded. Sipped beer. 'You're right,' I said.

'But you don't care?'

'Of course I care.'

'You could bloody well die!'

'I could get hit by a bus tomorrow.'

'And how are you going to pay for it?'

'I've got some money, sponsorship maybe.'

'And if that doesn't materialise?'

I had sold my London apartment. The proceeds would buy the boat. I wasn't yet sure about the rest of the costs, but my belief was unshakeable.

'I'll find a way,' I said. It was lame, but also the truth. 'If I am meant to do this, it will happen.' I felt a little foolish. I had constructed a budget and I was some way short of the required funding. 'Look, none of this should come as much of a surprise.'

'I thought the Clipper thing had got this out of your system.'

'It didn't.'

Louise was eating mechanically. I poured her more wine. 'You don't know anything about sailing, well okay, a bit, but you don't have the experience to do this.'

Now, on this point, she was right. I had never sailed single-handed but single-handed sea trials constituted part of my preparation plan. How did I explain that it was about feel, the assessment of my skills, the ability to develop? People had stood at the summit of Mount Everest without ever having seen snow before.

'I told you about this before we got married, before we had the children.' Our second son, Gabriel, had arrived two years before on 18th October, our fourth wedding anniversary.

'Well, you should have done it then, before they were born or do it later, after they've been through school.'

'I wanted to, remember?'

'I thought it was all pie in the sky.'

'It isn't – and if I leave it till after the boys are through school, I'll be too old.'

'Chichester's your big hero…'

'So?'

'He was in his sixties, right?'

'I can't wait that long.'

We talked around the subject through the rest of dinner, the best part of two hours.

To her eternal credit, Louise finally said, 'If you have to do this, then okay. If you really have to, then I'll support you as best I can.'

I smiled, as much to hide my guilt as to show relief.

'There is one condition,' Louise said.

My smile vanished. 'Only one?'

'I'm being serious.' Louise's eyes filled with tears. 'You have to promise.'

'Okay.'

'I mean it.'

'Okay, I promise.'

'You wear a lifejacket with a safety harness. Whenever you're on deck you wear a bloody lifejacket and make sure you're strapped on!'

CHAPTER 4

WHAT IF...

THE BROKER IN GIBRALTAR sent the specifications of the Trireme. She was robust and well equipped. Her underwater profile was near ideal, ticking many of the boxes on my wishlist. Her deep 'V' bow would be an effective wave-cutter. The fin keel lowered the centre of gravity, aiding stability and sea-keeping qualities. A skeg-mounted rudder added strength and protected the prop. The main disadvantage was the short keel. The boat would struggle to make a decent tacking angle going upwind. Topside, her decks were flush to the hull, allowing breaking water to spill off quickly. The low-profile coach-house minimised windage and a centre cockpit allowed quick access to all points on deck and greater security in big weather. At 38 feet, she was manageable single-handed but still had sufficient waterline length to produce decent speed (the longer the waterline length, the faster the hull speed). Constructed entirely of mild steel save for the aluminium rig, the Trireme 38 was near perfect. She lacked a cuddy to protect the helm, solar panels, a wind generator and support bars around the base of the mast, but these I could add. I decided to go to Gibraltar and have a look at her. I booked a flight for 8th March 2004.

I bought a copy of David Lewis's book, *Ice Bird*. A New Zealander by birth and medical doctor by training but a restless spirit by nature, David Lewis was the first to sail solo to Antarctica and his boat was steel, 1/8th inch plate all round. It was interesting reading given that I would inevitably encounter pack-ice conditions in the Arctic, along Russia's Northern Sea Route. In his book, Lewis also raised the question that everyone asks themselves at some point in their lives, *'What if?'*

In 2002, Louise and I considered the possibility of emigrating to New Zealand, principally to give the children a more outdoors life. In January 2003, we flew to Auckland. The two weeks we spent there were among the happiest we had together and we returned to England resolved to take things further. Medicals were conducted, applications filed, supporting evidence compiled. By August, the New Zealand government had approved our application. If Louise was prepared to give it a go, then I would sacrifice my aspirations for a circumnavigation – a small price to keep my family together. In the end, Louise didn't feel that we were strong enough together to survive the move. We abandoned the plan and decided instead on divorce. During the time we were in Auckland, David Lewis died.

One evening in late March 2004, Louise said, 'I've been thinking about your sailing.' Her eyes were downcast. 'It's very irresponsible.'

'I know it is; at least I can appreciate that argument.'

'What am I going to do?'

We had come quickly to the crux. 'Listen, it's still some time away. I'm not going to be here one minute and gone the next.'

She seemed sad, lost almost.

'I want to read you something.' I fetched *Ice Bird*, quickly explained who David Lewis was and found the page I wanted. I waited a short beat so I had her full attention and began to read. '"...*there is a compulsion to question and explore and to refuse to be satisfied with accepted explanations or assumed limitations placed upon endeavour. The imperative is present in individual men and women – in varying degrees, of course. The chosen or cursed ones are devil-driven; the call comes to them and they must answer.*"'

I looked at her for some reaction, but Louise stared at me for some sort of explanation.

'I guess I'm cursed,' I said. 'The truth is I've got no choice. What's the alternative? Every day to be regretting that I didn't fulfil myself in the way I need to, so that I can live in the moment and not always in some other time, unable to focus on the task at hand, be it job, children or whatever, and doomed to living with the misery of failure.'

'What failure?'

'I don't really expect you to understand because it's not the kind of thing you aspire to. You can't feel it. It's a bit like men and pregnancy. We can't feel it. We can imagine it perhaps, but it's not the same thing.'

'That's a stupid analogy.'

'Maybe, but you get the point. Look, if I'm hard about it, the divorce is your choice. If that's what you want, you have to take the consequences. You have to adjust to a new life on your own. It's nerve-wracking for you, but it's temporary. The thing here is the children.'

'I know. That's what I'm talking about.'

'When they are men, I'll ask them what they would have had me do. I'm confident now of what their answers will be. So I'm going to go.'

'And if you don't go?'

'Then I'll spend the rest of my life asking myself the same question over and over and never finding the answer.'

'What question?'

'*What if…*'

* * *

Le Breuil-en-Auge is a sleepy Normandy village between Deauville and Lisieux. From the village, a lane meanders up the hillside among the trees like a frozen stream and tops out into open farmland. At the apex of the hill, a driveway curves through flat lawn fringed with high hedgerows to a picturesque house of classic Normandy design – native columbarge of exposed timber frames in-filled with brick and whitewashed plaster sitting on a plinth of local stone and set beneath a steeply pitched slate roof.

We visited as often as we could, not for the place but to see Christian and Tracey Foures and their two sons, Alexandre and Louis, who spent weekends recharging here after their busy work and school week in Paris.

It all started in 1998, six months after Louise and I were married. With the implosion of my position at the company and me suffering a ragged combination of stress and depression at the shocking betrayal by someone I had known all my life and who I thought I knew, Louise decided we needed to regroup. We flew to the Maldives. At Mahé Airport, an attendant from the hotel led us and two other couples to a small quay nearby where a launch waited, its twin diesels humming in the gathering heat of morning. To escape the exhaust fumes, we climbed to the flying bridge while the other passengers headed for the cabin. Several minutes later, a head popped up sporting a thatch of unruly hair, wrap-round shades and a wide grin. A slender, arrestingly attractive woman followed him. The man made a comment in French and Louise, a fluent French speaker, struck up a conversation with him. The Frenchman introduced himself as Christian. His wife Tracey was English. We became friends immediately during the forty-minute transfer to Kuda Huraa, a fourteen-acre island of tropical splendour.

Our weekends in Normandy were to become a highlight of our lives in the ensuing years and we quickly fell into a practised routine centred on culinary extravaganzas. Most notable were the *plateaux des fruits de mer* sourced from the Saturday market in Deauville and lavished with Tracey's homemade mayonnaise.

On this cold February evening, Christian and Tracey's welcome was as warm as the log fire roaring in the grate.

With the children exhausted with excitement and asleep upstairs, Christian slung a giant rib-cut of beef onto a wire tray to cook over the open fire. The wine was uncorked and Les Rosbifs and Les Grenouilles settled in for the evening.

With Christian's English halting at best and my French close to non-existent, Louise and Tracey switched easily between languages as double-act interpreters. As the story of my intended voyage unfolded, Christian was at once incredulous, awestruck, envious and delighted. He insisted on breaking open the champagne.

'C'est magnifique,' Christian kept exclaiming, endlessly refilling my glass. Together, the four of us slid inevitably and inexorably towards comfortable drunkenness in a way that is only possible with friends who are deeply loved and implicitly trusted.

The weekend was just what I needed to take my mind off the project and get away from the mounting stresses of getting divorced, moving house, ensuring the welfare of the children as best we could, buying a boat and committing myself to a venture that seemed increasingly improbable.

Three days later, we said our farewells to Christian and Tracey. It would be the last time we saw them.

* * *

Louise had been busy house-hunting and found a suitable property in her preferred village of Chearsley in the Vale of Aylesbury. She burst into my office clutching a wad of magazines.

'I got this for you.' She handed me a copy of *Yachting World*. I took it, thanked her and thumbed through the glossy pages. We talked houses for 10 minutes. I had recently decided on a new-build complex – no chain, ease of purchase, nothing needing fixing. 'That place you're thinking about is too far from me,' Louise said.

'Twenty minutes?'

'You can do better.'

'Okay, you find a better one and I'll have a look.'

'I have,' she said, standing. 'Let's go.'

We drove to Ludgershall, a 'horseshoe' village and supposedly one of the best examples of its type in the country. The house was semi-detached, three bedrooms, five minutes to school, ten from Chearsley. The sellers were planning to emigrate to Portugal. Whichever house I went for, it was only going to be a base while I planned the voyage, trained for it and then actually sailed around the world. I put in an offer and by six o'clock that evening the deal was agreed.

The *Yachting World* magazine was a £2.50 gift, but the gesture was far more telling and infinitely more valuable. It demonstrated a measure of acceptance on Louise's part. For that I was grateful.

The whole problem of some kind of shore-support operation had been occupying much of my thoughts. In *Yachting World*, I saw a two-page spread advertising the United Kingdom Sailing Academy in Cowes on the Isle of Wight, offering a variety of courses. The professional skipper training caught my attention. Seventeen weeks' duration and fully residential, the course was expensive but offered everything I needed to cover from time on the water to re-familiarisation with radio procedure, diesel engine maintenance, electrics, navigation – a consolidation of my disparate experiences, an extension of that knowledge and the possibility that I might persuade them to provide my shore base.

I discussed the option with Louise after the boys were in bed. She still bristled every time I brought up the sailing, but I had a longer-term strategy. What if Louise acted as my shore support? This was more wild fantasy than realistic possibility, but Louise could bring so much to the project, an outlet for her outstanding organisational abilities (which I'd witnessed that very afternoon) and her previous public relations experience and, the children, by extension, would be more closely involved. There were downsides. Louise had no experience of sailing. She had never managed a project like

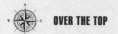

this and more immediately, her inclination towards the venture and me was likely to become hostile if I pushed too hard. I tried to dismiss the idea. She would *never* agree to it.

I didn't fly out to Gibraltar. By 16th March, I had made two firm decisions. First, the Trireme was too expensive and though I might eventually raise sufficient sponsorship to stretch my boat budget, I didn't want to overspend at this stage. Second, I would attend the UKSA in October.

The day I had been dreading crept slowly out of the future until one day, I woke up and it had arrived: Wednesday 7th April – moving day, the end of my marriage and the break-up of the family. It was a tragic day for little Benji and Gabriel. I hoped more than anything that Louise and I could make a better go of things apart than we had managed together. One question circled endlessly in my mind – would my voyage, with all its attendant dangers and absences, shatter the delicate balance of our friendship?

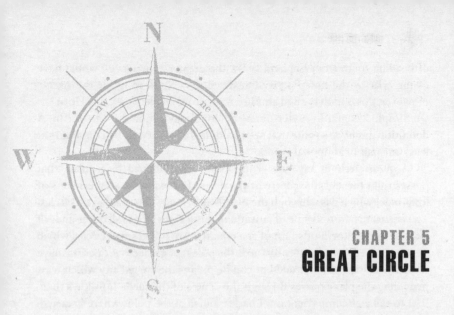

I SPENT THE NEXT FEW WEEKS settling into the house in Ludgershall, waiting for the shock of my altered situation to hit. Maybe the relief of being free to get on with the job in hand was overriding my sadness. Who knows? The mind is a complex machine. The pain of it all would manifest itself down the line but for the moment, I was content to focus on the boys and the voyage.

I concentrated my internet search for a boat in France and Holland, the biggest European markets for steel yachts which, if I was going to venture into the ice, was the only material to go with – aluminium was too soft and fibreglass a non-starter. Late in the evening on Monday 17th May, I sat back with a feeling of quiet excitement. I was looking at my computer screen, at a picture of a Flot 40 Mk II, built in 1990 and lying in Lorient on the Brittany coast. After searching through hundreds of boats, this one fitted the bill. I emailed asking for specifications and more pictures. It wouldn't take a lot of work to adapt her for my purposes. Much depended on the build quality and whether I believed she was strong enough to withstand the pummelling of a 30,000-mile passage through some of the most treacherous waters in the world.

I had to decide on a start date to bring perspective to timings and costs. My choice of route was fundamental to when that date would fall. The advantage of heading south from England lay in the greater experience I would have of the boat by the time I arrived at the Bering Strait to tackle the Arctic. However, this option created another monstrous challenge – Cape Horn.

Simple geography determines a circumnavigation of the earth. A definition might be a route that approximates a great circle by containing at least one pair of antipodal points.

A great circle is any line around the earth defined by a plane that passes right through the centre of the earth. For example, all meridians of longitude (which pass through the North and South Poles) are great circles. The equator is the only line of latitude that is a great circle (all other lines of latitude, either north or south of the equator, are called small circles which become increasingly smaller towards the poles). A great circle does not have to be a meridian of longitude but can be on a plane angled any which way, providing the plane passes through the centre of the earth. It follows then, that to sail a circumnavigation, I had to finish at the point where I started, always moving in generally the same direction.

Sailing south from the start meant I would have to finish by sailing back to that point from the north. Following a great circle route necessitates crossing the equator twice (going in opposite directions each time) and bisecting all meridians of longitude.

In *Gipsy Moth Circles the World,* Sir Francis Chichester described the essential element of what he termed a 'true' circumnavigation as a track where '...*the vessel passes through two points on the earth's surface which are diametrically opposite each other...*'

The best way of visualising antipodal points is to imagine a globe pierced with a stick passing through the very centre of the sphere. The entry and exit points are antipodal. The reasoning for at least one pair of antipodes on the vessel's track resides in shaping the track to conform as closely as possible to a great circle – a perfect ring around the earth. Land masses prevent a perfect track over water, so antipodes approximate an actual track to a great circle. The more pairs of antipodes along the track, the closer the track conforms. Many circumnavigations ignore this fundamental rule, but for me it was a necessity.

The final requirement of a circumnavigation is that the distance travelled should be at least 21,600 nautical miles, equivalent to the distance around the circumference of the earth. This requirement inevitably results by adhering to the antipodal principle.

To bisect every meridian of longitude, I would have to round Cape Horn westwards, from the Atlantic side to the Pacific. Cape Horn is the most feared stretch of water on the planet – the currents move east and the prevailing winds are from the west. To go westwards, I would be sailing into the teeth of the weather, effectively 'uphill' rather than running downhill with the wind behind. To take on this challenge with my limited experience was arguably crazy. However, the decision became a matter of elimination. To bisect every meridian and transit the Arctic via Canada's Northwest Passage meant going round the Cape of Good Hope, the southern tip of Africa. But – and this was a big *but* – would a route that missed out Cape Horn leave me with a gaping chasm of discontent? I didn't have to think for long. Yes, it would. So, if it was sensible to leave the Arctic phase until the latter part of the voyage, then a westward rounding of the Horn became inevitable.

I considered the reverse option, of travelling north to tackle the Arctic first. This would mean a June departure, which would not leave enough time to prepare properly, unless I delayed until 2006 and my finances wouldn't stretch to that.

I needed three months to reach Cape Horn by January, mid-summer in the southern hemisphere. My start date was therefore set for sometime in October 2005.

Now I had to create an identity for the mission. Ideas for names had been chasing around my mind. A circumnavigation was clearly *global*. If successful, I would achieve the 'first' vertical from which I deduced the word *Alpha* (and even if I wasn't successful, the attempt was still a 'first'). To conjure the thrill of adventure I came up with *Expedition* and my great hope was christened: the Alpha Global Expedition.

* * *

Wednesday 2nd June was blisteringly hot. I visited the UKSA in Cowes. After a tour round the facilities, I had a long chat with the chief instructor, Francis Knight. Elements of the 17-week course that were not directly relevant to me could be substituted with more useful material. I told Francis that I had a specific mission in mind for which the course at UKSA was a training step. He generously accepted that without probing further. Another reason why the UKSA appealed to me was that my time there would serve as a preparatory period for Benji and Gabriel to get used to my not being around quite so much. At least they'd be better equipped to handle my actual departure when it came.

On Monday 7th June, I met my accountant to set up a limited company in the name of Alpha Global Expedition Limited. The process threw out an unexpected opportunity.

Despite trying to ignore the possibility of Louise helping me on the expedition, I couldn't. She'd be perfect. Before we were married, she had worked in the hotel trade, in public relations, rising to represent some of the finest hotels in London. She was extrovert, capable, quick and a natural communicator.

I asked Louise if she would act as company secretary. She agreed. Perhaps this reflected a softening in her attitude towards the expedition and me. And, perhaps, if I trod carefully, I might eventually persuade her to get more involved.

On 16th June, I packed up the car and headed for France. In Lorient, *Ninae*, the Flot 40, was immediately recognisable with her broad yellow hull strip. She looked squat and solid as if hunched on the water in permanent anticipation of an elemental onslaught. She had never strayed far from her home waters so although the boat was older, her low mileage showed in her good condition.

I spent a couple of hours going over the boat, above deck and below, looking at systems, lifting floorboards, inspecting the bilges and the inside of the hull plating. I could see no sign of rust, no water, no damage. The interior was beautifully fitted out and fully insulated. The professionally installed electric, electronic, engine and plumbing systems looked to be in similarly good condition.

We took the boat out into the bay, hoisted sails and I spent 40 minutes playing with her. The helm was heavy and because of her weight, she could not point close to the wind without losing considerable speed but, with the wind abeam, she made 4–5 knots in a 12-knot breeze so performance was okay. However, more importantly, my feeling towards the boat, that inexplicable chemistry, wasn't there. Despite her good condition, her inventory, the meticulous build quality and her undeniable strength, I felt a grudging reluctance emanating from *Ninae*. My initial euphoria was evaporating and I left Lorient disappointed to begin my search anew.

Back in England, I drove into London for a meeting with Generate Sponsorship, a small agency marrying sponsors' money with suitable events. To approach bigger brands with credibility, I needed the help of people who knew their way round and could tap into their contact database, prepare a proposal document in the right format and press buttons with potential partners. My problem was cash flow and my dilemma acute; unless I invested in a professional sponsor document with a qualified contact list, I reduced my chances of success.

The UKSA left a message for me on Wednesday 21st July – if I had a boat, they had a berth for her. Well, I didn't have a boat, but the UKSA's willingness to provide berthing, if and when I did find a boat, was a great relief.

With no sponsorship and cash flow strained, I had to consider one final option: release equity in my house. This option had always been off-limits, but pitted against this sentiment was the question of my commitment. This expedition represented much more than just an adventure. It was a statement about my life, my principles, beliefs and character. Did I have the conviction and the courage to follow those beliefs? Did I have the guts to follow a dream or, by giving up, did I consign myself to the garbage bin of mediocrity?

This whole challenge was about so much more than getting on a boat and sailing it. The journey to get to the start line was proving every bit as arduous. I could have faced bald facts – I did not have sufficient funds, I did not have enough experience, I did not have enough time. Equally, I could borrow the money, get on with it, see if sponsors materialised and if they didn't, well…I'd find a way!

Or would I? Instead, I descended into crisis, paralysed by indecision. At the same time, I suffered a delayed reaction to the divorce, spiralling into a deep depression. On top of this, a friend with whom I had entered a property deal two years previously had bunked out and was now refusing to pay a substantial sum owed to me. I had been relying on this money. Now, my cash flow was groaning under ever greater strain.

My efforts at raising sponsorship did not yield results and Generate's work to secure corporate sponsorship had similarly come up empty. By the end of the summer, cash flow was desperately tight. The only solution was to mortgage the house and borrow the money.

I seemed to have gone nowhere.

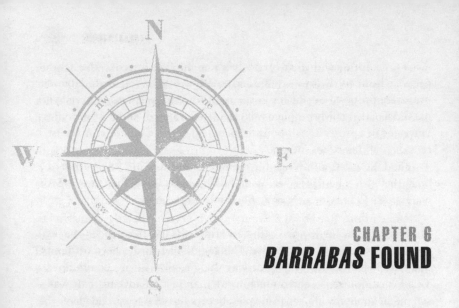

CHAPTER 6
BARRABAS FOUND

A NEW CHAPTER OF THE Alpha Global Expedition began on Monday 4th October, my first day at the UKSA. I spent Saturday with Louise and the children then, at 11am on Sunday morning, Louise took the boys off to a birthday party at our friends, the Laidlaws. Sam Laidlaw would come to play a pivotal role in the expedition.

I packed up and left, after first locking myself out of Louise's house while my computer and wallet were still inside. I clambered over the side gate, tried to force the kitchen door, breaking the glass in the process and finally got in through the landing window. It was not an auspicious start. For the first time since the divorce and through all the tribulation of the last two months, I felt alone.

I stayed with my aunt Rosemary on the Isle of Wight on Sunday night and at 10.30am the next morning drove to the UKSA. All the new arrivals were apprehensive in the unfamiliar surroundings. Refamiliarisation with all things marine was refreshing and revitalising. Conversely, being away from the boys was tough.

Among the other members of my crew on 'Starboard 5', Chris Elliott at 48 was the oldest. He'd lived in France for 25 years. A complex man capable of great sensitivity, softly spoken, courteous and likeable, Chris was the first to approach me and introduce myself during that first day at the UKSA. He was married to a French woman but after 10 years, they were now flirting with divorce. Chris was at the UKSA to train for a career change from his previous life as a freight agent. We had the 'divorce' conversation early on and as a result established a kind of bond. I could not know then that Chris's input would change the course of the Alpha Global Expedition.

Nick Musgrave was exactly my age. A former management trainer with Citibank, he was in New York during the 9/11 catastrophe. That experience, together with the humdrum tone of his existence, persuaded him to leave his job, sell his apartment and look for a new direction.

None of the 'Starboard 5' team or anybody else directly connected to the UKSA knew of my plans. Chris had twigged something mainly because I was always asking the instructors about steel boats and short-handed sailing. Despite my uncertainties about *Ninae*, I was having a spectacular lack of success at finding another suitable boat and like the dismal hankerings of a man after an old girlfriend, I called Bretagne Yachting, the broker in Lorient. *Ninae* had been sold. I was downbeat. Had I missed an opportunity? What I was really after was the Trireme I had found in Gibraltar a year before (which had also been sold).

During a weekend break, Chris went to France. On the evening we all returned to the UKSA he bounded into my room.

'I've found you a boat!' he announced, clutching some French sailing magazines.

'Really?' I said, trying to sound enthusiastic. How could he have found the right boat if he didn't know my plans?

Chris flicked through the magazines. 'Here,' he said, his finger tapping at one of the photographs in the brokerage section.

I recognised the boat immediately. It was a Trireme 38! But her hull was bare metal even though the caption described her construction as 'acier' – steel. Bare steel would rust. I assumed a print error in the caption. She must be aluminium, I thought. Aluminium or not, Chris had inadvertently come across *exactly* the right boat. I sat back, stunned.

There was a telephone number next to the picture. 'Can we call and find out?' I handed Chris my mobile.

The boat's owner, Bernard de Castro, answered. Chris began talking in faultless French.

'Ask him about the material – is it aluminium?' I whispered.

I heard Bernard laugh. 'Non, non,' he said. 'C'est Inox.'

My mind reeled. Inox! Stainless steel!

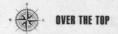

Marcel Bardiaux, 1960. I never thought I'd find such a boat. Never! And yet, out of nowhere, here she was, magically placed before me, a small colour photograph in a French sailing magazine. I knew with that peculiar, inexplicable certainty that I had found the boat to partner me on my voyage around the world.

Bernard de Castro sent detailed specifications of *Barrabas* and more pictures. The price was way over my budget, but she had everything I was looking for: safety bars at the mast, a stern frame supporting solar panels and wind generator, a large cuddy protecting the helm and companionway, six gel batteries as opposed to four on the Flot 40, and diesel-fired heating. All this would have cost 15,000 euros to add to the Flot 40. Given that the Trireme was two years younger, had a stainless steel hull and mast, a superior underwater profile and a practically brand new engine – a powerful 60hp Lombardini diesel with less than 65 hours' running time – *Barrabas* looked like a fair deal by comparison. I studied the pictures and the data long and hard. Bernard, a master welder, had taken six years over the build. It was obvious that *Barrabas* was over-engineered and incredibly strong. She ticked every box. What appeared as scratches on the bows turned out to be a remarkable feature – etchings of Neptune hurling a trident with a sea dragon rearing up behind, worked into the steel with an angle grinder by a French sculptor, the attitude of the cuts varied to reflect light and create a 3D effect.

Over the following fortnight and after many telephone calls to Bernard with Chris acting as interpreter, the time had come to make an offer. If *Barrabas* was the boat for the mission, I had to secure her. Bernard told us he was travelling from his home in Burgundy to Montpellier on the south coast of France where he kept *Barrabas* to see two other potential buyers.

The time had also come to tell Chris about the Alpha Global Expedition. He listened with bewilderment that transformed to elation when he realised that his contribution had been crucial. It was important that Bernard knew what might be in store for *Barrabas*. Chris called him. To our surprise, he had already put off one of the other potential buyers (who must have been dithering) on the basis that he felt I was serious. Now he was thrilled at the prospect of *Barrabas* sailing a circumnavigation. I agreed the asking price, subject to survey. It was a massive leap, but buying *Barrabas* felt right. The boat would keep me safe and bring my goal within reach. The responsibility on her would be huge. She had to be up to it. But I knew she would deliver, even though I had never set eyes on her. I remembered seeing *Ninae* for the first time. I'd felt deflated, my heart didn't skip a beat, my pulse didn't quicken. The relationship had to be strong, passionate. I felt that with *Barrabas*.

I had pledged money and with that pledge, the project came alive. I booked return flights to France for Chris and myself to have a look at the boat early in the New Year.

With Christmas approaching, I was keen to get away and have some time at home with the children. Louise and I gave Benji his sixth birthday party in early January at Chearsley Village Hall. Afterwards, I heard Benji say to Louise, 'I am so happy Daddy could come to my party.' He then looked at her and asked, 'Will Daddy be at my next birthday?'

'Your next birthday is a long way off, Benji,' Louise said. I looked at Louise and felt a void open within me. Here in a land-locked English village, the idea of sailing around the world seemed so ludicrous, so far removed from the basic reality of life and that reality stood before me etched in the innocent face of a six-year-old boy.

Travelling back to the Isle of Wight on the last ferry that night, I felt homesick for the familiarity of Louise and the boys. A thought kept replaying in my mind...*commitment is following through on a decision long after the mood has changed*. I wrote something similar in a card I left for Louise. These moments of indecision were part of the endeavour – never give up, just keep going.

The 'Starboard 5' crew met up at breakfast and we moved onto the UKSA's catamaran for the fifth sea phase. I was acting skipper and decided to sail to Portsmouth. We moored up for lunch before sailing across the Solent into Bembridge. The weather was cold and blowing Force 6, the catamaran's limit. My mobile phone had been ringing, but with the diesels running, I hadn't heard it. The boat's mobile phone rang. James Mitchell, the instructor, answered. He listened and then handed the phone to me.

'Hello,' I said.

'Adrian, it's Sarah.'

'Everything okay?' I asked the UKSA receptionist.

'Louise rang – there's nothing wrong with the kids, she said to tell you that straight away, but could you ring her back urgently.'

I hung up and punched in Louise's number.

'Adrian?'

The instant Louise answered, I knew something was terribly wrong.

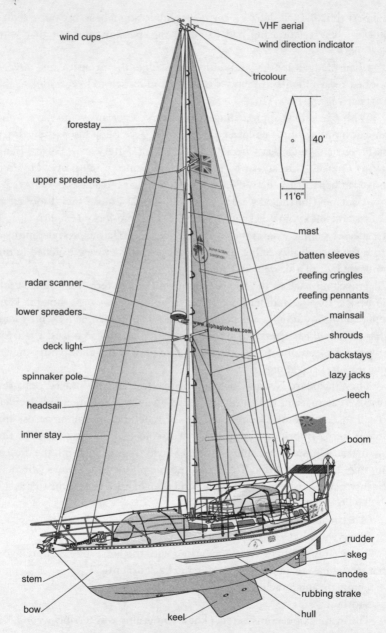

wind cups

VHF aerial

wind direction indicator

tricolour

forestay

40'

upper spreaders

11'6"

mast

batten sleeves

radar scanner

reefing cringles

reefing pennants

lower spreaders

mainsail

shrouds

deck light

backstays

spinnaker pole

lazy jacks

headsail

leech

inner stay

boom

www.alphaglobalex.com

rudder

skeg

anodes

stem

rubbing strake

bow

hull

keel

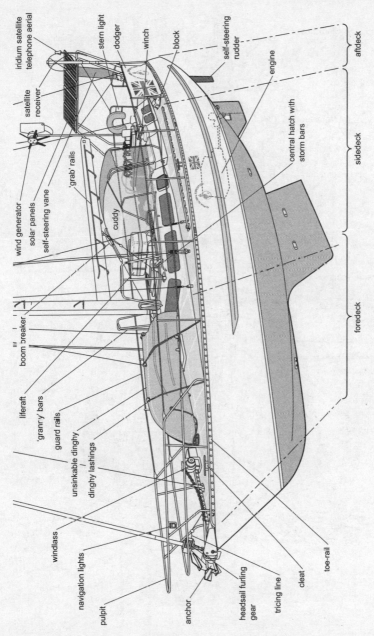

iridium satellite
telephone aerial

stern light

dodger

winch

block

self-steering
rudder

engine

aftdeck

satellite
receiver

sidedeck

central hatch with
storm bars

foredeck

wind generator

solar panels

self-steering vane

'grab' rails

cuddy

liferaft

boom breaker

granny bars

guard rails

unsinkable dinghy

dinghy lashings

windlass

navigation lights

pulpit

anchor

headsail furling
gear

tricing line

cleat

toe-rail

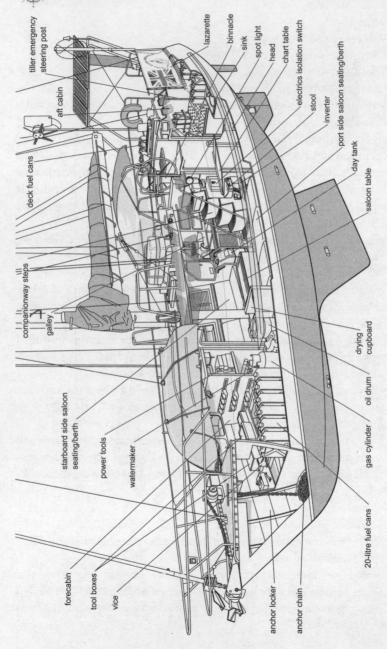

tiller emergency
steering post

aft cabin

deck fuel cans

companionway steps

galley

lazarette

binnacle

sink

spot light

head

chart table

electrics isolation switch

stool

inverter

port side saloon seating/berth

day tank

saloon table

drying
cupboard

oil drum

gas cylinder

20-litre fuel cans

anchor chain

anchor locker

vice

tool boxes

forecabin

watermaker

power tools

starboard side saloon
seating/berth

'What's up?'

'Where are you?'

'Out on the water. You okay?'

'There's no easy way to say…'

'Just tell me what's happened.'

A momentary silence then Louise said, 'Christian, Tracey and Alexandre have been killed.'

My hand dropped and I felt my throat constrict. Louise's voice sounded tinny. I raised the phone back to my ear. They had decided on a last-minute Christmas holiday to Thailand for a week. They were on the beach after breakfast when the tsunami hit. Louis, their younger son, had miraculously survived. Details were sketchy. She knew no more than that. My immediate thought was to get back to Louise as fast as humanly possible.

Someone produced a cup of sweet tea. I went on deck. The shocking deaths of our friends were incomprehensible, but their families… their grief was unimaginable. And as for Louis… he was only eight years old.

James called Red Funnel Ferries and asked if they could hold the 5.30pm sailing from Cowes to Southampton. We bombed across from Bembridge and made it back to the UKSA at 5.20pm. I jumped off the boat, sprinted to my car and got to the ferry terminal at 5.40pm. The boat was waiting. I drove like a maniac and finally arrived at Louise's house at 8.20pm. It was a long, difficult and painful evening that left us both wrung out.

Next day, I took Benji to school, the beginning of the new term, and then I drove to Southampton Airport. By some strange irony, Chris and I were flying to France that afternoon.

Port Camargue near Montpellier was an enormous, purpose-built marina development, the largest of its type in Europe. The weather was clear and sunny. Chris knew exactly where to go following Bernard's instructions.

We parked up.

'Nervous?' Chris asked.

I didn't reply immediately, just nodded. I was more excited than nervous. 'Let's go,' I said taking a deep breath.

Barrabas was impressive – meaty and beamy, her hull sides flared just behind the foredeck like the nostrils of a panting racehorse. She radiated solidity, strength and integrity. I sensed an instant chemistry, as if *Barrabas* knew why I had come.

Bernard de Castro greeted us effusively. A small man in his sixties with the physique of a jockey and a swarthy complexion pointing to his Spanish ancestry, Bernard bristled with energy. He was not in any way extrovert and the language barrier prevented me from getting to know him better but I could tell he was honest. No one who could build a boat like this could be anything but honest – the toil, the dedication, the craftsmanship, the care and attention to detail. These were hallmarks of strength and fortitude, qualities instilled in *Barrabas*'s construction every bit as tangible as the welds and steel of her hull. I liked him immediately. Bernard wanted to know more about the Alpha Global Expedition, specifics on the route, the ice, Cape Horn.

'This is exactly the type of voyage that *Barrabas* was built for,' Bernard said. I wondered whether he dreamed of sailing a circumnavigation. If he couldn't do it then perhaps seeing the boat he had spent six years building go around the earth might, in some vicarious way, be a fulfilment of sorts.

Bernard had created *Barrabas* with a 'belt and braces approach' as he put it, over-engineering the rig and deck fittings to a specification suitable for a yacht twice the size. Internally, the bilges were clean and dry with no signs of corrosion. As for visual appeal, *Barrabas* was striking: the artwork on the bows, the gleaming metal of her sides and her sleek, classically French lines.

I had researched stainless steel. Its obvious advantage is that it does not corrode at the rate or to the extent of mild steel. Chromium in the steel mix reacts with atmospheric oxygen, forming a tough film of chromium oxide on the surface protecting the metal beneath. Bernard gave me the grade of steel he'd used: 316 L (Ti) – low carbon content ($< 0.03\%$) with titanium. During welding, carbon atoms can migrate towards the heat source (carbide precipitation) creating areas of weakness, which ultimately become brittle and fracture. Other elements such as molybdenum introduced into the steel mix prevent carbide precipitation, but the best carbon 'anchor' is titanium.

To stop external carbon contaminating the hot steel during welding, Bernard had used inert Argon gas. I studied the welds above and below the waterline. There was no evidence of corrosion or precipitation.

Prohibitive cost rules out stainless steel as the material of choice for boat-building. Bernard had managed it because he worked for the French stainless steel manufacturer, Ugine. The company supplied the material at an affordable price and tested every piece for purity. As a master welder, Bernard defrayed otherwise exorbitant labour costs by doing all the work himself.

The famous French naval architect, François Charpentier, designed the Trireme 38 as a mild steel boat but because of the greater tensile and compression strength of stainless steel, Bernard was able to reduce plate thicknesses and save a significant amount of weight. The result was that *Barrabas* was lighter and stronger than the design specification.

The other huge advantage of stainless over mild steel is its malleability. On impact, stainless is more forgiving and will bend and fold before tearing and splitting. In ice-strewn waters, this property was critical, particularly in the absence of specific ice-strengthening modifications to the hull.

We spent the rest of the afternoon going over the boat, Chris interpreting between Bernard and me. At 6pm, we left Port Camargue and found a hotel in Grau du Roi. I woke at 4am thinking about *Barrabas* and the commitment I was about to make. On top of this, my mind was full of the tragedy that had befallen our friends, but somehow their deaths were acting as a spur, forcing me to realise even more clearly that nothing in life is certain, to dally is to waste, to prevaricate is to squander and to dream but not to act leads only to regret.

The following day we picked up where we'd left off, checking through the boat's systems, with me constantly firing questions and Chris doing a masterful job as interpreter. We ate lunch together in a nearby restaurant where the conversation continued with talk of parachute anchors, maximum angles of heel, other technical points and something else that intrigued me.

'How did you come up with the name, *Barrabas*?' I said.

Bernard nodded as though he'd expected the question. 'I was a young man, conscripted to fight in Algeria…'

The French military drafted the 22-year-old, an anti-authoritarian but a good soldier, assigned him to Special Forces and dispatched him into the desert in a small troop to gather intelligence. At a deserted oasis, he found and read a book, *Barabbas: The Story of a Believer Without Faith*, written in 1950 by Pär Lagerkvist, a Swedish writer who moved to Paris and lived in France and Italy. The author won the Nobel Prize for Literature in 1951. Bernard admired *Barabbas*'s maverick character. 'When I built the boat, she was a maverick also. It seemed right that I call her *Barrabas* too.' Although, whether accidentally or deliberately, Bernard chose an alternative spelling of the name.

'Do you still have the book?'

Bernard nodded. 'Oui. It's on the boat.'

'If I buy the boat, will you let me have the book?'

Bernard smiled then shook his head. 'Non,' he said.

I understood his need, a part of her that he could keep forever.

Chris had to get back to England. I drove him to the train station in Montpellier and returned to the boat for lunch with Bernard, a boeuf bourguignon made by his wife, Odette. I was a bit anxious given that Bernard's English was as bad as my French but over a bottle of Merlot, we managed, with the help of an electronic dictionary, to talk about the boat, my plans for her and the expedition. Lunch lasted an hour and a half. We talked about the deaths of my friends Christian and Tracey, our approaches to getting the most out of life, my reading of Chichester's book when I was fifteen, and his plans. 'Perhaps I will build another boat, this time from aluminium,' he confided. Afterwards, Bernard went off for a couple of hours so that I could have time on my own with *Barrabas*.

It was a beautiful afternoon. I climbed to the top of the mast, poked around below, had a nap in the back cabin and just existed with *Barrabas*. I imagined myself sailing her (I couldn't take her out on the water because there wasn't a breath of wind) and felt comfortable with the prospect. *Barrabas* seemed to be saying to me, calmly, devoid of any hysteria, 'Let's do it. I'm ready.' I got the feeling that the boat, like a thoroughbred, was straining at her mooring lines, wanting the big challenge to prove herself and win the fulfilment which, like me, she sought.

'Are you still interested?' Bernard asked when he returned.

'I've been sleeping in the aft cabin.'

He laughed, seemed unsurprised and understood that *Barrabas* and I had already established the beginnings of an intimate bond. We discussed details of the purchase transaction, agreed a price and a completion date of 31st January. He then asked, 'How can I be certain?'

I thought for a moment then said, 'Parce que je dit.'

Bernard raised his eyebrows, his mouth turned down at the corners, he cocked his head to one side and gave a small Gallic shrug and, with that, we shook hands and the deal was done.

* * *

It was late January 2005. The Yachtmaster practical examination was imminent. We picked up the external examiner, Mike Hindley, a former test pilot, from the harbour master's quay at Warsash on the River Hamble. After watching two of the others being put through their paces, I realised

Mike wanted to see confidence. We were in Wootton Creek on the north shore of the Isle of Wight when it came time for my examination. I barked orders for a stern spring and bow line, slipped the bow, drove back on the stern spring, forcing the bow out, and swung round in a tight circle, heading back out of the Wootton channel. The car ferry to Portsmouth was leaving dock. I hesitated to let her go and noticed a look from Mike, who was perched in the companionway. I knew what that look meant. I gunned the engine to get in front of the ferry. This met with a nod of approval. I ordered sails up and set course. Mike called me down below. A plane had gone down (hypothetically) and wreckage observed. Solent coastguard needed our help. Mike gave me a position on the chart to locate. I found a couple of transits, talking through my methodology as I plotted the transits on the chart. Outside the mouth of the River Medina near Cowes, he asked me to pick up one of the mooring buoys close by which I did under headsail. Mike simply said, 'Good, well done, you've passed' and promptly transferred the role of skipper to Nick Musgrave.

Back at the UKSA, I went to see the chief executive, David Green.

He reiterated the UKSA's willingness to offer *Barrabas* a berth.

The previous 48 hours had been momentous. After years of thinking and dreaming and months of planning and training, three major events occurred almost simultaneously – on Monday 2nd February, with the final transfer of monies to France, I had become the new owner of *Barrabas*; on Tuesday, I acquired my Yachtmaster ticket and on Wednesday, I secured the backing of the UKSA as my campaign base.

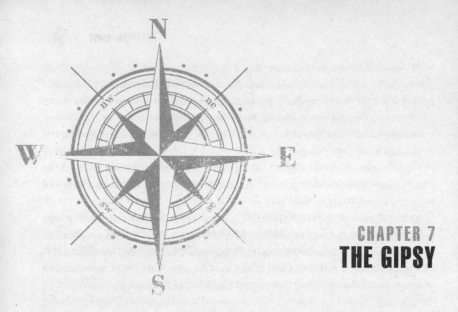

CHAPTER 7
THE GIPSY

BEFORE FINISHING AT THE UKSA, I asked Nick to help me crew *Barrabas* back to England. He agreed to join me in Montpellier in mid-March. I used the intervening time to begin the refit preparations.

My biggest concerns were the communications, navigation and weather systems. Costs would be high and I needed an expert to source hardware, programme the computers and supervise installation. I found Tim Thornton on the web at Marine Computing International. Tim would come to play an indispensable part in the Alpha Global Expedition.

I retained Generate Sponsorship to source supply sponsors from a shortlist that I'd compiled – work that could be ongoing while I was sailing *Barrabas* back to the Isle of Wight. By Wednesday 9th March, I'd done as much as I could to get the various balls rolling towards sponsorship and the refit. Louise drove me to Stansted Airport. When we said goodbye, her voice held a tremor.

'Be careful,' Louise cautioned.

It was great to see *Barrabas* again. On board, I slept well, feeling that same sense of embrace as when I'd met *Barrabas* for the first time in January. I had the next few days to familiarise myself with the boat before Nick arrived. I took an hour to figure out how the head (toilet) worked, went shopping for provisions and decided to go through *Barrabas* from stem to stern to sort through tools, spares and gear and discard rubbish.

Louise called on Friday morning.

'Is there some part of you that doesn't quite believe that I'm actually going ahead with this project?' I could hear the excitement in my own voice.

'Now you're in France, the reality is beginning to sink in, yes.'

She was worried about being left with the children and not having me around as a support system.

'It'll be okay,' I said. 'I'll be back before you know it.' I knew something that Louise did not – that she was strong, much stronger than she believed herself.

That conversation was pivotal. Up until then, Louise's attitude to me and the expedition had been detached and critical. That hostility seemed to be dissolving. She was beginning to believe that I could and would do this and, more importantly, she was beginning to accept that my commitment was real. I felt closer to her then than I had for a very long time.

Chris called.

'You still good for tomorrow?' I asked.

'No. I've got two job interviews, so I'll be with you Sunday.'

On Saturday morning, I worked my way through the engine and electrical systems and then drove to Montpellier to collect Nick from the airport.

Chris arrived at the yacht club on Sunday at 11am. Nick and I drove across to meet him and together the three of us had lunch at a quayside café. Back at the boat, we telephoned Bernard at his home in Burgundy and went through the long list of questions I'd compiled during my familiarisation with *Barrabas*.

Chris left early on Monday morning. My telephone rang. It was Louise. She was tearful. Christian and Tracey's bodies had been identified in Thailand and returned to France. The funeral was taking place that afternoon in Honfleur. Alexandre's body was still missing. We assumed he'd been swept out to sea.

Nick and I went through the topsides. We spent time scraping the hull as best we could with a makeshift scraper on the end of a pole.

'Is there a plastic water bottle I could cut in two to see under water?' I asked Nick, pulling items out of the lazarette.

'Or we could go buy a face mask,' Nick suggested.

'Bernard must have used something to see underneath.'

I reached into the lazarette and pulled out a bucket stuffed with rags.

'Nah,' Nick said. 'He wouldn't have thought of something like that.'

I emptied the bucket and lo! Bernard had cut the bottom out of the bucket and screwed in a Perspex pane, caulked with a silicone sealant. We laughed like drains. Bernard, it seemed, had thought of everything!

We woke to thick fog on Wednesday 16th March, but the weather was favourable for our departure the next morning. The voyage to England would be an opportunity for me to gain an understanding of *Barrabas*, her sailing abilities, her sea-keeping qualities, her idiosyncrasies, her moods. The learning curve would be steep. How would I handle *Barrabas*? Our bond would be forged during the next few weeks.

Nick and I enjoyed good sailing towards the Iberian islands, feeling secure on *Barrabas*. On Sunday 20th March, with dolphins cavorting in front of the bow, we sighted the mountainous silhouette of Mallorca through the heat haze. It was a magical moment for me. *Barrabas* and I had travelled our first steps together. Passing the Canal de Mallorca with winds gusting to Force 5, *Barrabas*'s speed over the ground nudged 11 knots. I was amazed. There are no currents in the Mediterranean so her speed was purely wind-driven without assistance.

On approach to Gibraltar, *Barrabas* sailed into the 'Vendiale', a seasonal westerly wind. The sea state became agitated, with steep, breaking water, the first heavy weather we had encountered, but *Barrabas* stayed composed. I was quickly developing a keen sense of the boat and getting a measure of her mood.

'How does she sail?' I'd asked Bernard at our first meeting.

'Treat her well and she will behave. Treat her badly and she will bite!' he'd replied, grinning.

We arrived at Marina Bay, Gibraltar, to refuel, re-provision and get our laundry done. I could see that Nick was tired. A decent night's sleep in port would do us both good. We slipped out of the marina the next day, then anchored off Algeciras to await the tide that would carry us through the narrow strait between Spain and North Africa.

The weather turned foul off Cape Saint Vincent, Portugal's southwestern corner. Force 8 winds ripped around the headland, churning the seas to white water. *Barrabas* stayed steady and solid under shortened sail, not rising to the temptation to ride high over the waves and slam her bows. We trundled up the Portuguese coast in light winds, mostly under engine. It meant another refuelling stop, and south of Cape Finisterre and with no charts, we tentatively put into Camarinas. It was a beautiful spot, an enclosed bay surrounded by verdant, forested slopes dotted with white sandy beaches.

We moored up at the Camarinas Club Nautico, eventually locating the yacht club manager, Carmen Rodriguez. I bought two Cokes and noticed her take what looked like a crème caramel out of the oven. Speaking in halting French, I joked that this was our lunch. Carmen grinned, placed chicken curry and rice in front of Nick and myself, followed by the dessert, which turned out to be a delicious cheesecake.

As we went past Cape Finisterre, light following winds provided an opportunity to see how *Barrabas* performed under spinnaker, but ominously we were picking up radio warnings of a Force 10 storm moving into the area. Barometric pressure began falling and by the early hours of Friday 9th April, winds had accelerated to Force 9. Nick had been hand-steering since 2am – five hours by the time I came on watch at 7am. I could sense immediately that *Barrabas* was overpowered. Nick was screaming through the wind that he had almost broached twice.

'Heave-to now,' I yelled.

'Too dangerous!'

I yelled at him again to gybe the boat. 'Do it now!'

Barrabas came round beautifully, the sails crossing the deck, opposing the force of the rudder turned in the opposite direction and she stopped amongst the seas breaking all around us. Amidst the fury of the storm, *Barrabas* was an oasis of calm. Nick lashed the helm and we quickly shortened sail.

At 4pm, we raised the storm staysail. As night fell with no let-up, I decided to run a 30-minute watch system to combat fatigue. What an introduction to the boat's ability to handle rough weather! She behaved magnificently, never slamming her bows on the big waves. The storm eventually blew itself out by the following morning. I ordered Nick below to rest. Ten minutes later he appeared at the companionway looking sheepish.

'I've blocked the bloody head!'

I grinned at him. 'It'll be dirty work.'

He spent 20 minutes slopping out the toilet into a bucket. A wave hit the boat, heeling her over. A barrage of cursing came from below. The bucket, full of effluent, had slid away from Nick, hit an exposed frame and spilt its contents all over the floor and into the bilges. He gamely spent the next two hours cleaning up, sluicing out, washing floorboards, filling and evacuating the bilges while I steered through the aftermath of the storm. The heads had blocked because he'd used it without water in the bowl. I decided to take the pump apart myself and learn the system. Nick had done enough. It took me another hour.

Through our various trials, my primary concern with *Barrabas* was her inability to sail close to the wind. That limitation could affect our attempt at Cape Horn with the wind coming at us in monstrous conditions. It was a concern that would sit and fester for the next 10 months.

In the early morning of Monday 11th April, off Ile D'Ouessant, close to the northwestern corner of France, the engine suddenly died. During my watch from 2 to 7am, I had monitored the fuel situation, revising my consumption estimate from 3 litres per hour to 2.5 litres per hour. Instead of refuelling the tank at 6am, I'd decided to leave it until after breakfast. There was no wind and the tide was taking us towards the rocks near the coast.

I broke out the reserve fuel, bled the engine to rid the fuel system of any trapped air and restarted the engine. It gunned and died. After five attempts, the engine was refusing to start. We were now only half a mile from the treacherous rocks of Ile D'Ouessant.

Nick kept watch while I went below to strip the fuel system. A blockage in the fuel feeder pipe from the tank was obstructing fuel flow. I blew it back, taking in a mouthful of diesel in the process but cleared the blockage. This was our last chance to get the engine started otherwise I would be forced to call for help. The engine fired first time, even though when I pushed the throttle forward, increasing power to 1,800rpm, she began to sputter and complain. It had been a narrow escape. While Nick helmed, I sat at the chart table, designing a more robust fuel system – more filters and a secondary fuel tank – to ensure that I didn't lose the engine like that again.

That night, in dense fog, we crossed the shipping lanes of the English Channel, navigating with radar. At one point, 17 ships were within three miles of our position.

At dawn, the English coast was a welcome sight; peaceful Dorset countryside rolling down to a still and languid sea. I wondered what it would feel like to see the English coast at the end of a circumnavigation and for a moment, I dreamed. After a brief stop in Weymouth to take on more fuel, we made it into Cowes at 2am on Thursday 14th April and picked up a mooring buoy at the entrance to the Medina River, the same buoy that

Mike had asked me to pick up during the Yachtmaster examination. After breakfast the next morning, I motored *Barrabas* downriver and tied up at the UKSA.

My first voyage on *Barrabas* had ended after 2,000 miles. It had been quite an undertaking, but I never really stopped to think about that. It was only afterwards that I realised the passage had really been a trial: a crash course in heavy weather tactics, emergency reefing drills, systems maintenance and radar navigation in the hardest school of all – the open sea.

* * *

The *Oxford Mail* published an article about my upcoming voyage while I was sailing *Barrabas* back from France. BBC Radio Oxford picked up the story. Louise drove me to the studio for an interview with Anne Diamond, once a national TV presenter and now hosting the breakfast show. The follow-on was that BBC regional TV wanted to send a film crew to the boat. Although media attention was beginning to build, I still had no sponsorship funding.

With the Alpha Global Expedition unexpectedly launched in the media, the immediate necessity was to organise an expedition website. I wanted the expedition to benefit charity so that the voyage wasn't solely, and selfishly, serving my own personal aspiration. I nominated two charities – Save the Children and the Oxford Children's Hospital – one a global organisation to reflect the global nature of the voyage and the other, an important paediatric centre close to where I lived near Oxford.

Generate had been busy with the list of suppliers I'd provided. There were expressions of interest from Hydrovane, DMSTech and GUL. I spoke to all three companies and arranged to drive down to the GUL factory in Cornwall to pick up sail clothing in anticipation of the BBC film crew.

Tuesday 26th April turned out to be a lovely day, perfect for the long drive down to GUL's offices. En route, I pulled off the M5 motorway for coffee and sandwiches. I was sitting in the car putting sugar in coffee and unwrapping food when I was startled by a loud rap on the window. A woman in her sixties stood by the driver's door. I assessed her quickly – peroxide blonde hair, bad teeth, threadbare clothing – but she radiated a certain energy. Perhaps she just wanted directions.

The engine was off so the electric windows weren't working. I opened the door.

Her eyes were a piercing blue. 'You're going to live to 92,' she said without hesitation.

The woman had my attention. 'And..?' I asked.

'You'll be in good health all the way through – perhaps a little illness at the end.' The woman paused. 'D'you mind talking to a gipsy?'

'Not at all,' I said, shaking my head.

The woman took hold of my right hand in her left and her right index finger began an intricate dance around my palm. 'You have two sons, they're both healthy and they'll both do well.'

I didn't say anything, giving her no clue. I wasn't wearing a wedding ring.

'This journey you're planning – it'll be the best thing you'll ever do.'

That stunned me.

The woman went on. 'You're worried about something?'

'Lots of things – money mostly.'

Her finger went back to its dance. 'You'll be getting some money.' The woman searched skywards for a moment. 'In August.'

'How much?' I was trying hard to keep my tongue from my cheek.

The woman thought for a moment. '£28,000,' she said and began to turn away.

'Wait a sec.' I scrabbled in my pocket, found a ten-pound note and pressed it into her hand. I could ill afford it, but something compelled me. The woman looked at me for a moment, not smiling, then turned and wandered away among the parked cars. More than three months later, I would have reason to think of the woman again.

I carried on to the GUL factory. In the factory shop, I tried on oilskins and mid-layers and came away with two sets of each that GUL agreed to sponsor.

* * *

Marine Computing International, Tim Thornton's company, had imploded. A client had reneged, bringing about a cash crisis for the small firm and, in the aftermath, Tim had lost his three staff to other job offers. I drove to the MCI office on a small industrial estate near Southampton to find Tim sitting among a chaos of strewn papers and abandoned desks. Despite his personal disaster, Tim's enthusiasm for the Alpha Global Expedition was undisguised. As a yachtsman, meteorologist and technophile, his expertise was obvious. We discussed the specifications for the weather and communications systems and I left Tim to design the system architecture.

By mid-May, it was time to go to work on *Barrabas*. The Medina Yard on the Isle of Wight, located just up-river from the UKSA, was owned by Sir Peter Harrison, the money behind Team GB which had challenged for the America's Cup in Auckland in 2003. Craig Nutter, a former Team GB crewmember, managed the yard. Craig did what he could to accommodate my limited budget. With *Barrabas* safely in her cradle, I spent nine hours with the jet-wash cleaning her undersides (a yard record!). I enjoyed being there – the people, the place and the atmosphere; and Cowes, the centre of the British yachting scene, was home to every imaginable boating service and supplier.

My first stop was Spencer Rigging, the oldest established riggers on the island. I'd decided to replace all the standing rigging – the array of steel wire stays that support the mast. Mark Spencer agreed 'to do something' on price and promised to get Ray Field, his most experienced rigger, to do the work. The rigging loft was like a stage set, harking back to the days of square-riggers with its tarred wooden floors and smell of caulk. As a modern-day addendum, centre-fold spreads papered almost every square inch of wall space.

Richard Pierrepont of RHP Marine was next on my list. His services company could provide battery installation and electrics as well carrying out the modifications to the engine fuel system I had designed during the trip back from France.

Louise telephoned me on Friday 20th May.

'I was with Bob and Tina at their new art gallery in Thame and we came up with a publicity idea.'

I was curious. Tina Hadley was a professional photographer whom we'd commissioned for our wedding and the boys' christenings.

'I talked to Bob and suggested that he sponsor the AGX [Alpha Global Expedition] by donating a limited-edition print as a raffle prize for people donating to the AGX charities with £5 or more. Local press are interested. On the back of it, the gallery gets good exposure. What do you think?'

'I think it's a great idea,' I said, feeling elation far in excess of the benefits of a little local publicity. Was Louise becoming 'engaged' in the expedition? She had never before referred to the voyage as the 'AGX'.

We talked about the boys' upcoming half-term break and agreed for the three of them to come to Cowes.

Louise and the boys arrived on Friday 27th May. We spent a wonderful time together, taking the boys to the beach, going for walks along the seafront and visits to arts and crafts centres, riding on the steam railway and eating bowls of moules mariniere at a beachside restaurant at St Helen's. At the weekend, we visited Sam and Debbie Laidlaw at their holiday home in Bembridge. Sam took a real interest in the expedition, driving over to Medina Yard to have a look at *Barrabas*.

It was a great few days and a chance for me to take my mind off the daunting amount of work that I needed to complete on *Barrabas*. Antifouling turned into a big job. Layers of epoxy primer, tie-coats and antifouling added and removed unequally over the years had left *Barrabas*'s hull surface uneven below the waterline. The only way to get the paint off was to sandblast the hull using small-bore Olivine grit. The problem was that if I took the hull back to bare metal, I'd need more paint than I'd planned. I spoke to Darren Gittins at Blake Paints. Darren spoke to his technical department and came back with a spec for stainless steel – three layers of epoxy primer, a tie-coat and two coats of antifoul. He reduced the price on the epoxy, provided the antifoul at no charge and agreed to get the paint to the yard in time for the blasting.

Generate had been in touch with Kemp Sails. On Friday 3rd June, I left a message for Matt Atkins, the general manager. Matt phoned me back and I gave him the link to the test server to have a look at the expedition website that had just come on-stream. He consulted with Rob Kemp and they came back with the offer to sponsor the sails for the AGX. It was fantastic news. Matt told me the AGX was exactly the kind of project to promote Kemp within their prime market of cruising rather than racing sails.

Barrabas's new paint job was finished by mid-June. Her undersides were now beautifully smooth. I hand-painted a white bootstrap between the maroon antifoul and the gleaming bare metal of her sides.

Towards the end of June, the twin pressures of time and financial constraints were mounting. If I was going to make the departure date in October, I was going to have to forego a lot of the work I wanted to do – no back-up generator, no watertight forward bulkhead, no new handrails welded on deck, no new running rigging organisers to take all lines back to the cockpit. Even without these items, I was close to my bank debt limit. My mood plummeted. Everything seemed to take on massive proportions, even the tiniest jobs. Through it all, I kept repeating to myself, '*I have to deal with this – nothing is a problem! It's all about attitude.*' I was becoming psychologically weakened, vulnerable to outside influences, the opinions of others who did not see the expedition from a similar perspective. People are generally well intentioned, but often blind to the point of view of others. The battle to stay true to myself became a constant and wearying skirmish.

At the UKSA, I introduced myself to Paul Burnett, who taught the advanced engineering course. We discussed the problem I'd experienced with the blocked fuel line off Ile D'Ouessant. Paul identified the line filter in the uplift pump as the probable reason why the engine was struggling at higher revs.

Water is heavier than diesel. In a diesel tank, a film of water can collect at the bottom either from condensation or water contamination in the fuel. A certain type of bacteria or 'diesel bug' thrives in this environment, proliferating to form a black sludge. If this sludge gets into a fuel system, it can block fuel lines, clog filters and incapacitate injectors. This sludge had caused the problem on *Barrabas*. I needed a more robust system to ensure that fuel reaching the injectors was clean. The Arctic phase was uppermost in my mind. *Barrabas* would probably be under engine for significant stretches because of light winds and drifting ice.

The system I'd designed en route back from France was to fit two Racor filters, each capable of filtering 500 litres per hour, the first situated between the main tank and a new 'day tank' and the second between the 'day tank' and the engine. A third filter, already on the engine, would make a final clean before fuel reached the injectors. An additional advantage was that a day tank increased my fuel capacity by 80 litres.

I was looking for an expert's opinion on the filter/day tank idea and Paul thought it excellent. Craig agreed that it sounded like a plan.

Back on *Barrabas*, I checked the uplift pump as Paul had recommended (a small pump on the engine that pulls fuel from source and pushes it towards the injectors). Just as Paul had predicted, there was a level teaspoon of black sludge in the filter.

I finally met Rob Kemp and Matt Atkins when they sailed to Cowes to compete in the Round-the-Island race.

'What did you have in mind for the sails?' Matt asked.

'You know my route, Cape Horn and the Arctic?'

Matt nodded.

'In a nutshell, the sails have got to be bulletproof, heavily reinforced at the tacks, clews and heads (the three points of any triangular-shaped sail) and reinforced reefing cringles.'

'So, all attachment points.'

'Yes. Also the mainsail should have four reefs instead of the usual three so I can use the fourth reef instead of a separate storm trysail.'

We agreed the design details and Rob and Matt went to work measuring up for several hours.

I had a number of transatlantic telephone conversations with John Curry in Vancouver, a former accountant who had bought Hydrovane, originally a British company whose manufacturing base was still in England. Hydrovane was, in my opinion and in the opinion of others (including a few round-the-world yachtsmen), the best self-steering system in the world. John agreed to sponsor the AGX.

The Hydrovane arrived at the UKSA for collection in early July, packed into seven wooden crates. I took great care with the Hydrovane. Vertical and horizontal alignments had to be true, otherwise the resultant forces of wind and water acting on the vane and rudder would be unbalanced. A single lower bracket fixed on the underside of the sugar scoop and an 'A' bracket coming off the transom supported the shaft. The two stainless steel tubular bars of the 'A' frame were too long and needed trimming. With a hacksaw, it would have been an hour of sweat. I decided on a simpler approach. Craig introduced me to a self-employed welder named Michael Ferguson. Fergie (as everyone knew him) cut the stays to length. I asked him about other welding and metalwork that I needed done, not least boring out the thru-hulls to take the instrument transducers. He came to the yard that afternoon to rim them out.

A crucial piece of equipment arrived from Katadyn in Switzerland – the water-maker. I fitted the unit in the forward part of the hull, making use of two defunct thru-hull fittings, which had once been plumbed to a toilet.

By mid-July with so much still to do, my major worry was lack of time alone with *Barrabas* on the water. Perhaps the delivery trip from Montpellier would be the only sea trial I would have.

To make space for the day tank, I removed the old diesel stove heater. For heating, I fitted an Eberspacher system, running one of the hot-air outlets into the portside forward cabin locker to use as a drying cupboard. (On the voyage, the drying cupboard worked superbly – almost as effective as a domestic tumble dryer.)

The constant worry about money, combined with the long hours I was putting in on *Barrabas*, eventually took their toll and I went down with a severe bout of 'flu. Generate was working on promoting a new marketing initiative with Timberland and had entered my name as a contender for the inaugural Timberland scholarship. The award was not a scholarship per se but more a marketing initiative to promote the rugged nature of the brand's products. On Tuesday 19th July, I drove down to Timberland's HQ to meet the marketing team, struggling through the hour-long meeting with a thundering headache and a sore throat. Afterwards, I drove home and collapsed into bed with a soaring temperature.

Early on Wednesday morning, I was in the car again driving to Romsey in Hampshire to pick up the five new American Lifeline AGM batteries, which DMS Technologies' had agreed to sponsor. These were powerful batteries, each of 210 amp/hour capacity, one for engine start and the other four to provide power to the rest of the boat – the house bank.

Still feeling the after-effects of the 'flu, I met Ray Field, who came to the boat with the new standing rigging. I had been in two minds about replacing it but confirmation that I had made the right decision came when we dropped the forestay and found severe wear at the masthead attachment. Ray figured that the forestay was close to parting. If it had failed at sea, the mast could have come down!

Ever since the art raffle, which had been modestly successful, Louise had been taking a greater interest in the project and had begun contacting the national and sailing media. We decided to take a short break in Dorset with the boys. We set off on Monday 25th July and spent an afternoon on Studland Beach until Benji soaked himself in the freezing sea and we had to go back to the B&B. The weather was awful, cold and overcast. On Tuesday, we all went to a small chocolate factory then onto Lulworth Castle. The weather deteriorated to constant rain, but through the gloom came some outstanding news: I had won the Timberland scholarship and was being awarded £30,000! It had come just in time. My last bank statement showed I was down to my last £100. Without the scholarship, I would have been forced either to beg for more money from the bank, delay departure while I figured another way to raise funds, or abandon the expedition altogether.

By the end of July, I was through the bulk of the heavy work and, after more than two months ashore, I re-launched *Barrabas* on Saturday 31st July, sailing across the Solent and up Southampton Water to Shamrock Quay. A company of electronic engineers recommended by Tim were on stand-by to fit the navigation and communications systems.

While this work was going on, I re-covered the cuddy with exterior-grade clear polycarbonate sheets, moulding the bends and curves using a hot air gun.

* * *

Cowes Week is the biggest regatta in the world. The island was inundated with boats, sailors and spectators. I was pleased to be on the mainland, but Timberland reckoned Cowes Week (where the company had a stand) presented a good opportunity for a full press launch of the Alpha Global Expedition.

On Thursday 4th August, Louise and I went over to Cowes. The whole experience was surreal. The Alpha Global Expedition still seemed like no more than an 'idea', a formless dream. When we arrived in Cowes, the marketing manager, Niamh Lyon, whisked me off to the Timberland store and kitted me out with new clothing. Louise, to her delight, got a new pair of shoes. Timberland's PR agency had lined up a series of interviews – *Isle of Wight County Press*, Cowes Radio, ITV Meridian, *Yachting World*, Isle of Wight Radio and Solent TV.

At 4pm, Niamh presented me with a 'giant' cheque for £30,000 in front of a large crowd. In my mind's eye, I could clearly see the lined face of a woman with a piercing blue gaze who had read my palm in a motorway car park.

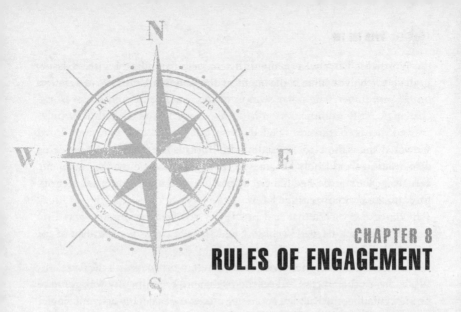

CHAPTER 8
RULES OF ENGAGEMENT

BY MID-AUGUST, the end of the refit was in sight. Tim came down to *Barrabas* to install the software onto the purpose-made computer and my laptop that would act as a back-up. I stripped out the fore cabin and built in a workshop. This space, where I could store tools and spare parts, would be useful, not only from an organisational perspective but as an area where I could drill, saw, file and fix things without messing up other parts of the cabin. I fitted a small vice onto the workbench and finials for my toolboxes to keep them in place. I also read *Two Against Cape Horn* by Hal Roth. Roth's account of his time in the Cape Horn area did nothing to quell my fears.

By the end of August, *Barrabas* was back at the Medina Yard. Fergie welded new block mounts at the base of the mast and fitted the storm bars that I'd designed to prevent the hatches being ripped off if *Barrabas* rolled in big seas.

During the early part of September, I snagged the boat, fixing a constant stream of niggly problems. Benji spent some time with me on board *Barrabas*, driving up and down the Hamble River. The sight of a small boy at the helm of a heavy steel boat seemed to amuse everyone who passed. By 8th September, the refit was finished except for the fitting of the new sails.

Permission from the Russian government to sail in their Arctic territorial waters along the Northern Sea Route (NSR – previously called the Northeast Passage) remained the major outstanding logistical issue. I wrote to the consular department at the Russian Embassy in London on 6th September. The polar section of the route presented an awesome challenge. NSR Administration had only ever allowed a handful of fully-crewed yachts to transit. I needed a visa, but I could only get one if I had special dispensation to be sailing in Russia's territorial waters. This dispensation would only be granted if various government departments agreed, including the Federal Security Bureau, Russia's internal security force, formerly known as the KGB.

One of the yachts that had previously received permission was Eric Brossier's French-flagged *Vagabond*, which made an eastward transit of the NSR in 2002.

I emailed Eric to get his advice on how best to proceed with the Russians. While these other yachts had set the precedent, the difficulty was going to be in persuading the Russian authorities to let me make my attempt single-handed, without an ice pilot on board, a mandatory requirement for every vessel, regardless of size, sailing the NSR. But if I carried an ice pilot, I would effectively be sacrificing my single-handed status.

Eric's response shocked me: *'Hi Adrian… we needed permission from Russian government to sail the NEP (Northeast Passage) in 2002. It took me three years to get it… Good luck, Eric Brossier.'*

The unpredictable nature of the North Polar ice, its extent and drift, exposed any logistical planning to uncertainty. I exchanged correspondence with Lars Kaleschke at the University of Bremen's Institute of Environmental Physics. Lars wrote to me in September: *'The sea ice coverage has a high inter-annual variability and the pattern is hard to predict if not impossible… permission of the Russian administration could be the most uncertain factor…'*

The lateness of my application to the Russian government would prove a serious error.

Barrabas was moored at Port Hamble Marina. On 12th September, I set off for Poole, where Matt and Rob, driving from the Kemp sail loft in Wareham, met me to fit the new sails. A BBC film crew arrived in the afternoon and, with Matt on board, we took *Barrabas* out onto the water to try out the sails.

* * *

During the preceding few weeks, Louise had become increasingly involved with the expedition, finding supply sponsors and having fantastic success:

Nivea, Ecover, Heinz, Cadbury, Mornflake, Clipper and Creative (MP3s) had all agreed to supply products. The Alpha Global Expedition seemed to be gaining momentum, an energy drawing support from both companies and individuals.

It was Thursday 20th September when Louise announced, 'I've made a decision.'

I was standing in the hallway of her house. 'Which is?'

She paused, gathered herself and said, 'I'm going to be the expedition manager.'

I was overwhelmed and hugely, massively relieved. I wanted to fling my arms around her, but instead I said, 'It'll be a lot of work.'

'Who else is going to do it? Someone has to manage the website, look after the charities, deal with sponsors and probably a host of other things we haven't thought of.'

'I agree. Thank you.' What more could I say?

'I have some rules.'

I frowned but stayed quiet.

'When it comes to PR, what I say goes. If there is water involved, you deal with it. In other words, you sail the boat, I'll do everything else. Agreed?'

'Agreed.'

'Right,' she said, 'the next job is to sort out a weapon and get a firearms licence.'

The risk of piracy attacks was a real danger to small boats passing close inshore along the coasts of West Africa and Brazil. I would be sailing through both these areas. I'd researched the incidence of pirate attacks on small boats. Yachts are soft targets: low freeboards and unarmed crews usually carrying valuables on board: money, jewellery, passports. Another risk would come from polar bears if *Barrabas* ever got stuck in ice.

'And we should announce a departure date.'

We decided on 18th October, Gabriel's birthday. It would have been our eighth wedding anniversary.

I was still waiting for two pieces of equipment from the United States. Ever since the harrowing disasters in the 1979 Fastnet race (15 fatalities) and the 1998 Sydney to Hobart race (six fatalities) when massively powerful weather systems wreaked havoc with the race fleets, discussion had ranged widely about the best way to stabilise a small boat in survival conditions. After months of research on the merits and disadvantages of deploying various types of drogue from the stern and parachute anchors from the bow, I settled on a Jordan Series Drogue (JSD). Designed by Donald Jordan, an aeronautical engineer and yachtsman and developed in conjunction with the US Coastguard, independent research concluded that if all the boats in the '79 Fastnet and '98 Sydney-Hobart had been equipped with JSDs fewer lives would have been lost

I contacted Don Jordan for his opinion on parachute anchors, first used by American fishermen after the Second World War. Surplus parachutes, deployed from the bows of the trawlers and coastal fishing boats, had the effect of slowing the boats in big seas. The problem was, the anchors 'snatched' when they inflated (with water), exerting huge loads on the attachment points.

Don Jordan sent me an email on Sunday 18th September: '*I am now 90 and no longer answer questions. However, this is an emergency. YOU MUST carry the drogue on this wonderful adventure. The chute is a technical monstrosity. It has 30 times the drag of the drogue and acts like a mooring on the bottom. In a breaking wave strike, it would develop loads that no gear could stand. I wish you well. Don.*'

As a result, Dave Pelissier of ACE Sailmakers in Maine was making a JSD for *Barrabas*, tailored specifically for her displacement.

I also wanted a second piece of critical survival gear and I was not going to leave until I had it – a solid, unsinkable lifeboat (in addition to the inflatable life raft already on *Barrabas*) small enough to stow on the foredeck, with oars, a collapsible sailing rig and watertight stowage compartments for emergency provisions and additional survival kit. After weeks of searching, I couldn't find anything in the UK. In America, David Hulbert had designed the Portland Pudgy. I contacted him. Development of the Portland Pudgy was at the end of the prototype stage and not yet in production. I explained my situation. David agreed to manufacture a one-off specifically for *Barrabas*.

But how were we going to get the lifeboat to England? Louise contacted DHL and the company not only offered to airfreight the survival craft from the US but act as the expedition's official courier. Over the coming months, DHL would prove to be an invaluable sponsor, responding to rapidly changing situations with cheerful efficiency.

Louise came up with a sparkling idea – obvious really, but then all the best ideas are. As I was raising money for the Oxford Children's Hospital, could the hospital supply the medical kit? She put the idea to Janet Sprake, Head of Fundraising, who came up trumps. David Skinner, Head of Accident & Emergency medicine at Oxford's John Radcliffe Hospital, agreed to put the kit together, including prescription antibiotics and surgical equipment and to be my shore-side medical liaison (David was also a keen sailor and kept his boat in Chichester). The offer included access to his full team, which ran a 24-hour rota and would be available to me if ever I needed advice or, worse, needed to perform any surgical procedures on myself.

The final preparations were frenetic. On 1st October, my 45th birthday, Louise and I took time out and spent the day with the boys at Legoland. Fergie was busy fabricating stainless steel cages to house additional 20-litre fuel cans on *Barrabas*'s aft deck. I finally found an underwater collision repair kit from Alan Molyneaux, whose company supplied the Royal Navy. Barton Marine came on board as a supplier with new blocks for all the running rigging, and Martin Amy at Kelvin Hughes, the country's largest marine chart supplier, was busy collating my chart portfolio, including Russian charts sourced from the Russian Hydrographic Office in Moscow, covering the Northern Sea route.

Sam Laidlaw called in early October. As former vice-president of Chevron Texaco Oil and now Centrica's chief executive, Sam's contacts included people in the high echelons of Russian business and heavyweight political figures in Moscow. He extended an open invitation – call if we needed any introductions. Despite my repeated letters, emails and calls to the Russian Embassy in Kensington Palace Gardens, I hadn't received any response. After Eric Brossier's comments, any expeditious route through the bureaucratic maze was welcome. I emailed Sam to say that we'd give the Russians a little more time but, more likely than not, I would take him up on his offer.

By the second week of October, Louise's garage was stacked with provisions: tinned fruit and meat, cooking oil, dried pasta, chocolate, vitamins and supplements, sauces and spices, porridge oats, rice, biscuits and ready mixed bread flour. Clipper had also supplied organic tea (bags), coffee and drinking chocolate. Running out of tea and coffee would be disastrous. I drank prodigious amounts of the stuff but I can't drink either without milk. I bought 60 litres of long-life milk and 60 tins of Carnation evaporated milk. I began ferrying these supplies to Port Hamble, storing them around *Barrabas* in cupboards, lockers and beneath the cabin floorboards.

Time slipped away. Job lists seemed to grow ever longer. Louise and I were exhausted and, after a long discussion, we decided to defer departure to 28th October. Even with the 10-day postponement, it was still a race to get a tick against each item on my final checklist.

I visited Doug Florent at the Oxford Gun Club on Monday 10th October. Doug recommended a pump action shotgun with a plastic stock to limit seawater damage. That afternoon, back at Louise's house, Brian Brewster, the Thames Valley Police Firearms Officer, stopped by to interview me and fill out the various documents I'd need for a firearms licence. While we were form-filling, the JSD arrived from Maine.

The next day, I was back on board *Barrabas* with Fergie to weld the fuel cages on the aft deck and the transom.

Sky News contacted Louise the following day, 12th October, after she'd issued a press release about the new start date. They wanted to shoot a pre-departure interview.

Tim Thornton gave me a series of tutorials on the computer on board *Barrabas*. Afterwards I went back to Louise's house, loaded up the car with more supplies then rushed back to *Barrabas* to meet up with Dick Everitt from *Practical Boat Owner*, who was planning a big spread in the magazine.

Meanwhile, Louise was busy sourcing fifty 20-litre fuel cans to give me an extra 1,000-litre capacity. She eventually got them at trade price.

On Saturday 15th October, the 'Pudgy' emergency dinghy was air-freighted to the UK from Maine and delivered to *Barrabas* at Port Hamble. I collected my charts and almanacs from Martin Amy at Kelvin Hughes in Southampton, then raced back to Port Hamble in time to meet the DHL lorry. Steve Walker, one of DHL's managers, the driver and I broke open the crate. The small lifeboat was bright orange and weighed 70kg and, when we positioned it on *Barrabas*'s foredeck, it fitted perfectly! The final delivery came from Marlow Ropes and I spent the remainder of the afternoon replacing most of the running rigging.

On 18th October, I again wrote to the Russian Embassy in London, hoping for some indication that my application to sail the NSR was at least being considered by the relevant departments in Moscow.

The UKSA had agreed to supply my fuel at cost. So, on Friday 21st October, Fergie brought his van over from the Isle of Wight, collected the new fuel cans, took them back to the island, filled them and returned them to Port Hamble for loading. With *Barrabas* laden down with an extra tonne of fuel, I drove back to Oxford and met Louise at the BBC Radio Oxford studios for a live link-up with Johnnie Walker's 'Drive Time' show on BBC Radio 2. I was shown into a small studio room, hooked up to mikes and headphones, then left on my own. I was dirty from working on *Barrabas* all day. 'Wow,' I thought to myself, 'a year ago, the Alpha Global Expedition was just an idea in my head. Now I'm about to talk to eight million people!'

Louise was suffering from a severe bout of 'flu, the consequence, I surmised, of exhaustion and stress. She soldiered on, accompanying me to John Radcliffe Hospital the following day to pick up the medical kit from David Skinner. I sat with David in a treatment room for 20 minutes while he explained the contents: painkillers, motion sickness tablets, antibiotics, fracture casts, morphine, anaesthetics, tissue adhesive and surgical instruments.

* * *

John Reed, the secretary of the World Sailing Speed Record Council (WSSRC), visited Louise and me on board.

It was Louise's idea to have my voyage monitored in some official capacity. I'd never heard of the WSSRC. I tended to baulk at officialdom and the WSSRC sounded exactly like the type of bureaucratic organisation I'd spent my life trying to avoid.

'So, John,' I said as he clambered aboard, 'what do I need to do to comply with your rules? For that matter, what are your rules?'

I was expecting him to produce a checklist and spend a couple of hours going over *Barrabas* while firing questions at me. At the very least, I was expecting to be asked to sign a declaration that my logbooks would accurately reflect any and all events, actions and occurrences on the voyage. To me, one critical aspect of any verification procedure would be to record the number of hours on the engine (to check against the number of engine hours recorded at the end of the voyage and, if different, for it to then be incumbent on the sailor to satisfactorily explain that difference). I was also expecting fuel samples to be taken for subsequent comparison with fuel samples taken after the voyage to determine whether additional fuel had been shipped during the passage.

John made a cursory examination of the cockpit and briefly looked at the winches to ensure they were 'manually operated and not electrically powered.'

'Is that it?' I asked, trying to hide my surprise.

'Yes.'

'Don't you want to see below?'

'Not necessary.' Then, with a totally straight face, he said, 'There's a fee for the WSSRC – £1,500. You can pay by cheque or cash.' He'd been on my boat for less than 10 minutes!

Louise and I looked at each other, then she laughed out loud. I was incredulous. Louise couldn't see his face. I could and I could tell he wasn't joking. I batted the issue aside. 'Let's forget about any fee for the moment. What exactly are your rules?'

John Reed talked for several minutes, then looked at me expectantly.

'So, if I've got this right,' I said, 'any form of assistance that includes going into port renders me no longer single-handed?'

'That's right. You can anchor, but you can't tie up to a structure connected to the land.'

'And if I hail a passing ship and they sling a pint of milk over the side which I then retrieve…'

'You're assisted and therefore no longer single-handed.'

'But if I have a problem with the engine, for example, and I need the engine to charge the batteries and I need the batteries to power navigation instruments and communications like the satellite phone for safety purposes, can I call an engineer and get the engineer to tell me how to fix the engine?'

'That's fine.'

'That's *not* assistance?'

'No.'

I was flummoxed.

'So, according to the WSSRC, Joshua Slocum and Sir Francis Chichester were not single-handed?'

'No.'

'Even though at all times while their vessels were underway, actually creating their tracks around the world and they were the only ones on board, you're telling me that they were not, in fact, single-handed?'

'That's correct.'

There had been no mention of the antipodal principle. When I asked him about it, he looked perplexed. I explained what antipodal points were and their relevance in shaping a vessel's track to a great circle.

'Are you saying that the Vendée and other such round-the-world races don't comply with the antipodal rule?'

John shook his head. 'No, but those races are run according to our rules.'

'So, what about non-racing events like mine?'

'Well, they're difficult to monitor.'

'So how do you monitor them?'

'We just apply our rules.'

'But those are race rules.'

'Those are the rules.'

I was amazed. 'So, if I've got this right, the only way, according to your rules, that a single-handed circumnavigator can be a single-handed circumnavigator is if he or she sails non-stop. In doing so, there is no necessity to conform to the antipodal rule but they can take any type of assistance so long as it is not physical, in which case it doesn't count as assistance, even when that help might be the difference between a sailor being able to continue their voyage or having to abandon?'

To insist on rules that retrospectively voided the vast majority of recognised and generally accepted single-handed circumnavigations was akin, at best, to a badly tailored suit of clothes – ill-fitting – and, at worst, woefully inadequate. I also felt that to list record voyages, fastest and firsts, whether circumnavigations or otherwise, based on ability or willingness to pay, could not possibly be right.

Forget the WSSRC. I would sail based on common sense principles. I would start and finish at the same point; bisect every meridian of longitude; cross the equator twice in opposite directions; sail a minimum distance of 21,600 nautical miles and record at least one pair of antipodal points on

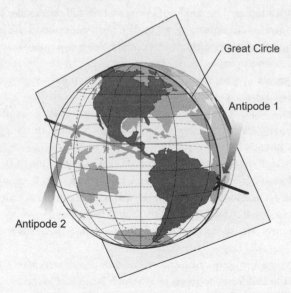

Any two points diametrically opposed on a Great Circle are antipodal to one another.

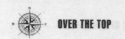

my track. Finally and crucially, I would be the only person on board while *Barrabas* created her track around the world.

* * *

With two days until departure, I collected my shotgun from the Oxford Gun Club. It had arrived that morning from Italy in tandem with my firearms licence from Thames Valley Police.

Despite repeated requests for an acknowledgement that my application to sail the NSR had been received at the Russian Embassy, I had still not heard back from the consular department.

I cannot remember too much of my last evening. Louise had booked the children and us into a B&B in Hamble. *Barrabas* was tugging gently at her mooring lines on the events quay at Port Hamble Marina. I stowed the gun and ammunition on board. There still seemed an infinite list of small jobs yet to complete but I dismissed them. I remembered once hearing someone say that if you waited until every last 'T' was crossed, every 'I' dotted, you'd never leave.

We had supper at a pub in the village. The atmosphere was warm and congenial. An open fire crackled, casting cosy orange light over thickly hewn wooden tables. The tinkle of conversation fell on me like warm rain but Louise and I were unusually silent. We both understood the magnitude of the voyage ahead but neither of us could quite grasp the reality of it.

I slept soundly enough. At 10am, we were at the boat. Press and television crews arrived, filming and interviewing me for two hours. What I really wanted to do was hug my children and slip quietly away. Louise had collected a five-day weather forecast from the marina office – southwesterly winds at Force 7 (wind speeds of 28–33 knots). It would be choppy, but no more than 'uncomfortable'.

Matt Atkins then stepped on deck to crew for me until I reached the start line. I kissed Benjamin and Gabriel, pressed my cheek against the soft skin of their faces, closed my eyes and breathed their scent deeply.

'I promise I will come home safely, boys,' I whispered.

I reluctantly released each of them. Louise stepped towards me. Nothing needed to be said. I hugged her hard.

I had only a few items of personal nostalgia onboard: two soft toys to symbolise the children – a green bear which Benji had loved as a baby and a red dog which Gabriel had barely let out of his sight. Louise had given me a Rolex Explorer II as a wedding present which whilst having an obvious practical application – I kept it on Universal Time Coordinated throughout the voyage – served as a reminder of all she was doing for me. Finally, I had my Heuer Autavia, bought in Hong Kong all those years before to keep me aware of the pledge I had made to myself and which I kept on local time as I made my way around the world.

We slipped the lines and *Barrabas* turned her bow away from the pontoon, taken on the ebb tide, the low rumble of her diesel engine walking her sedately towards the river mouth.

A TV crew from Sky News buzzed around *Barrabas* in a rigid inflatable boat (RIB). Someone yelled at me for a comment. I shouted back, 'So far, so good – two miles down, 30,000 to go!' With the mainsail up and the headsail reefed, Matt clambered onto the RIB. Moments later, *Barrabas*'s bow breached the start, a line between Calshot Spit buoy and Hillhead, and in that moment, 1.53:34pm on Friday 28th October 2005, decades of dreaming, years of planning and months of preparation condensed and crystallised into performance.

I was alone.

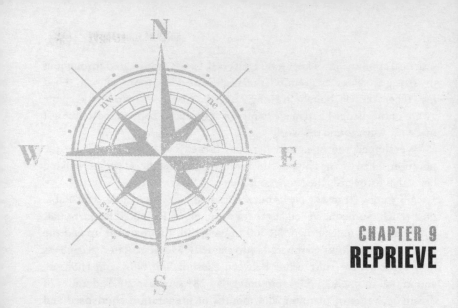

CHAPTER 9

REPRIEVE

I EASED *BARRABAS* tentatively eastwards through the Solent, past the sea forts and through an anchorage area where ships rode at their chains in the dwindling afternoon light. Hand steering, to prevent myself thinking about the children I had left behind and the months at sea ahead, I concentrated on weaving a zigzag course down the eastern side of the Isle of Wight. Close to the shipping lanes in which ferries plied between Portsmouth and France, I kept focused on tacking *Barrabas* into open water in a gathering southerly Force 6, eventually rounding Saint Catherine's Point on the south side of the Isle of Wight at 2am. With the wind holding from the south, I put *Barrabas* onto a beam reach and set the autopilot.

Below deck, the night light over the chart table cast a dull red glow while the lights of the island twinkled through the open companionway. I rested through the night, snatching a catnap now and then. By the murky dawn, the Isle of Wight had faded to a green-brown insinuation on the horizon. At 8.15am, I ate my first meal – porridge and fresh coffee – and for the first time in my life felt seasick.

The weather forecast spelled an ominous deterioration through the day to Force 8 conditions. A pang of concern skittered through me. Yesterday's forecast had specified Force 7 at worst. I shortened sail in winds gusting to 35 knots.

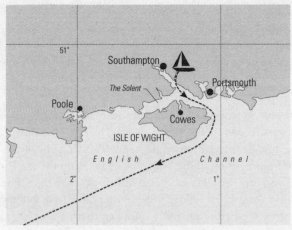

Barrabas heeled over, her side deck flush with the surface. The air vent for the freshwater tanks was on the starboard side deck. Worried that seawater might find its way into my 400-litre water supply, I fitted a length of hose to the vent pipe and lashed it to the guardrail but I was soon to discover that my remedial action had come too late.

Adrian: Saturday 29th October 2005[1]
I know I keep thanking you for all you have done so far. It would have been extraordinarily lonely not to have had you there in an active capacity. Whatever the eventual outcome, I am really proud to have come this far and your involvement means it is a shared experience rather than an episode that would otherwise have been locked in my head...

By early Sunday morning, even the most pessimistic forecast had not predicted conditions worsening to Storm Force 10. If these conditions had been on the five-day forecast Louise had given me on Friday, I would have delayed the start. At 4pm, I tacked to give myself sea room. Since my departure, I had gone 48 hours with little sleep.

---

1 All emails from me are to Louise unless otherwise specified.

I heard ships on the short-range VHF radio requesting anchoring to ride out the weather. Throughout the night I crabbed my way slowly, painfully, westwards and out of the Channel.

And then I was swept off the deck.

* * *

I grab at the boat, kicking to raise my body out of the water. By some miracle, the shock cord securing the spray dodger to the guardrail has slipped beneath the middle finger of my right hand. It's a thin line, 4mm diameter. The forward momentum of the boat quickly takes up the slack in my arm, tugging through my shoulder joint, hauling me through the water. The cord tensions. How long will it hold? Come to that, how long will my shoulder hold? The drag is twisting my body round so that I am facing backwards, my arm stretched up and out behind. The dislocation and surgery have left my right shoulder weakened. Either the shock cord or my shoulder is going to fail. No question. It is a matter of which will go first. Either way, it will be the end. I try pulling myself towards *Barrabas*, crooking my arm at the elbow to save the strain through the shoulder. The lactic acid burn comes quickly. It's no good. I have to straighten my arm and I feel the shoulder beginning to rip.

I am now level with the transom. Two brackets protrude beyond the edge of the aft deck. These brackets are designed to take the bridle lines for the drogue and capable of withstanding many tons of tensile force. If I can reach the starboard bracket, I will have a secure hold.

I lunge for the bracket, bringing my left arm out of the water. Kicking is hard and ineffectual in my waterlogged boots. I miss the bracket by the width of a hand. The effort yanks at my shoulder. It is going. At best, I have one more attempt. The shoulder will not tolerate any more. I am becoming exhausted, strength flowing out of my body. I repeat the manoeuvre, giving it everything I have. My fingertips brush past the bracket. Now I have nothing left. Cold is beginning to bite. My shoulder will fail at any moment. The shock cord has frayed, its outer sheath ruptured. A few rubber bands are all that are holding me.

Then I see the lanyard trailing through the water behind the Hydrovane's rudder. I can scarcely believe it – a lifeline! I stretch towards it with my left hand and close my fingers tightly round it. Then I release my tenuous, one-fingered grip on the shock cord. Pressure through my right shoulder evaporates. I actually laugh at the relief, swept aft of *Barrabas*, bodysurfing behind her. My right hand finds the lanyard. Now I have a two-handed grip.

Barrabas slows momentarily and I move past her transom, my body twisting round so that I am facing backwards once more. Quite suddenly, quite mysteriously, I feel a pressure against the back of my thighs, my buttocks, the small of my back. It is shaped and solid like an armchair. I slide sideways on this cushion of water, around the self-steering assembly towards the port side. I have been gathered up by another wave. Air trapped in my oilskins may be giving me added buoyancy. In an instant and with infinite gentleness, I am lifted and come to rest sitting on the sugar scoop while *Barrabas* bucks and lolls and surges on the angry sea.

I sit there disbelieving, uncomprehending, shivering.

Delivered.

* * *

Lack of sleep was beginning to melt time. The aftershock of my close call with death had left me exhausted. By the end of the day, I'd had enough. Winds had moderated slightly but were still blowing at Force 8 from the southwest, pinning me down in the western approaches of the English Channel.

Would it be better, safer, to find an anchorage, catch up on sleep and tidy the boat while I waited for a better weather window? I decided to make for the Helford River (Cornwall). My decision did not elicit any emotion from me – this was the situation. I had assessed conditions and forecasts from the perspective of safety and practicality. I was neither upset at the delay nor relieved at the prospect of rest. If I did experience any type of reaction, it was relief at my detachment. I was reassured that, despite suffering fatigue from long hours of sleeplessness and a near-death experience, my mind was functioning rationally and not emotionally.

* * *

Barrabas fretted at her mooring buoy. Close by, a collection of stone houses huddled together on the north bank of the Helford River.

I kept looking at the spot on the starboard side deck where I'd been standing when the wave swept me off the boat. I measured the distance between that spot and the aftermost part of the boat's structure: 1.83 metres, 2.5 metres if I included the full extent of my outstretched arm. The

GPS had recorded an average boat speed at the time of 5.2 knots, equivalent to 2.6 metres per second. From the moment I hit the water, the boat would have travelled past me and out of reach in less than one second. One second!

I looked at my hands and flexed my fingers, then felt the pulses at my wrists and wondered at the fact that I was still alive when I could so easily have been out there, floating face down in the sea.

* * *

I used my time in the Helford River to complete small jobs: stocking the lifeboat with food, a hand-held GPS and batteries, flares, manual water maker, a tarpaulin and mini-parachute anchor. I surveyed the contents of the 'grab bag' stowed at the base of the companionway steps and re-packed it with emergency medical supplies, water, signalling mirror, more batteries, a handheld VHF radio, knives, torch, a thermal survival aid and a SAS survival guide, waterproofed pencil and paper and matches dunked in hot wax to keep them dry. The 'grab bag' was a waterproof, plastic container with a screw top and a rope handle. All boats at sea have one, or should have, and, if there is an emergency where the crew has to take to the life raft, the bag is 'grabbed' on the way out by one of the crew.

Storm damage was relatively minor but I needed to reconstruct the restraining bars for the fuel cans in the fore cabin and rewire the solar panel array to bypass the solar charge regulator that had burnt out – short-circuited by seawater. On deck, I replaced the headsail sheets and rigged a new headsail furling line.

My main concern was water – seawater had contaminated all four water tanks. I pumped them dry. A few litres of bottled water would suffice until I was once again at sea and could operate the watermaker.

The newly installed Eberspacher diesel heater was not working. The diagnostics programme indicated a fuel issue. I stripped the fuel supply system working from the pump to the tank. With the standpipe out and the valve open, I could not blow through. Figuring a blockage, I fed a piece of wire up the standpipe – still no joy. I fed the wire through the valve end. There seemed to be an obstruction. I disconnected the valve, shoved the wire through until it hit the obstruction, jiggled it about and to my amazement a small brass screw popped out. It had orientated itself so the head was blocking the valve in the open position. How had it got there? A mystery; a demonstration of the law of boats – *if it can, it will.* After an hour reassembling the system, I switched the heater on, waiting anxiously but with rising euphoria as the cool air blowing onto my hand from the vent became warmer and then hot.

On shore, Louise had support from David Skinner as medical advisor and Tim Thornton to deal with technical issues. Ricardo Diniz now joined her, although Ricardo was in Lisbon. Some months later, Ian Johnstone-Bryden would join the team and go on to produce a number of detailed reports about the expedition for his website, Broadly Boats. For the first of these reports, Ian asked Ricardo to describe how he had become involved:

As a keen sailor, I am aware of most projects that happen around the world. One day I got a Google alert about somebody trying to do something new. Well, there aren't many 'new' projects left these days! What could he possibly be doing? Less than 90 people have sailed around the world alone. And here was a guy from the UK about to go for it vertically!

The hardest part in any of my voyages has been the trials and tribulations before departure day. Getting to any start line takes a lot of cash, huge determination and dedicated consistency. I admire people who have the guts to get over that stage, let alone manage the bit at sea. After a few more moments reading the website, I could sense the amateur side to everything and had even more respect for the venture. Adrian's ex-wife was expedition manager with a bunch of mates advising him as he went along. I took my hat off to all of them, especially to the ex-wife! I wrote her a quick email suggesting she ignore all emotions for now and let the expedition get into the flow, as all these projects do so much sooner than one would expect. Funnily enough, Louise thought the mail was for Adrian but replied anyway. We kept in touch. I provided some advice; in particular, meteorology.

I began providing more information, from suggestions to make their website more interesting to daily 'tips of the day' sent directly to Adrian's satellite phone. This must have been strange for Adrian. Suddenly, out of the blue and less than a week into his trip, a stranger from Portugal was almost co-managing his show. Above all, I just wanted to help in every way possible. I was not worried about Adrian or his boat. I knew he would get into the rhythm and the boat would take care of him. My major concern was the mother of two young boys and her mental stability managing all this. Louise is not a sailor. She has never been in this seat before.

* * *

On Monday 7th November, I dialled the number in Lisbon that Louise had emailed to me.

'Ricardo?'

'Yeah.'

'Adrian…'

'God… how're you doing? Ric, by the way.'

'Okay, Ric. Cold, wet, knackered, pissed off…'

'The usual, then,' Ric laughed softly.

'There will be good days,' I said.

'There will be good days,' Ric affirmed.

'Louise has brought me up to speed on your involvement with the expedition. Great to have you on board!'

'Great to be on board.'

'I need to get out of here.'

'I've been looking. What weather system do you have?'

'Maxsea software. I can download weather reports through the sat phone. I've just pulled down one for the next six days.'

Ric had studied the weather. 'I figure the 9th.'

'Okay, I'll go with that.'

Adrian: Tuesday 8th November 2005
The weather window has arrived, bringing northwesterly winds which should get me towards Cape Finisterre on Spain's northwestern corner. I am anxious to be clear of Biscay with its notorious seaways. I leave from the Helford River at first light.

Louise: Tuesday 8th November 2005
You are very much in my thoughts as you spend your last night so close to home. So many people are behind you with this – feel that energy as you go on your way.

Stay warm, keep your safety harness on, drink three litres of water a day, sleep as much as you can, take your vitamins, eat well, write your diary, use the video cameras, enjoy your music and know that we three Flanagans will be counting the days till you come back safely.

Friday 11th November in the Bay of Biscay turned into a bitch. The weather built to yet another mindless fury. The boat took a real pounding. At 3pm, I decided to tack eastwards and wait until evening by which time, according to Ric's information, I would get northwest winds that would then push me towards the northwest corner of Spain. I set the Hydrovane. It works by staying in the same position relative to the prevailing wind – should the wind direction change, the Hydrovane will follow it round and the boat will then turn. At exactly 4pm, I watched our course change from 150° (east of south towards France) to 210° (south southwest towards Madeira) in 10 minutes. At last, the northwest winds that would push me southwards!

I waited for the depression to hit and when it did, 45-knot winds kicked up a mean, breaking sea. Sitting on the banquette, bracing myself with my feet against the folded sides of the saloon table and nursing a mug of hot, sweet tea, I ate the leftovers of tuna spaghetti from the previous day and tried to get some sleep.

My latest weather file showed conditions worsening in Biscay but the situation looked calmer closer inshore. The north Spanish coast was 10 miles south. I gybed onto a southerly heading and sure enough, the seas became flatter, protected from the wind by the Spanish mainland. At 6.40am, I gybed again onto a westerly heading to take me past Cape Finisterre and out of the jaws of hell that is Biscay in a storm.

I nosed round the headland, exposing *Barrabas* to the untamed Atlantic winds. The seas, herded remorselessly from the great open spaces of the ocean into the confined, rapidly shoaling continental shelf, built into lines of large waves. I took the helm to guide *Barrabas* through the onslaught, angling her bows to the approaching waves. The water rushing past her keel was slewing her round. I had to apply tremendous pressure through the wheel onto the steering cables to hold her steady. As *Barrabas* slewed for the umpteenth time, a loud cracking sound ricocheted from somewhere below decks and the wheel suddenly went loose in my hands. One of the steering cables had parted! Rushing to the Hydrovane, I used the self-steering rudder to turn *Barrabas* through the wind and backed the sails, stopping her in the water. I had two spare cables, cut to length and fitted with turnbuckles. It took an hour to replace the failed cable and make the tension adjustments. I worried that only one spare cable might not be enough to get me round the world. Then, I had a small *Eureka!* moment. I could cannibalise the guard rails if I had to – four lines of 4mm wire rope, two each side of the boat, running through the stanchions from the after frame to the pulpit.

With the lights of the Spanish mainland twinkling in the darkness, we navigated along the coast. The depression moved eastwards. The wind moderated and swung round behind us and, at last, we had perfect sailing conditions to drive us south.

A school of dolphins came and danced with *Barrabas*. I watched them for a while but I was too tired to stay on deck for long. For the last six days, I had only been able to manage catnaps. Conditions had been too dangerous to sleep for any decent length of time. I went below and crawled into my sleeping bag. I set the radar and got up every two hours to check the course and look out topsides for fishing nets marked by flashing yellow or white lights. On my second foray topside, I was within a mile of a trawler, but it moved off to the east.

It was getting warmer! Fresh from sleep and jubilant at our progress and the improved weather, I shed one of the two base layers I was wearing.

Adrian: Tuesday 15th November 2005

At last, a beautiful day's sailing – blue sky, fair wind, dolphins. Currently following the Portuguese coastline, but tomorrow will head towards Madeira. I managed to do the washing up this afternoon.

During the storms I was afraid, but I expect to be. Not to experience fear in those conditions would be to underestimate the power of the sea to destroy on a whim. Also, I had averaged probably no more than an hour of sleep a night, so I was becoming seriously fatigued. However, my main concern was with the massive hits Barrabas was taking. To be below and literally hurled across the cabin because of the force of wave impacts again and again and again, seemingly without end, began to make me wonder just how much more punishment she could take. The steering cable exploding was just an example of gear failure because of the stresses on the boat. There might so easily have been show-stopping damage such as structural failure in the rig. I just needed to get the hell out of there. Barrabas was magnificent. She took everything the sea threw at her. Without hesitation, she would raise her proud bow for the next punch. When waves were smashing over her deck, she seemed to quiver as if to shake the water off. You can tell Bernard that my belief in the boat was realised during that onslaught.

Louise: Tuesday 15th November 2005

I feel like a new woman since I know things are so much safer and better for you now. Next weekend I am going to Lisbon to stay with Ricardo and his wife, Lucia.

I leave next Friday. Ricardo is bemused at our fondness for Mateus Rosé! I am very, very excited! A Czech outdoor magazine contacted me today for photos. News of your exploits has spread around the world! Boys very well and asking about you – told them about the dolphins and they loved it.

Ricardo: Website Report, Tuesday 15th November 2005
40.26 North 009.03 West (Portuguese waters)

Just west of Adrian's position the bad weather was still producing gale force winds. The sea state was so rough and confused that two of the new, super advanced boats in the round-the-world Volvo Ocean Race suffered severe structural damage and had to seek refuge in Portuguese ports.

For me, sitting on the deck of my brave little ship, feeling the sun on my face, surrounded by a smooth and glittering sea with a gentle breeze stoking our passage southwards, I was simply glad to have come through my first experience of single-handed open water sailing. It had been nothing less than baptism by fire.

Quite how far news of my voyage had spread around the world was impossible to gauge, but it did reach one man in Holland, Henk de Velde. A sailor and circumnavigator himself, I was surprised not to have heard about him, more so given the contents of his initial contact with Louise.

Henk de Velde: Wednesday 16th November 2005
Dear Louise,

Also my team is always very small. When I am on my way the other side of the team is one other person.

I did exactly the same voyage Adrian has planned, single-handed (except some weeks with a Russian ice pilot) but not non-stop. I stopped in Argentina, Chile, Easter Island, Hawaii, Dutch Harbour, Provideniya, Tiksi, Murmansk, Tromsø, Holland – it took me 3½ years (including 10 months in Siberia) and 6 months repairing in Hawaii and waiting for the ice to go in the Bering Sea.

One thing: non-stop is almost impossible and I do not talk about ice but Adrian needs a Russian ice pilot (compulsory in Russian waters and the Russians consider the whole northern Arctic Sea north of Russia their territory). They will want him anyhow to clear in (probably Provideniya) and out (Murmansk).

Adrian must know that the way towards a goal is as important as the goal itself.

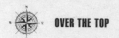

Henk de Velde was born on 12th January 1949. After a career in the merchant marine, he took to sailing, circumnavigating several times, first with his then wife, Gini, on a seven-year voyage between 1978 and 1985 then later as a single-hander.

It was his sixth voyage that interested me. In 2001, aboard his steel monohull, *Campina*, Henk set out to sail a vertical circumnavigation. Passing westwards through the Strait of Magellan and with a plan to sail Russia's Northern Sea Route, Henk did get permission from the Russian government to attempt the passage. Six yachts had previously received similar permissions: three Russian, one German, one Irish and one French (Eric Brossier's *Vagabond*). Henk's *Campina* was the seventh. Other than *Campina,* all these boats were fully crewed, but the Russian government insisted that *Campina*, like all the others, take a Russian ice pilot on board.

I knew that to complete my voyage non-stop was improbable – storm damage or circumstances beyond my control might yet force me into port, but I was determined to maintain the single-handed aspect. I reaffirmed the vow I had made to myself at the outset: no one would be with me at any time while *Barrabas* was making way through the water. I still needed to secure permission from the Russian government and then convince them to allow my attempt on the NSR *without* an ice pilot.

* * *

I hadn't yet developed a routine, hampered by the amount of maintenance and problem-solving that had dogged me from the start. My only routine was my bowl of porridge each morning with brown sugar and evaporated milk, followed by two cups of freshly brewed coffee.

Another problem occurred the following morning coinciding with the deteriorating weather, though this one was of my own making. I'd switched on the watermaker, but forgotten to open the outlet seacock to discharge the excess brine and relieve pressure in the system. The watermaker had blown out its valve. The trouble-shooting flow chart suggested that the pressure recalibration was a 'return to factory' job. I'd have to see what I could do myself.

Adrian: Saturday 19th November 2005
Awful weather – very squally, winds gusting to 30 knots. Watermaker bust. I collected rainwater in a bucket hung on the after end of the boom so I'll be OK for the next couple of days.

A second message to Louise from Henk dissipated my nagging doubts over the adequacy of my preparations.

Henk de Velde: Saturday 19th November 2005

I just read the news on Adrian's voyage about repairs. Just to tell you it's part of the game. I had to repair my broken boom in Iceland, I had to repair my engine in Argentina and recheck it in Chile. I had to repair all electrics on Hawaii. I had to repair sails in Dutch Harbor. I had to repair the transmission in −40C in Tiksi. I had to repair my rudders in Murmansk.

Give Adrian my best wishes. At heart I am with him.

I progressed slowly against the building seas and headwinds. An unstable patch of air just west of my position was displaying all the characteristics of a hurricane in its early stages. Ricardo was watching developments. *'We are monitoring this system very closely. Although pretty certain that it will not build into a serious storm, we want to keep Adrian moving towards the safest part of the cell, and that is exactly what he is doing.'*

I bashed on through Sunday, head to wind, managing to hold my course south of west. I considered how I was feeling. Fear had diminished, my respect for the sea had not, but curiously being single-handed did not seem strange or unnerving – on the contrary, my solitude felt natural.

Below decks, tied to the mast support post, Benji's green teddy bear and Gabriel's red dog, kept me company. Some part of my mind lingered constantly on the boys as if I had two hard drives running simultaneously in my head.

I was not yet in tune with the sea, though increasingly my feeling for the boat was becoming instinctive. I went about the deck checking and re-checking the rigging. I still felt very much the interloper, spending so much of my energy fire-fighting, managing mini-crises and dealing with heavy weather instead of simply being part of the way of things.

With less than two litres of drinking water on board, I went to work on the watermaker. I wasn't overly concerned. I had plenty of tinned fruit (in juice) on board: 150 tins. Aside from the nutritional value of the fruit, I had stowed so much of it precisely for this reason – a fall back if my water stock depleted and, because it was tinned, its extended shelf life meant that I would not be in any immediate danger. Plus, I had plenty of long-life and tinned milk as well.

The thread on the watermaker valve was damaged. I filed the edges carefully, then screwed it back into the watermaker unit, trying to visualise how tightly it had been screwed down before so that I could get the pressure setting correct. It was guesswork but, after an hour pitching around in the confines of the fore cabin, I tried the watermaker. A few minutes later, beautiful, fresh drinking-quality water began dribbling from the end of the product tube. It was a huge relief. Now I could get on and sail the boat. I ran the watermaker for four hours until my two 10-litre jerry cans were full. For several minutes, I sat on the companionway steps looking at the fresh, clean water, occasionally leaning forwards to heft the cans. Never before had the vital necessity of water been so apparent to me.

Louise: Monday 21st November 2005
Can you fill me in on batteries, watermaker, state of mind, are you eating and taking vits? Are you okay?

I leave for Lisbon Friday and come home Monday. Big snow predicted this week. It is freezing here. The new website [which Ric had redesigned] *has been incredibly well received. We now have a visitors' book… I am coping very well – the boys are not driving me half as crackers as I thought.*

With the storm spent and northeast winds chasing me south towards Madeira, I emailed Louise.

Adrian: Tuesday 22nd November 2005
…after all the hoopla with batteries, watermaker, steering, weather and so on, finally I can give you that good message I've been waiting so long to send. All systems on board restored to normal working – makes you pretty self-reliant this single-handing business – electrician, rigger, sailor, navigator, washer(wo)man, cook, diesel mechanic.

Today the weather is perfect. I am sailing fast and straight on a direct line towards Madeira 200 miles away. I've taken some nasty bangs – deep bruise on the sole of my right foot, which makes putting weight on it a bit painful. I was thrown across the cabin twice in recent days and on both occasions hit my left forearm midway between wrist and elbow… I thought I had broken it – felt nauseous for about 30 mins.

I am doing my first lot of laundry today – socks and base layer. I will hoist them up on a halyard to air dry. I'll also have a wash this afternoon and a shave.

I am eating pretty well – usually porridge and coffee for breakfast with a cooked meal mid-afternoon (high carb – pasta or rice with something). All this supplemented with tinned fruit, dried fruit and chocolate plus the vits etc.

Please give my boys a big hug and kiss. Green bear and red dog are my constant companions.

* * *

Louise and I met Nikki and Paul Howe during our honeymoon in 1997, at a Tuscan farmhouse where we were all staying. We'd been friends ever since. I knew they were following my voyage and a straightforward message from Nikki created a new awareness in me.

Nikki: Wednesday 23rd November 2005
We are so pleased to hear that you are making really good progress now, despite the setbacks. We are now in the throes of Christmas preparations (all that shopping again… Ugh!), but fortunately weather has been fantastic, cold, bright and crisp…

The infinity of space without walls, the absence of crush, the unconstrained vista where I could see the curvature of the earth – all these were now beginning to influence my perceptions. I was too recently into my trip to have gained a completely different perspective but too removed from normality not to be changed.

Christmas shopping? The idea seemed at once familiar yet distant, bizarre yet mundane. I later recognised this altered perception as a precognition, the first tremor, a forerunner to the seismic shift that would compel me to redefine my understanding of my world, from the inside to the outside.

Trying to engage the Russian government was proving almost impossible. We still didn't know which department to contact or, more specifically, who to call directly. I'd been at sea for almost a month. Time was not on our side. I asked Louise to speak to Henk.

Henk de Velde: Thursday 24th November 2005
Louise,
If Mr Nikolai Monko is still in his post then he is the only one to give permission. But it's also good to contact MSCO (Murmansk Shipping Company). They do the routing of the ships including icebreakers and will give Adrian direction where to go or not!

Was Nikolai Monko still head of Northern Sea Route Administration, and if so, had my application landed on his desk yet? If it had, was the application being processed? If approval came, I would need as much time as possible to then persuade Nikolai Monko, or whoever was now in charge of NSR Administration, to let me go without an ice pilot.

I spoke to Louise and she decided to chase things up with the Foreign Office. Louise has a special ability to get people to listen and then act. That evening, I received a message, forwarded by Louise, while I ate a supper of spaghetti with tomato sauce and sausage, listening to Roy Orbison crooning in the background.

Laurie Brock: Russia Section, Foreign & Commonwealth Office, London: Thursday 24th November 2005
Hi Louise,

Steve Hunt (Deputy Head of Russia Section) is preparing a letter about your ex-husband's trip to send to the Russian Embassy here in London…

With the calmer conditions, the boat in order and my routine of inspections, checks and maintenance beginning to create a routine of sorts, I began to relax. The books I had on board made an eclectic mix. I'd picked some off my shelves at home and some Louise and others had given me. From this limited library, I selected Campbell Armstrong's *Mambo*.

Louise: Friday 25th November 2005
Well here I am in Lisbon! Already hit the shops and only came away with a small gift for the boys. Ric picked me up from the airport… Lucia his wife and baby Miguel have just come home after being away for the week so haven't spent much time with her yet. Ric has shown me how he updates the website every day… wow! I´ll be at technical HQ for the next few days. So glad I came.

CHAPTER 10
ENLIGHTENMENT

Louise: Saturday 26th November 2005
Impressed by your progress! I am having a fabulous time here – eating, chilling, sitting behind my computer on your behalf – but that is my life now and I'm enjoying it.

Louise was recharging but I was listless, unable to summon either the energy or enthusiasm for the smallest task, hardly bothering to stick my head above the companionway to make visual checks for shipping. The emotional drain of buying and refitting *Barrabas,* plus all the ancillary effort of finding sponsors and the wrench from the children, had finally caught up with me.

I forced myself to set about tidying the fore cabin and the aft deck. The pair of boots I was wearing when I went over the side still reeked. I soaked them in the galley sink in fresh water and laundry liquid.

A thought lifted my spirits. From the Helford River only a few weeks before, I was now between Madeira and the Canaries, heading towards Brazil, blown only by the wind. I was crossing an ocean. It seemed incredible, fantastic. But a deep depression in the west was beginning to move east towards me. The forecasters described the system as a tropical cyclone – exceptional for this time of year and latitude. It was going to be another howler.

Louise: Sunday 27ᵗʰ November 2005

My few days here have just flown by – I can't believe I have to go home tomorrow. We went out for a very nice dinner last night with JP who is Ric's dad. JP used to work for BBC Radio in the UK for many years and now has a radio show in Portugal. (He is going to continue to plug you on his show.) They leave to go out for dinner at about 10pm here. Haven't got to bed before 12.30 yet. Turned into a pumpkin the first night and still look like one!

***

Louise had been in touch with Eric Brossier on board *Vagabond* somewhere in the high Arctic, asking his advice.

Eric Brossier: Sunday 27ᵗʰ November 2005

Hello Louise,

    The most important thing is to have a Russian partner, an official company, who will ask the permission for you. Otherwise, it might be really difficult to get proper permission to sail the Northern Sea Route. Good luck, Eric.

The second night of the storm was horrific, although I felt less worried because I was now confident of *Barrabas*'s capabilities. She seemed stable as the centre of the depression passed over us. The wind tore the Windex (a small wind vane) from the mast top – a nuisance because I'd used it constantly as a visual aid to trim the boat. Sleep was impossible, so I settled on the starboard banquette below decks and began reading *Between a Rock and a Hard Place*, about the traumatic experience of climber Aron Ralston, trapped by a falling boulder in the Canyonlands National Park in Utah in 2003. Close to death, he had cut through his elbow with a penknife to free himself.

Louise: Monday 28th November 2005

And how are you today? Heard on the TV that a tropical storm is approaching the Canaries – you are doing so well – when I look at the map I can't believe how far you've gone.

The morning broke blue and bright, warmed by the African sun. The wind had dropped to 10 knots. I prepared the spinnaker – an involved process, especially single-handed. Effort has to be co-ordinated because control of the spinnaker occurs at both the mast and in the cockpit, so I had to execute economic manoeuvres and scuttle between foredeck and cockpit. The hoist was good and the spinnaker unfurled with a magnificent smack, blossoming like a giant flower of pinks, blues and turquoise.

Barrabas dug her shoulder in and jolted forward, slicing the water at 8 knots. I didn't know it then, but we had weeks ahead of us before we would encounter another storm, south of Buenos Aires. I listened to Albinoni's concertos while the azure dimmed to indigo and myriad stars lit the night sky like fairy lights tossed onto tar. The two saloon banquettes doubled as my bunks and depending on the heel of the boat, I chose starboard or port, whichever was on the low side. A cooling draft blew in through the open central hatch drying the inside of the boat.

By next morning, I was refreshed. With daytime temperatures climbing to the mid-twenties, I had little need for clothing. I had a good rub down with baby wipes and wandered around the deck naked, enjoying the delicious unfettered sensation while the sun and breeze dried me. With *Barrabas* slicing through the water, I felt a surge of euphoria. I had never experienced freedom like this before, freedom spiced with the thrill of adventure. Despite the freedom, I still hungered for the trivia of home.

Louise: Thursday 1st December 2005

Carol Thatcher doing quite well in the jungle programme, George Best died when I was in Portugal, Tony Blair becoming less popular by the millisecond, Jeffrey Archer trying to get back into politics and David Cameron saying it will never

happen, Rod Stewart's girlfriend had a baby, Britons stranded in the Canaries
after a deadly storm ripped through the Spanish resort!

With *Barrabas* sailing comfortably in the warm breeze, her course controlled
inch-perfectly by the Hydrovane, I fetched the fishing rod, casting a lure on
a wire trace with 50 metres of line trailing behind the boat, enough for the
lure to sink a few feet beneath the surface and spin to attract fish.

Individual packets of ready-mixed flour in three shades – white,
wholemeal and granary – should have made bread-making simple but my
attempts at baking met with limited success. I eventually figured out the
best mix and, on my third attempt, produced a good loaf. I cut three slices
of the still-warm bread, coating each piece with a generous layer of Nutella
chocolate spread, then settled on my bunk to finish Aron Ralston's book.

I'd had a few weird premonition-type experiences recently and
another happened while I was reading. I put the book down, imagining
Aron's location as similar to the Spielberg film, *Temple of Doom*. When
I resumed reading, Aron referred to the film on the very next page. It
freaked me out!

A line in his book embedded itself in my mind. *'Our purpose as spiritual
beings is to follow our bliss, seek our passions and live our lives as inspirations to
each other.'* I lay for some time thinking about that. It was the second tremor,
nudging me closer to the realisation that the power to achieve, to do, to be
as we want, is within each of us. The secret is in that realisation and then in
the discipline of nurturing belief in ourselves. Through all of the criticism
I had received from some sections of the media, friends, family and even
strangers about the foolhardiness of the expedition, I saw that it was not
just stubbornness that had compelled me but a silent, contained, hidden
power that is everyone's to command.

What was beyond my power at the moment was getting my application
processed and approved to sail the NSR! The question of the Russian
permissions hovered in my mind like the whine of a mosquito in the dark.

Louise: Friday 2nd December 2005

*I haven't contacted Mr Monko yet but will write to him as his telephone
numbers don't seem to be working. I will also chase the Foreign Office on their
letter to Moscow. I will also call Sam Laidlaw and ask him to speak to the
Murmansk guys.*

Sam: Friday 2nd December 2005

Louise, I have a meeting on Tuesday with a very influential Russian and have told his staff in advance that I will be raising the subject. I will let you know the outcome. Best, Sam.

The wind corridor I was following towards the equator was taking me close to the Cape Verde islands off the west coast of Africa. On 3rd December, Ricardo posted a piece onto the website: *'For the next few days we will not be updating Adrian's position. All is okay and we know where he is, but we just don't want the pirates off the Cape Verdes to know too.'*

I woke at 2am (local time), covered only with the silk liner of my sleeping bag. The saloon hatch was open, peeling slices from the warm trade winds. *Barrabas* rolled beneath an ocean of stars. I watched through the open hatch. The moist, dusty smell of land scented the air. Santo Antao, the westernmost of the Cape Verde islands, lay due east of my position less than 80 miles away. I went on deck. Beneath the blanket of night, the sea seemed compressed. Cloud obscured the southern horizon, creating the effect of timeless infinity while *Barrabas* cut her path of white luminescence.

I made a cup of tea sweetened with a spoonful of cane sugar and drank it with two slices of the delicious spongy bread I'd baked the previous day. The fishing rod was in its holder and lashed to the railing on the aft deck. I checked the line, fibres of fish tissue hung from the hook, the lure bitten through. A large fish had taken the bait then broken free. I replaced the lure and cast it back into the dark water. Later, after daybreak, I noticed the end of the rod straining. I tested the line for tension and with a brief spike of exhilaration felt an increase in drag. Slowly, I reeled in. Beneath the indigo veneer, a silvery dart zigzagged. The jackfish was about the size of a decent trout. At lunchtime, the fish – gutted and marinated in oil and lemon – sputtered in the pan. Its red meat blanched to chocolatey brown with the texture of soft chicken. I ate the fish with curried rice. It tasted wonderful.

As well as email, I called Louise at least once a week as a way of simulating proximity to the children. Benji sounded sad and I could not really understand what Gabriel was saying but it was great just to hear their voices. They were about to go off to see the latest Harry Potter film. Louise reassured me that Benji wasn't sad, just into his Playstation, which I'd interrupted.

I caught another fish, bigger than the last at about four pounds. In the broiling mid-morning sun, I squatted on the aft deck gutting and filleting the fish, clad only in a quick-dry towel wrapped around my waist like a sarong. *Barrabas* glided smoothly though the turquoise sea. In the steady northeast trades, sailing was easy. The constancy of the wind left me with little to do to trim the boat. Out of the shipping lanes, my time was my own. So far on the voyage I hadn't been bored. I often avoided tasks simply to bask in the sun or watch the sea and think. Sometimes I brought cushions into the cockpit. Shaded from the sun by a cover I'd rigged over the cuddy, I would lose myself in books punctuated with bouts of napping.

Below in the galley, I fried the fish in olive oil and garlic, then prepared a 'Cape Verde' fish curry (which I made up as I went along). After frying, I diced the fish, then poured in a jar of Nando's coconut curry sauce adding raisins, cane sugar, garlic purée, crushed pineapple, peanuts and crushed chilli. Setting the gas to low, the curry simmered away for fifteen minutes while I cooked plain white rice in the pressure cooker. It tasted wonderful.

Ricardo advised I alter course to head southwest, which meant putting the wind directly behind the boat on a dead run. I decided to gull-wing the sails by setting the spinnaker pole and sheeting the headsail through its outboard end. Then I let the boom carrying the mainsail out wide on the other side. The rig worked like a dream, generating 5 knots of boat speed in 10 to 12 knots of apparent wind (the actual wind speed minus the speed of the boat). The gull-wing arrangement was as close as I could get to a 'trade wind rig' – two similarly sized headsails both flown from the forestay and each poled out on opposite sides of the boat.

Adrian: Tuesday 6th December 2005

My greatest emotion at the moment – amazingly, I don't have one. I've surprised myself by remaining completely 'normal' and not pitching between highs and lows as I was anticipating before I left. My mindset is 'just get on and do the job'. I don't feel emotionally deprived, psychologically vulnerable, mentally taxed, spiritually bereft or physically stressed (though I have been mentally taxed and physically stressed on this voyage already). I suspect all these things will come in time.

Taking advantage of the steady trade winds to get as much sleep as possible during the night, I was jolted awake at 3am on 7th December by a thunderous crash. I was off my bunk and on deck in less than three seconds. Had we hit something? Had some part of the rig failed? I inspected the rigging using a torch but couldn't see anything wrong. There were no objects visible in the water and the ship's starboard hull looked okay (the side from which the noise had come).

Still worried, I went below to brew up and discovered the problem. One of the gimbal screws on the cooker had sheared. The cooker had collapsed down into its well sending the heavy pressure cooker and the kettle crashing to the galley floor. At least it was nothing serious! I fixed the cooker, had my tea and went back to sleep.

Some of the necessary regular jobs were so tedious that I developed a reward system to prevent myself ignoring them altogether. The worst categories were:

1) jobs involving lifting floorboards – inspecting the batteries, wiring, bilges, transducers;
2) anything which meant having to reach into almost inaccessible recesses – cleaning the engine pan, checking fuel stored in the lazarette;
3) cleaning cupboards.

Rewards were small but meaningful – chocolate, a cigarette, an extra spoonful of sugar in tea or coffee. For a really dirty job, I gave myself a really big prize like doing nothing for the rest of the day.

Now confident in my watermaker and with plenty of fresh water stowed, I gave myself a deck bath, my first of the voyage, washed my hair and had a shave. Here's how it usually goes: you get up in the morning, have a shower, go to work. While you're on the train or in the car or on the bus, you don't think about the shower you had. It's normal, you take it for granted. At least, that's always how it was with me. Until *that* deck bath. It felt so great! Cleansing, cooling, luxurious. My morale skyrocketed. I felt bright and shiny all day (inside as well as out). I'll never take a shower for granted again. Ever!

At night in the trade wind latitudes, I often heard thuds on deck. At first I wondered, 'What the hell is that?' When I went on deck, I found the cause and the casualties – flying fish colliding with *Barrabas*. It became routine in the morning to walk around the deck clearing the fallen. The most I ever

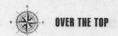

found in a single morning was twelve. They are edible but full of small bones and unbelievably stinky. I wasn't tempted.

Adrian: Wednesday 7th December 2005
Stumbled upon a really outstanding breakfast variation. Made porridge the other day and had some cold plain rice left over. So mixed it all up and produced PORRICE – really good, sort of chewy. Have begun reading Ewan McGregor and Charley Boorman's book about their motorcycle trip.

Louise: Wednesday 7th December 2005
X Factor *still going – left in are good-looking chap Shane, Brenda, Journey South (an ex-plumber and electrician) and Andy, the ex-bin man. Carol Thatcher won 'I'm a Celebrity…'* She is amazing. The nation saw her pull down her pants and pee next to her bed because she didn't want to go to the loo in the dark on the first night. When she parachuted in she was sick on herself.

It was becoming unbearably hot. The heat confined me below decks most of the time. I was not wearing clothes. Even going on deck for a pee (Carol Thatcher and I might have something in common after all) meant I was covered in sweat by the time I made it back below. I loved the evenings best with the air cooled and the sun blocked by the sails.

The tropical convergence zone or Doldrums is a transition area running along the equator. The spin of the earth causes reversal effects between the northern and southern hemispheres – the northeast trades of the northern hemisphere become the southeast trades of the southern hemisphere. The high surface temperature forces air to rise, leaving a windless tunnel or fickle breezes. Thunderstorms are frequent. Beneath massed banks of cloud, the wind can scream furiously in its desperate quest to escape upwards.

A grey veil of rain advanced from the east. The wind picked up to 25 knots. Carrying full sail, *Barrabas* was overpowered. I had to reef the sails so, naked, I tried to furl the headsail but the furling line jammed. I rushed to the foredeck to free the line while *Barrabas* buried her nose in the waves. Racing back to the cockpit, I got the headsail in, then dashed to the mast to shorten the mainsail. My course was due west, not where I wanted to go. I put the wheel hard over to port to get onto a more southerly heading. No response. I immediately thought, 'The steering's buggered again!' I lashed the wheel then stepped down onto the sugar scoop to look under the stern.

Seawater soaked my head and shoulders. The rudder was amidships. I clambered back on deck then ducked below to the aft cabin to check the steering mechanism. The pin connecting the quadrant (cable wheel) to the rudderpost had sheared, disengaging the rudder. To make up a new pin would take 30 minutes, but I figured that if one had sheared, others would too. Better to fashion a more permanent solution, a key, and that meant cutting a groove into the solid stainless steel of the rudder post. It would take much longer and be more involved but I could take advantage of the Doldrums' intermittent winds and flat seas to get the job done.

The temperature below deck crept past 40°C. As I set to work dismantling the steering system, sweat dripped off my nose like a leaking tap. I removed the quadrant, 2½ feet in diameter and weighing 20kg. Using an angle grinder, I cut a groove in the forward part of the rudderpost and a groove on the quadrant where the two opposed, each groove two inches long and a quarter-inch wide and deep. I cut the key from a small block of steel with a hacksaw. The stupefying heat limited work to ten-minute periods. It was a painstaking task. First, I was losing so much fluid in sweat that I needed to drink regularly. Second, the motion of the boat meant I had to brace myself using muscles in my legs, arms, back and neck. Third, the inverter kept cutting out because the angle grinder was pulling more power than the inverter could deliver. On average, I was getting one minute's use of the grinder per 10 minutes. The job took up most of the day and by the end I felt as if I'd run a marathon, twice.

The result was not pretty, but it was functional. By 5pm we were sailing again, albeit at 2 knots but going in the right direction.

My passage through the Doldrums ended on Monday 12th December with the arrival of the southeast trade winds, though we were still in the northern hemisphere, 200 miles from the equator.

Life on board gradually distilled to bare essence: my space, physically restricted to 40 feet; my choices, limited to what I had in the cupboards; my options, confined to my own imagination. Contrarily, these reductions brought enrichment. The simplest tasks expanded to greater significance. The true value of existence became more apparent. For example, having a shave; not an activity usually capable of engendering euphoria, but a shave, when a rarity, produces a greater sense of cleanliness and when cleanliness is critical to the maintenance of health, given that I could not simply wander off to the nearest hospital should anything go wrong, the significance, value and enjoyment of it escalated. All this seemed further enhanced in the rarefied circumstance of near-total isolation. BBC Radio Oxford called on the satellite telephone at 8.30am the following day, accentuating the contrast between my existence at sea and normal life at home. During the brief lead-in, I listened to the tail end of the sports bulletin and the local weather report. Here I was, close to the Atlantic equator, listening to Oxford United's latest football score!

With the stable weather and energy-vapourising heat, I was racing through my reading material.

Adrian: Wednesday 14th December 2005

Reading a lot – so what have I got left? Authorized bio of T E Lawrence, The Tibetan Book of Living and Dying *(philosophy),* No Second Chance *(thriller), an Umberto Eco novel –* The Island of the Day Before. *Then there's the* Oxford Dic of Ships and the Sea *(I'll do that cover to cover). I'll re-train myself on astronavigation. Plus the crosswords/word game books… then there are the instructions on the fire extinguishers, labels on the milk bottles and food tins, the computer help directory…*

Sam: Wednesday 14th December 2005

Louise, I spoke to my friend about permissions for the Arctic Sea transit. I am sure he will help although he did warn that it is risky and nearer the time, we should shout. Best, Sam.

Louise had emailed a copy of a letter written by the Russia Section at the Foreign Office to the Consular Department of the Russian Embassy in London. We now had definitive action from the British government. The identity of Sam's 'friend' remained veiled but at this stage it didn't matter.

I crossed the equator at 10.14am on Saturday 17th December. My offering to the gods was modest – bread (stale) and a box of chocolate-filled squares (a breakfast cereal that I'd tried and didn't like much). I figured Neptune should have been pleased to see his portrait floating by, etched on *Barrabas*'s bows.

I had demarcated major milestones, each representing an approximate 25% progression to the Bering Strait: first, the Atlantic equator; second, Cape Horn; third, the Pacific equator and the fourth, the Bering Strait itself. I felt huge pride in Louise and *Barrabas* as I mentally ticked off the first of these milestones.

Thunderclouds moved in around me. I counted eight mini-squalls going on. I was getting good at dodging them, but a big one ahead was going to get me. I decided to take a deck shower! As the rain came, I lathered up. The wind beneath these clouds can pick up dramatically if only briefly. I was carrying full sail when the wind suddenly kicked up to 25 knots. The boat heeled over, forcing the side deck underwater. I decided, mid-shower, to shorten sail. Soap streamed into my eyes, stinging like crazy. The wind strengthened, driving the rain horizontally. It was like taking a shower in a grit blaster. Shortening the mainsail involves working six separate lines between the mast and the cockpit: three reefing lines, the topping lift, the boom breaker and the mainsail halyard. So there I was, blinded, being hit by what felt like slow bullets, trying to keep my nether regions out of the firing line and execute the sail-shortening manoeuvre. By the time I was done, the rain had passed, leaving me covered in suds. I tied a rope around my waist, dived into the warm ocean and clambered out onto the sugar scoop at the back of the boat. Two cups of fresh water as a rinse and I was done. Then the full rigmarole with the lines in reverse to get the mainsail up again and we were off. Thus was my introduction to the southern hemisphere.

The next day, Sunday 18th December at 11am, I smoked my last cigarette! My supply was limited by design, but naturally, as soon as the faintest urge for a smoke came, I went off and searched all the cupboards and compartments in the aft cabin just in case a packet had become dislodged and hidden itself away in some crevice. I didn't find any.

Louise had decided to take the boys to Mauritius for the Christmas holidays.

Louise: Sunday 18th December 2005
Benji's been unwell. High fever yesterday but slept it off (until 8am) and he's much better today. We were out this morning and the boys bought their Christmas presents from you with the money you left them. Gabriel got a remote-control car and Benji a Star Wars game for his Game Boy – should keep him quiet on the plane on the way to and from Mauritius! They are thrilled at the extravagance. They got a few other bits as well as they had £35 each to spend (£20 from you and £15 from Father C). We came home and I cooked our usual Sunday roast – they are now absorbed with the car/game. A little later, we'll light a fire and watch The Polar Express. *Can you see Brazil?*

Adrian: Sunday 18th December 2005

I can't see Brazil and I don't want to get much closer than I am now. Pirates are a risk all the way down the South American coast, but particularly off Brazil. Remember a few years ago, a NZ yachtsman Sir Peter Blake was gunned down – that was in Brazil. Slightly different set of circumstances, but all the ingredients are available to create the risk: busy shipping lanes, ease of access to guns, a 'life is cheap' mentality imposed through brutal poverty blah blah blah. A few years ago a Swedish guy, single-handing, was making his way round the world stopping here and there. He was in the Caribbean and set off for South America. He has never been seen or heard of since. The yachting fraternity suspects pirates.

By the end of the month, I would have experienced my own close encounter with pirates, but for the moment, my mind was on other things. The Russian question was always there, of course, and, in addition to that, Rose Dale, a friend and Louise's neighbour, had given me a book, *The Tao of Pooh*, by American writer, Benjamin Hoff, which described the principles of Taoism through illustration with characters from *Winnie the Pooh* (a bit of a weird mechanism but there you go).

My personal philosophy, defined over many years, essentially mirrors Taoism: the recognition of an inner voice that always speaks the truth, awareness, inner quiet, adhering to the laws and forces of nature, living in the 'now' (which I've persistently failed to do), minimal effort (not laziness, though in my case, that was often true) by not forcing a situation but instead letting events unfold naturally. I always knew that my ill-defined philosophy was informed by Eastern influence – naturally enough, having spent so much of my youth in Hong Kong, Japan and Thailand. On some instinctive level, I understood these principles but it took a slim, childishly written book to crystallise them into a fuller understanding.

When I read *The Tao of Pooh*, the timing was coincidental but crucial. I was just beginning to sense, feel and appreciate the pulse, rhythm and heartbeat of the ocean and the natural world. I was receptive to the idea of change and growth and I felt myself integrate more fully into the energy around me, taken up in its arms and swept along in its flow.

The 'how' and 'why' of adventure is difficult to articulate. To me, it is a *sensing* within an individual, a particular mode of expression and a means of discovery that certain people seek out because of an overriding need to see for themselves what lies beyond, rather than the mute acceptance of the experience of others. It was the same with the Alpha Global Expedition – I had to do it. The thrill of it, the expectation of danger and even the hunger for it would reveal 'truths', answer questions like: how would I cope? What would I find? I could never imagine or simulate this experience. I had to live it. As the days passed into weeks and months, it was becoming evident that the Alpha Global Expedition was delivering 'adventure' on a number of levels – physically of course, but also mentally and even spiritually. I was changing, maybe even evolving.

Louise and the boys flew to Mauritius for the Christmas holiday. I was happy for them but felt slightly depressed not being with them despite my recent 'enlightenment'. On the upside, I was cheered by a message from Aron Ralston just before Christmas.

Aron Ralston: Tuesday 20th December 2005
Adrian,

That's very cool that you're writing to me from the middle of the Atlantic! I'm writing to you from Aspen, Colorado, where it's snowing right now. I hope your expedition goes off with grand adventure and you handle it all with grace. Although the story will be better if you make some big mistakes along the way that nearly cost you everything but you find a way to make it happen anyhow (isn't that what adventure is all about?!).

I looked through your expedition website and it looks like you're well prepared and outfitted. That titanium stainless steel boat you've got looks hot!

Cheers, and obviously all the best wishes in the world for safe journeying and passage through the pack ice next year for you!

I hadn't told Aron nor reported on the website that I'd already made one seriously major mistake, which had almost cost me my life.

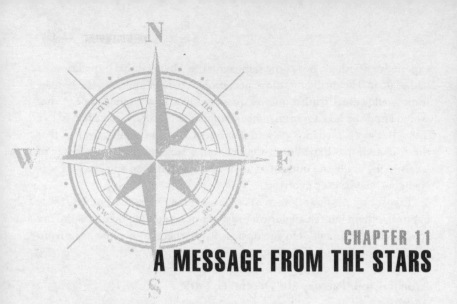

CHAPTER 11

A MESSAGE FROM THE STARS

Adrian: Thursday 22nd December 2005

I hope you're settled into the hotel and have infused your circulatory system with pina coladas. Having one of the best sailing days so far – making a good line down the coast of Brazil. I am about 200 miles offshore. This wind should hold as far as Buenos Aires.

Louise: Thursday 22nd December 2005

Having a fabulous time. Gabriel in the pool floating with arm bands albeit in the shallow end but taking his feet off the bottom and he did that immediately! They are in their element. Everyone so friendly – food wonderful – archetypal Indian Ocean stuff – white sand, swaying coconut palms, turquoise seas. The manager is letting me use his secretary's computer for emails.

Don't forget to open your Christmas presents. Mine you will find boring until later in the trip. Matt's you will think is the best present you have ever received in your entire life – I know you… so let's see if I'm right!

I thought to myself, 'The best present Matt or anyone else could give me at the moment would be a pack of cigarettes…'

* * *

Time ran seamlessly. I felt that I was now 'into' the voyage. Conditions were beautiful: a 12-knot southeast wind, blue sky and blue ocean. *Barrabas* was now pointing her bows towards the Falkland Islands.

Christmas Day. Louise telephoned. I spoke to the children – Father Christmas was due to make an appearance on the beach, arriving by speedboat. The boys were beside themselves with excitement.

The winds lightened, intensifying the heat. I hoisted the cruising chute, a lightweight sail, to try to maintain boat speed in the gentle breeze. Sweat ran in rivulets down my back and chest. The deck was too hot to stand on for long so I retreated below to send a plethora of emails. When it came to opening the presents, I followed a practised routine from childhood: look, smell, weigh, shake, rip. A hot-water bottle and thermal socks from Louise and the boys (I felt real gratitude towards Louise later, when I used the hot-water bottle constantly in the Arctic). From Rob and Matt at Kemp Sails, a mini bottle of champagne, Christmas pudding, an issue of *Maxim* magazine and – lo and behold – a packet of cigarettes! I was delirious with joy, dancing around the cabin, yipping and hollering. I immediately sent an email to Rob and Matt…

May the blessings of a thousand angels fall upon you. I ran out of cigarettes a couple of weeks ago (by design it has to be said, but nonetheless…) so when I opened the box… well, the choirs of heaven began to sing… and the high-end (no pun intended) reading material… outstanding (again, no pun intended). The accompanying calendar now adorns the chart table…

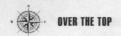

Sky News called twice for live interviews. My parents in South Africa watched on TV while they ate their Christmas lunch.

I trailed the champagne from the back of the boat to cool it down but it had all the effect of a dunking in a warm bath.

Boxing Day was difficult and I knew it would be hard for Louise, remembering the deaths of Christian, Tracey and Alexandre on the first anniversary of the Asian tsunami.

I didn't know the exact time that they died, but I calculated that it must have been about 10am where they were in Thailand. Taking account of time differences meant that was 2am UTC. My position, at 33° west longitude, put me two hours behind UTC. It was midnight, local time on Christmas Day (2am UTC on 26th December) when I went on deck. Suddenly, I felt a powerful urge to look upwards. The sky was unblemished. The stars dazzled. As a child growing up in Thailand, I had watched the stars from the beach house in Pattaya. Now, whenever I saw the three stars in a line that constitute Orion's Belt, I thought of Tracey, Christian and Alexandre. Directly above *Barrabas*, Orion's belt appeared to be mounted on top of the mast. At that exact moment, the brightest shooting star I had ever seen blazed across the heavens, moving from compass south to compass north. I checked the time. It was 2.04am UTC. I heard splashing all around *Barrabas*. The night was very still – the wind light, the sea smooth. Dolphins were cavorting and diving. The dolphins played for 10 minutes, their bodies drilling torpedo wakes of green phosphorescence through the dark water. Then, as suddenly as they had come, they were gone.

Louise: Tuesday 27th December 2005

Gabriel proclaims, 'I want to stay here forever!' Our routine is as follows: wake up between 7.15 and 8.15. Get ready and go for breakfast. We eat fruit: mango, watermelon, pineapple, papaya, all fresh off the tree. Bacon, eggs, waffles, pancakes, great fresh coffee, hot chocolate. Then I go and bag a sun bed by the edge of the pool for later (my god, I must be German). Boys go to kids club at 10. I go to my own private office they have given me and attend to emails etc for about an hour or so. Then I go to the pool and read (magazine, book or Daily Mail, *which comes about every three days). Get boys at about one or two. Order poolside service – by a process of elimination from wading through the poolside menu we are down to a huge box of chips (great ones), virgin pina colada for Benji and me (sometimes mine's not so virginal) and freshly squeezed OJ for Gabe. We swim and play until four-ish then go for a walk down the beach – Gabriel wading up to his waist in the sea sans armbands. Then back to the room about 5.30–6 shower/bath, TV, colouring, toys and then dress up for dinner at 7.30. Huge buffet – different every night (Benji v adventurous). Last night we lay on a hammock outside our room and looked at the stars. Lights out at 10.30. Wake up next day and do it all again!*

Despite the exuberance of her email, I knew Louise would have been thinking of Christian, Tracey and Alexandre as well and guessed she'd chosen not to mention the anniversary to prevent me becoming maudlin.

Bright light loomed just below the horizon off my starboard bow. 3am. I climbed halfway up the mast and glimpsed a white light. The boat was moving towards us fast. A beam swept through the darkness, a searchlight playing over the inky surface. The vessel closed to four miles then turned and maintained station off my starboard side following a parallel course. After 20 minutes, it fell back until it was lost over the horizon astern.

The radar was never on while I was outside designated shipping lanes and far enough offshore to avoid fishing boats or during daylight hours, unless mist or fog reduced visibility. I should have put it on once I'd seen the vessel just before dawn. I didn't and it still wasn't on at midday. I was below deck. Some intuition urged me to go topside and, as I stepped up into the cockpit, I got a hell of a shock! A boat lay 300 yards dead ahead. A sudden rush of adrenalin fizzed around my body. I guessed the vessel weighed 100 tons. She was wallowing, engines off, no wake from her stern. Immediately, I thought 'gunboat' – one of the Brazilian navy boats that protect the oil rigs that Ric had mentioned (although I hadn't seen any rigs). She looked sleek, fast. The binoculars told a different story. Streaks of rust trailed down her sides, no markings. A fishing boat, then? I couldn't make out any gear running out from her stern, no equipment on deck to evidence an offshore trawler. *Barrabas* was on a collision course. I unlashed the wheel and steered away. The boat was now very close, 150 yards. I could clearly see aerials and scanners bristling from the pilothouse but no sign of life on deck. Laundry flapped languidly in the hot air, strung between the pilothouse and the upper deck. Sea gipsies? Why would sea gipsies be 300 miles offshore? Or was it pirates?

Was this the same boat that had been tracking me earlier? Had they motored round so I would sail right past them, giving them the chance to eyeball the yacht by daylight? It was too much of a coincidence that I should appear to be tracked and shortly after, literally run into a boat 'parked' on the ocean. The aerials clinched it. If the boat was not a protection vessel or a commercial fishing vessel, why the degree of electronic sophistication?

I brought *Barrabas* to within 50 yards of the inert ship, close enough so that whoever was in the pilothouse could read the Alpha Global logo and expedition website address on the mainsail. I reasoned that a pirate vessel would be equipped with internet access. A check would confirm that I would be unlikely to have money or valuables on board. Maybe my thinking was far-fetched. Would a bunch of murderous pirates do research on an English website? Maybe not, but what alternative did I have?

As we passed, I looked back. An eerie sight – a dead ship on the high seas. That sixth sense, honed through 61 days alone on *Barrabas*, was unequivocal. This was a pirate vessel – menacing and deadly. The modus operandi of pirates in hotspots around the globe – the Malacca Straits, the Red Sea, Nigeria, Yemen, the Philippines, Brazil – was consistent when it came to attacks on small craft. Kill the crew, plunder the boat then sink it with the bodies on board, preferably in deep water, leaving no trace. I urged *Barrabas* to fly.

Within an hour, the vessel had disappeared below the horizon astern. I breathed easier. By 5pm, I had covered 30 miles since my 'near collision'. On deck, fixing the starboard spray dodger, I noticed a ship astern. Through the binoculars, I recognised the distinctive profile of the vessel – it was the pirate boat. Tension prickled my skin. The pirate vessel was tracking *Barrabas*. What other explanation could there be? Almost immediately, I considered the possibility that I would have to engage in a firefight if the vessel approached. I watched her disappear westwards then switched on the radar and picked up the contact. There were no other boats around.

That night I didn't sleep. At 1.50am, the bright glow reappeared in an identical position relative to *Barrabas* as the previous afternoon. I broke open the shotgun, loaded seven rounds in the magazine, chambered one and sat in the cockpit, the weapon resting across my knees while *Barrabas* barrelled along at 6 knots. An attack would most likely come before dawn. The radar's sweep picked out the contact off my starboard side, shadowing me as before. With the radar guard set to six miles, I stayed on watch. The radar alarm shattered the dawn at 4.30am. The contact was at nine o'clock, range six miles. I maintained watch but made no further sightings. By daybreak, I had lost the contact. A large tanker came across my bows, range four miles. The pirate boat had peeled away, perhaps drawn to another target, perhaps deciding that *Barrabas* was not worth attacking.

* * *

Louise: Friday 30ᵗʰ December 2005
We had a nice time out yesterday. We went to the nature reserve and went in an open top 4x4 on safari. Benji has got a sort of sick bug today and keeps throwing up but the nurse has given him some anti-throwing-up medicine – French stuff of course… they have a medicine for everything.

Hope the pirates have F***** OFF and that you didn't have to deploy any weapons?!

I don't think Louise had taken the pirate issue seriously and I was glad of that.

Cape Horn posed the next danger. I was still six weeks away, but the psychological barrier to entering this notorious stretch of water rose ever higher with each passing mile.

On New Year's Eve, out there, in my peculiar and isolated time continuum, nature performed a spectacular fireworks display, the sun detonating as it touched the western water, hurling golden shafts through the clouds and spilling crimson into the northern sky. I celebrated New Year with a tot of Navy Rum, the first alcohol I'd touched for over two months. It nearly blew my head off!

* * *

I began the New Year, like so many millions, with a resolution – to keep the boat tidy and not allow small jobs to accumulate into an ugly pile. Apathy had leaked into my days, perhaps a consequence of the easy trade wind sailing and the searing heat. The easy option had been to relegate small, non-essential tasks to a worksheet that I would get round to at some point.

I started with the galley, stripping the cooker, scrubbing, cleaning and disinfecting every piece until it was gleaming, bleaching the sinks, clearing black gunk from the drainpipes and emptying and wiping out the cupboards.

Light winds in the afternoon meant I could make overdue repairs to the mainsail without compromising progress southwards. I took the sail down, running the slides off the mast track. The top three eyelets needed re-stitching and the webbing link connecting the top car to the sail had chafed badly. I made a new one. Running downwind with the boom fully extended brought the sail into contact with the after-shrouds. After more than two months at sea, agitation had caused areas of chafe, especially to the top batten sleeve. I covered the worn areas with adhesive-backed sailcloth, swung *Barrabas* round into the wind and reset the main.

Dipping into a book of crossword puzzles and revising astro-navigation between chores became a tactic to conserve my limited reading material.

The brutal conditions we would encounter approaching the high southern latitudes were difficult to imagine. Big weather at 30° south showed on the weather files I downloaded but at our present latitude, just south of Rio de Janeiro, the sea state and wind were perfect. *Barrabas* hummed along, her sails goose-winged, the main tucked down at the third reef to avoid casting a wind shadow onto the headsail. I looked out to starboard, to the western horizon and imagined the land close by. A couple of days sailing in that direction and I could be in Rio. For a moment, the question flitted through my mind – should I go into port? What had been an idle thought took root and I found myself seriously considering the possibility. And then what? Call it a day? I realised how tired I was and how afraid at the prospect of Cape Horn.

I thought about my 'coping' strategies. I missed people because of my isolation. I missed the familiarity of surroundings and routines because my environment demanded continual adaptation. I missed the children as if part of my soul had died. However, these apparently negative sensations had a hugely positive effect. They focused my attention onto just how good life could be if approached with an open and positive attitude, discarding regrets as useless baggage, and worries over the future as unproductive distraction. Attitude was all-important. The greater part of the challenge was psychological – how easy it would be to slip between the cracks and become depressed by missing the boys, home, comforts, by thinking about the costs and worrying about the consequences if it all went wrong. I didn't have any photographs of the children pinned to the bulkheads (but I did have some on the laptop) and I avoided dwelling on the past – disciplining myself to exist in the moment. But suddenly, I was weakened, tempted to end the voyage, and I found myself in a crisis of confidence. Could I carry on? Could I face the Horn? Seemingly out of nowhere, this crisis became almost overpowering. For the next 24 hours I battled the fatigue, the doubt and the fear until the crisis was past.

For several days, I'd been fantasising about fresh fish. The line had been trailing but no takers. After 'morning chores' (cleaning out saloon cupboards) I pulled the line in to set a different lure; in fact, a series of lures I had bought in Spain during the delivery trip from France. These lures, designed to run close to the surface, might change my luck. Perhaps the previous lure had been too deep.

Splashes disturbed the surface all around *Barrabas*. Had I wandered in among a shoal of feeding fish? I went aft to monitor the line while we passed through the shoal. Still no takers. Back on the foredeck, I noticed shadows darting around the bow. A dozen sizeable fish swam just ahead of the boat like miniature dolphins. I fetched the spear gun (Bernard's, he'd let me have it with the boat) and cocked the weapon onto the more powerful of its two settings. Lying prone on the foredeck with my head and shoulders protruding over the water, I could get the tip of the spear just above the surface. I took aim and fired. The spear ploughed a harmless furrow through the water in front of my target. The anchor chain was digging into my ribs so I rolled onto my side and re-cocked the spear.

The fish were zigzagging fast. My shot had to be millimetre-perfect. I selected the target and watched it for a while, getting an idea of the swim pattern. I took aim at a point over the water while the fish was on a zig furthest out from the bow. At the point I judged the fish would turn on to the zag, I fired. Then all hell broke loose. The spear and the fish had merged too quickly for me to see and now the fish was thrashing on the surface in a pink froth. I could see the entry point of the spear just behind its head. I walked the fish back slowly to the aft deck, not sure how deeply the spear had penetrated and lifted the fish. It was heavy, about four kilograms. The spear had exited though the gills.

I killed the fish and cut fillets, which I fried in olive oil then slow-cooked with peanuts, cashews, pepper and sweet chilli into a kind of fish satay.

I decided to ride the culinary wave – the fish satay was delicious – and attempted a sweet chocolate loaf. I ended up with something the weight and consistency of a house brick.

Louise called. She and the boys had flown home from Mauritius and just arrived back at the house. When I spoke to Benji, he told me he wanted me to come to his birthday party the following day, 6th January. I remembered what he'd said to Louise the year before. It was all I could do to stop myself from crying.

Adrian: Friday 6th January 2006

My darling Benji,

It is your birthday today – you are seven years old! You have given me so much happiness and I am sorry that I am not with you today to share your birthday with you, but I am thinking about you (as I do every day). Remember, you are my special, special boy. I have given Mummy some money so that you can go and choose a present for yourself. I love you, Daddy.

Despite the obvious contradictions, I liked to believe that the voyage of the Alpha Global Expedition would contribute to the boys' ultimate sense of belief in themselves. My chart portfolio included two world charts, one for Benji, and one for Gabriel. Each week I marked my position on the charts with annotations of what had happened during the previous seven days. I marked up Benji's chart on Sundays, Gabriel's on Mondays so that each would be unique.

We were by now 1,653 nautical miles south of the equator. The tropical sun beat down. With all the hatches and the companionway open, a draught eddied through the cabin. It was cooler below than on deck. I tied a torn teacloth around my head as a bandana to catch the sweat before it ran into my eyes. Dehydration became an issue. I had Powerade powder on board, which I mixed with water to make up an electrolyte fluid. Every 30 minutes I drank a pint. Even lying on my bunk reading, making little or no movement, my skin stayed damp with sweat.

CHAPTER 12
THE BIG STORM

BUENOS AIRES LAY 500 miles to the west. *Barrabas* was sailing beautifully. The weather and conditions bar the odd squally day had until very recently been consistent, warm and sunny. On 12th January, *Barrabas* found her 'slot' (as I call it) – the sweet spot that is so difficult to attain, the play between wind, water and rudder relative to the sails. It was the first time that *Barrabas* was truly in that groove and I knew it because she felt different. The wind was just aft of the beam and we may have had the benefit of a half-knot current. She was gliding effortlessly through the water. There was no bounce, no challenge from the water against her hull, no sandpapery resistance. The co-dependent forces at play to maintain the boat in the slot were too complex and too fickle to maintain for long but while *Barrabas* was perfectly tuned, it seemed as if the sea itself was grease and she was simply sliding downhill.

If the daily runs of the previous week continued, I estimated we might be rounding Cape Horn by the end of the first week in February. The southern hemisphere summer runs through December, January and February, with a significant variation in storm frequency during the different seasons, a 10 per cent storm frequency in summer against 40 per cent during winter.

In July 2005, while I'd been fitting out *Barrabas* at the Medina Yard, my father had telephoned. He'd seen Roz Savage being interviewed on

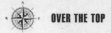

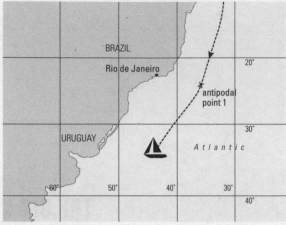

the local TV news. Roz was a rower, preparing to attempt a trans-Atlantic. I had emailed a message of good luck to Roz. She sent me one back, having looked at my website and we arranged to meet up a few weeks later, after Cowes Week. The tropical storm off the Canaries that had lashed *Barrabas* as we passed the islands in late November 2005 had disrupted the start of her race. She eventually got away on 30th November, but worse was to come when her shore-side weatherman went AWOL. We exchanged emails at sea and I offered to help by providing weather data. I'd been sending her weather forecasts twice a week since. By mid-January, she was halfway across the Atlantic.

Roz: Thursday 12th January 2006

And as Adrian predicteth, so it came to pass… thanks for the weather info. You must have some friends in high places – ever since you started providing my weather, it's been nigh on perfect, so thank you very much!

My 'friends' were the Gridded Binary Data (GRIB) weather files, a format capable of packing a huge amount of information into a small electronic packet that had proved so accurate for me and, so it seemed, for Roz. I could request and download the files and then view them ready geo-referenced through the MaxSea software. My habit was to request wind speed, direction and wave heights. My GPS communicated with the computer to show my position within the weather file so I could see exactly what was happening around me at any time for the period I had requested.

Later, as I approached Cape Horn, Ric agreed to take over supplying Roz with weather information. He was also using GRIB files and while his part in my voyage had moved to a more strategic role in route planning, his GRIB reports would give Roz the immediate information she needed. She would eventually make it to Antigua on 13th March after 103 days at sea.

Louise: Saturday 14th January 2006

Had a great time at the London Boat Show yesterday. Visited all our sponsors exhibiting, walked around handing out leaflets, met Andrew Bray (editor at Yachting World *magazine) and had coffee with John Curry and his wife, hung out with Matt and Rob and Toby (they are fab). In this month's* Practical Boat Owner *you have a triple-page colour spread and in* Sailing Today, *most of page 9.*

I sent an email to the Murmansk shipping company about a week ago and still haven't had a reply from them. I will keep persevering. The Russian Embassy hasn't even responded to the letter from the Foreign Office.

'Great!' I thought. Were we ever going to hear from the Russians?

The weather, like my frustration, built through Saturday and by Sunday morning *Barrabas* was running downwind with one reef in the mainsail. The seas began to heap. I kept checking the state of the weather from below decks while the Hydrovane held *Barrabas* on her course. At 8am, I prepared the cockpit lines to shorten sail. In only a few minutes, the wind escalated, whistling then shrieking and finally screaming. The seas, goaded by the winds, turned from ugly to monstrous, great walls of water rampaging up behind *Barrabas*'s stern. Very soon, in the dimmed lighting of this boiling theatre, their crests began to tumble over in great grinding cauldrons of hissing spume. The noise was intimidating, seeping into my skin and climbing up to invade my mind.

Barrabas was committed to her course. It was too late to heave-to and stop the boat. To do so in these seas would mean exposing the boat's side to the potential devastation of large breaking waves, risking a capsize or, worse, a complete rollover.

I checked the wind instruments – 42 to 45 knots constant. All too frequently, the readout registered 48, 49, 50 knots. As waves passed beneath the hull and gripped the keel, *Barrabas* slewed to windward. The sudden decrease in the angle of the wind-strike on the sail pulled *Barrabas*'s nose further into the wind, heading her up. The power of the pull began to override the Hydrovane's ability to steer the boat back on course and I had no option but to take the wheel and hand steer. I did so for hour after gruelling hour, watching behind as giant waves stormed past in a relentless sequence. Sometimes there was not enough space or time between waves to line *Barrabas* up correctly to take the next one on her port quarter. Physical and mental fatigue meant I began to mistime my turns.

Water cascading across the deck loosened the spinnaker, bagged and lashed at the base of the mast. The wind whipped some of the sailcloth free. It blew over the side and as soon as the sailcloth touched the surface, the water gripped it, pulling it free of its sock so that it was streaming behind *Barrabas* and acting like a drogue, slowing her down. There was no way I could pull the spinnaker back on board. The control lines for the sock snagged around the mast. With a knife between my teeth and clipped onto a strong point on the transom, I leaned far out over the aft deck and cut the spinnaker free.

The force I had to exert on the wheel as the water whipped the boat round, exacerbated by the fact that *Barrabas* was carrying far too much mainsail, required the total of my strength. I knew that the steering system would not take that degree of punishment for too long. I prayed for a break in the weather, a lull, just enough time for me to heave-to and shorten sail. No lull came. After six exhausting hours, I felt a slight release in the wheel beneath my fingers. I had become so attuned to *Barrabas*, to the way her heart beats, that when the first strands of her steering cable parted, I felt it as keenly as an earthquake. I gripped the wheel harder. The slight bucking came again and then the wheel went free, all tension gone as the cable failed.

The boat was now in serious danger. She was out of control. A wave pushed us skywards and, even as I sensed her nose heading up, I was unclipping my lifeline to go below and secure the companionway to prevent a massive flooding in case she rolled. Most boats, if rolled, will right themselves. If they lose the keel, they will still float. But *Barrabas* was made of steel – she would not float. If water swamped her while she was inverted in a full capsize, the weight of it would quickly exceed the weight of the keel. It would be her death knell.

I quickly called Louise. It was late morning in England. I explained the situation and gave her my co-ordinates. I asked her to be on standby.

If I hadn't called her back within one hour, she was to alert Falmouth Coastguard and relay my co-ordinates. Falmouth would then liaise with the Argentine coastguard.

Barrabas had headed up and turned beam onto the seas. If a capsize was coming, now would be the time. I had to get back up on deck and drop the mainsail. Now, side on to the 50-knot wind, the sail was thrashing with incredible violence. In the few minutes that it took me to get to the mast, clip on my lifeline, release the halyard and drop the mainsail, the severe flogging was enough to damage or even destroy most sails. Rob Kemp and Matt Atkins knew that *Barrabas* would experience frequent, extreme conditions and that the sails needed to be able to meet those demands. Incredibly, when I inspected the sails later there was no damage at all. For the second time, I whispered my thanks to them for their craftsmanship.

With the mainsail down and lashed, the wind took hold of the five square metres of headsail I had been flying to stabilise the bow. *Barrabas* pointed back downwind and the Hydrovane took over. Because the Hydrovane is completely independent of the ship's rudder, a steering failure does not render the Hydrovane useless, as it would most other self-steering systems that operate by controlling the ship's rudder. It was for that reason that I had chosen the Hydrovane.

Two hours later, I had replaced the failed steering cable. By morning, the winds had calmed to 16 knots.

The force of water over the deck had also ripped away some of the Treadmaster anti-slip decking. The wind generator had broken, with repercussions on my fuel reserves for battery charging. Without the wind generator, I would have to run the engine more often to keep the batteries charged. The inverter, which converts the ship's batteries, 12 volts to 240 volts shorted out, which meant I could no longer use any power tools. I did have a small back-up inverter of 300-watt capacity to charge the cameras and provide emergency lighting. Two 20-litre jerry cans had torn out from their mounts in the aft cabin, leaking 15 litres of diesel into the bilges. The shackles securing the tack of the mainsail to the gooseneck had failed but with the mainsail reefed down, there was no longer any load on the tack. I could repair that later.

A bad wrench to my right shoulder left me barely able to lift my arm. I diagnosed damage to the shoulder joint capsule. Luckily, the centre of a high-pressure system due to pass over would give me a few days of calm and time for my shoulder to mend.

My relationship with the sea changed. I respected it more but, curiously, feared it less. Faced with the sea's wrath, fear was a wasted emotion because it changed nothing. This was a time of change in the voyage, both in my perceptions and in the character of the ocean. It was bigger, more ominous and less quiescent. I wondered whether this was my mind playing tricks as we closed on Cape Horn. My relationship with Louise was about to deteriorate as well.

Falmouth Coastguard called on the sat phone at 10am on Monday morning, the day following the storm, triggering a bout of anger that I directed at Louise. Despite calling her back within the hour as I'd promised during the storm, she had already alerted Falmouth Coastguard. They were calling to check if everything was okay with me.

Falmouth Coastguard controls the international registry of EPIRBs (emergency position indicating radio beacons). Any distress signal activated anywhere on the world's seas is picked up by Falmouth. Knowing the GPS location of the signal, Falmouth will then alert the nearest MRCC (Maritime Rescue and Co-ordination Centre), which in turn puts a rescue plan into play. Before leaving the UK, I had notified Falmouth of my plans and we agreed that in any perilous situation Louise would alert them on my instruction so they would at least be prepared if the situation escalated. I was adamant that any alert would be a last resort, taken only if I was literally stepping up into the life raft (if I was 'stepping up' it meant the boat was sinking). There is an ongoing argument whether private boats engaged in non-commercial activity should rely on rescue services. Adventure demands total self-reliance. I decided that any alert would be in extremis only. My instruction to Louise had been to prepare her, not for her to act.

At 10.15am, Louise called – I told her I did not appreciate her acting unilaterally. We both shouted at one another. I said I did not want to talk any more and ended the call. It was the first time my psychological containment had really cracked.

My spirits lifted when a school of dolphins visited the next day while I was replacing a failed reefing block at the mast base (damaged by the spinnaker lines under tension). When I went below and switched on the computer, there was a message waiting.

Louise: Tuesday 17th January 2006
I hope you are not still angry – I did what I thought best to protect you, and our team are in agreement that I took the right course of action. Being furious with

me will not help anything. My priority is to help keep you as safe as possible – I am and have been all along totally committed to that and needless to say I am mightily relieved that the situation resolved itself.

I felt foolish, humbled. How could I be so bloody selfish, as if starting out on the Alpha Global Expedition wasn't selfish enough. I cursed myself out loud. Louise was looking after our children, worried sick about me and that situation was liable to become significantly more dangerous, at least until I was sailing northwards in the Pacific away from Cape Horn. Falmouth Coastguard had not been in the least put out when I spoke to them and had told me that Louise's actions had been correct. I thought for a long time about why I had become so angry, which led back to the concept of the need for self-reliance. I called her back, tried to explain and apologised.

Perhaps it was the tension of the storm, frustration that the Russians were not responding or having been at sea for almost three months. Maybe it was the looming threat of Cape Horn. Whatever the cause, from that point on, I began to feel restless.

Ricardo: Wednesday 18th January 2006
The southern oceans have begun their pounding. Let's guide you in nice and safe and with plenty of back-ups in the next few weeks.

I went on deck to change sail. Winds had dropped, slowing *Barrabas* to a crawl. I was at the mast. A noise of rushing air interrupted the familiar sound of water sloshing against the hull. I turned quickly. To my astonishment, a whale, perhaps 20 feet in length, floated on the surface, watching me. I didn't know what type of whale it was but, judging by its unblemished back, it was young. The whale circled around *Barrabas* in a figure of eight pattern, gliding under the bow, turning onto its back to show a white belly (I didn't think whales could do that). Then it was gone. My spirit soared. It was a wondrous experience.

Sam: Friday 20th January 2006
Louise,
The person I spoke to who runs Sovcomflot, the Russian state shipping company, has made the passage twice with an icebreaker. Whilst in principle he would be prepared to help with permissions, he strongly recommends against it as a very hazardous endeavour. In addition to the ice, the winds can be very tricky.

They recently had to abandon and evacuate a 15,000-ton tanker crushed in the ice. Not what you want to hear I know but better to be honest. I hope Adrian is doing OK, we are all thinking of him – his progress and determination are really inspiring. Love, Sam.

Despite the negative tone, I found the note from Sam encouraging. The influential Russian Sam had mentioned turned out to be Sergey Frank, who, aside from heading Sovcomflot, was also a former transport minister in President Putin's cabinet. He could undoubtedly exert influence, particularly as Nikolai Monko's department (by now we had learned that Nikolai was still in his post at Northern Sea Route Administration) formed part of the transport ministry. However, there appeared to be some misunderstanding of my intention. I was not planning a passage through ice in wintertime. If I was going to get through the NSR, it would only be possible in ice-free waters and that meant in high summer. I needed to clarify my timings and the anticipated conditions. I wrote an explanatory note to Sam, which included the following paragraph:

…Whilst at all times of year the Arctic is hardly an environment to trifle with, there are extreme differences compared with winter. Summer air temperature on the coast is +2° C as against –50° C in winter. The edge of the permanent ice is (usually) way off the north Russian coast. The extent of seasonal ice melt and growth depends on prevailing weather conditions. The problem is that inter-annual variability means predicting ice conditions is impossible. My plan is to approach the Bering Strait in mid-July. Meanwhile, my shore-side weather and routing team will have been monitoring the ice-melt pattern and the rate of the receding ice limit since early June. They will also have been monitoring wind patterns to determine the likelihood of a southerly wind. Historical data comparisons will generate a 'probability' scenario. In other words, because of the inter-annual variations in weather factors, I will only be able to determine the feasibility of a passage through the NSR when I get there in mid-July and the summer ice melt is well underway…

The air temperature was beginning to fall and for the first time since I'd been in the southern hemisphere, I was wearing a thermal base layer. I was still nervous about going round the Horn. Could *Barrabas* really do it? Could I?

After a month without a cigarette, I was feeling proud of myself. That night, as I was lying in my bunk and rolling to the motion of the sea, my mind drifted, conjuring memories, a kaleidoscope of images. In 1982, I'd spent a year travelling around Sri Lanka. It had been a wonderful trip, buzzing around the place on a 250cc motorbike. I remembered squatting by the side of the road, clad in sarong, many bangles and long hair, passing the time of day with some local builders when one of the men offered me a cigarette called a bidi. It was like smoking shredded tractor tyre. After coughing and spluttering, one of the other builders offered me something else, in a yellow box. Curious, I took the box from him – tea cigarettes.

Eureka! Tea! It's a dried leaf! By candlelight, I dissected a tea bag. Then I found the thinnest paper I had on board (a writing pad). With great care, I rolled a cigarette. The first drag was a bit papery, like a whiff of smoke from a freshly lit fire on a chilly night. Then the herb burned beautifully and I smoked the reefer-like creation. I learned later that Augustine Courtauld, who joined Gino Watkin's Greenland Expedition in 1930, became stranded on the ice-cap through the long polar winter. Three weeks before he was relieved, he ran out of pipe tobacco and tried smoking tea. He didn't like it much. After my initial try, I decided I didn't like it much either.

CHAPTER 13

ONE HUNDRED DAYS

MY REPAIR OF THE STEERING QUADRANT was holding well, but the steering cables would always be vulnerable in big seas. I had the emergency tiller but I needed a way of controlling it from the cockpit, so I spent the day designing and implementing a system of lines and pulleys leading from the tiller to the cockpit. If I pulled on the starboard line, the tiller went left turning the boat to the right, and to the left if I pulled on the port line. To try the system out, I neutralised the Hydrovane and steered manually, tugging on the lines and sending *Barrabas* on a mad zigzag over the water while I got used to the very different feel of the tiller.

As January drew to a close and *Barrabas* sailed further south, the weather worsened, with winds regularly gusting to 40 knots. Wind direction became less predictable as low-pressure systems whipped around the bottom of South America. For much of the time I was headed with the wind coming from the southwest, precisely the direction in which I wanted to go. I read and re-read the Admiralty pilot for the South Atlantic region. Admiralty pilots are books published by the UK Hydrographic Office, giving sailing directions for most of the coastal areas in the world, describing recommended routes and detailing geographical and navigational information. To enter the Cape Horn area through Le Maire Strait between Staten Island and Tierra del Fuego was not an option. Tides through the strait were fearsome and *Barrabas* did not have the speed to make it through

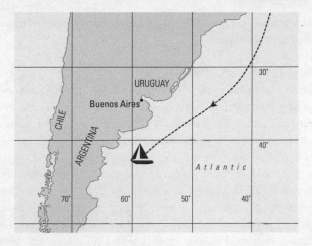

on one turn of the tide. Marcel Bardiaux had tried that. His boat had rolled, almost killing him. Dangerous overfalls extended 18 miles eastwards from the eastern tip of Staten Island. I would have to give the overfalls a wide berth, which meant adding 100 miles to the Cape Horn passage.

A message from Louise reminded me that Sunday 5th February would mark my 100th day at sea. She also attached another message, posted on the website:

Paul Mead: Tuesday 31st January 2006
I'm a very modest yachtsman from the east coast where I sail my production built Jaguar 25 out of a place called Pin Mill near Ipswich. I've been chasing a dream for the last 30 years (I'm actually 44) to sail the Atlantic single-handed... I've taken a keen interest in Adrian's voyage and found it very inspiring. It's so nice to come across an expedition that is based from the grass roots. The B&Qs of this world are great boats with great skippers but out of reach and touch to most people's imagination. I feel Adrian is carrying the baton out there for the common man and he has my vote over and above any multi-million pound expedition.

The process of adventure is complex, individual and impossible to fully articulate but sewn through with common threads: thrill, dare, challenge, need, discovery, unpredictability. What pattern any one person weaves from these threads is what makes adventure so irresistible. The challenge

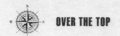

of my particular adventure was brought home when I received this message
from David Scott Cowper:

Wednesday 1ˢᵗ February 2006
*With regard to undertaking the Northern Sea Route, the Russians, up to date,
appear to have been insisting that a Russian pilot accompanies the crew on the
vessel sailing this route. The boats that have done it have all had fluent-speaking
Russians on board and those people had experience of the route. The first sailing
boat to pass successfully along this way was the German yacht,* Dagmar Aaen,
*under the command of Arved Fuchs. I know that he spent approximately 10
years devoting his life to obtain this achievement. The second was a boat called*
Vagabond, *under the command of Eric Brossier and he too spent many years
trying to obtain permission and again had to have a Russian pilot on board. The
other sailing boat was* Northabout, *an Irish contingent, again a Russian pilot and
fluent-speaking Russian had to be on board. These three boats had crews ranging
from six to ten people. There was also a Dutch yacht attempting the passage and
unfortunately he had to be rescued as his vessel received damage from the ice and
I think it cost his sponsors quite heavily in salvage fees* [David was referring to
Henk de Velde].

*For my part, I tried to obtain permission in the early 1990s and reconnoitred
the North East Passage on a Russian icebreaker in 1990 in the hope that I could
obtain contacts for granting permission. When again I tried in the years 2000 and
2002, the insistence was that a Russian pilot had to accompany me on board.*

Although we'd never met, David had phoned me before I left England to
wish me luck and offer advice. A truly remarkable man, David was the
first single-handed yachtsman to circumnavigate both west to east (1980)
and east to west (1982) via Cape Horn in his 41-foot yacht, *Ocean Bound*.
He was also the first sailor to complete a single-handed 'powered' vertical
circumnavigation in a motorised vessel, *Mabel E Holland*, a converted
lifeboat. During this powered voyage, David became the first seaman to
transit Canada's Northwest Passage solo (although it took him four seasons
to do it). While David's message might have been discouraging, I did not
feel discouraged. For some indefinable reason, my belief that permission
would come was absolute though I did not know when or how.

For the second time, a whale visited us, this time a pilot whale, about
15 feet in length, which took up station 65 feet off my port quarter and
accompanied *Barrabas* and me through most of the afternoon.

Just after midnight on Saturday 4th February, the wind went to the northeast. I set full sail to get *Barrabas* screaming along. She was sailing beautifully. True wind was touching 20 knots and though by no means extreme, caution suggested that I ought to bend in one reef, but I wanted to make hay while the wind blew in the right direction. My strategy to sail conservatively and avoid any unnecessary stress to the rig was for the moment abandoned. The tail end of the southern hemisphere summer meant the onset of worsening weather at Cape Horn. I had to get through as quickly as I could.

Winds built through the early morning and by 6.50am, the anemometer was recording gusts of 25 knots. Time to reef down. Whether we had an opposing current that day, I do not know, but *Barrabas* would not tack. I tried gybing. She refused to come round with the boom in board. The only way I could get her to swing her stern through the wind was to let the boom out wide, build boat speed then spin the wheel hard over to turn her and hope I could get the boom in fast enough before the wind smashed it across the deck. As she came round, I pumped at the main sheet to bring the boom back in board, but I wasn't quick enough. The boom slammed across and, although it was not a major slam, the gooseneck attachment smashed. I must have taken *Barrabas* through hundreds of gybes – a familiar, practised routine. The repair would take time, costing us valuable ground.

To replace the gooseneck, I needed to disengage the boom from the mast. I thought about the best way to do this without taking the mainsail off the boom and, with the boom weighing over 80kg, I also wanted to avoid any heavy lifting. After thinking about the problem for several minutes, I decided on a plan. First, I dropped the mainsail and lashed it down onto the boom. Then I untied the main halyard from the head of the sail and retied it around the end of the boom nearest the mast. I did the same thing at the afterend of the boom, using the topping lift. Using a block and tackle secured to the deck either side and halfway along the boom, I created a bilateral downward pull to counter the upward pull of the halyard and the topping lift. Now I had to devise a method of pulling the boom backwards to disengage it from the mast and create a sufficient gap in which to work to replace the gooseneck. I did this by rigging the storm jib sheets from the forward end of the boom through blocks fixed (at the same height) to the aft deck frame just below the solar panels and then down to the winches. By winching the jib sheets, I pulled the boom backwards and, critically, the up-hauls and down-hauls kept it level. With a new gooseneck fitted, I eased the jib sheets and re-engaged the boom. It slid home perfectly. Sometimes the only way to solve a problem is to think laterally and while the replacement of the gooseneck had not been particularly challenging, I was reminded of what one French racer in a Vendée Globe race had done when his engine failed to start. He needed the engine to charge the batteries. Without power, he would lose navigation and communication. Unable to hand-crank the engine, he set up a system of lines and pulleys, connected at one end to the engine crank and, at the other, to the aft-end of the boom that was set out wide. He then gybed the boat. As the boom crashed across, the lines transmitted a ferocious rotational force to the engine crank and up she started, thus saving his race.

The Falkland Islands lay 225 miles south-southeast. I planned to pass to the west of the islands. At 7pm, I crossed latitude 50° south, moving into the 'Raging Fifties'. Traditionally, a rounding of Cape Horn starts and ends by crossing the fiftieth parallel in two different oceans, southwards on one side, northwards on the other. My adventures at Cape Horn had begun.

I stayed awake until the clock tripped over into Sunday. I had been at sea for 100 days! As I sailed on, I came to appreciate just how small our world is – I had been a third of the way around it on a small boat going at walking pace in 100 days. The earth's vulnerability struck me – like a human body, every function depended on another. A failure in one would lead to the collapse of the whole.

Talking of human bodies, I was fine, bar the odd knock. My left wrist was causing me some concern. It ached constantly, the legacy of a motorbike accident years before. I had started strapping the wrist for support.

My diet became heavily carbohydrate-based as the temperature dropped: rice, pasta and bread with a variety of sauces created from the various condiments in the larder. I tended to eat a lot of the same thing, then get bored and go onto something else.

I slept as much as I could, keeping, as far as was possible, to a regular light/dark, day/night pattern.

My tension mounted with every mile south towards the Horn. It must have been very clear to Louise. Despite us both celebrating my 100 days at sea, we had not fully recovered from our argument.

Louise: Sunday 5th February 2006
Up till the time the boys and I went to Mauritius, we seemed to be pretty connected, with you wanting to be involved in what we were up to. Since we got back (I don't

know if it's just your power situation so there's less time to write) I am feeling totally unconnected to you. It is difficult when I spend a huge majority of my time doing things on your behalf and just generally thinking and worrying about you. It is a very unsettling feeling – probably difficult for you to understand. I know it's you doing the dangerous, scary stuff but that doesn't cancel out my issues and insecurities and things I am coping with just because my feet are dry. Today you are a quarter of the way through this and believe me it seems like you've been gone ages – the prospect of the same again three times over feeling the way I do today seems very daunting. Maybe I should be keeping this all to myself but as you know that's never been my way!

During the long windless patches, *Barrabas* drifted north on the Falklands current as if she was tethered by a great elastic band, progressing south then being pulled back, stretching out the time it would take us to get to Cape Horn. Every mile south had to be massaged from the wind and coaxed from a reluctant sea and it began to seem that the percentage of usable north, east or west winds would be unlikely to get us to Cape Horn before the end of February.

Adrian: Monday 6th February 2006
I appreciate everything you are doing – I know it is difficult for you. I am a bit stressed. Trying to get to Cape Horn is like someone telling you that in 10 days you have to go 15 rounds with Mike Tyson (and, by the way, you will be blindfolded and have you hands tied) and there is nothing you can do about it.

I worried about Louise and knew her well enough to understand that the loss of equilibrium between us would gnaw at her. Cocooned on *Barrabas*, I could distract myself much more easily.

Louise: Tuesday 7th February 2006
Thanks for the email. It is difficult for both of us. I will be as relieved as you when you're round the Horn so let's focus on that for the moment…

SEA MIST DESCENDED. The Falkland Islands lay abeam to the east. For the last few days, I had been using the gas burner to heat the inside of the cabin and strung a washing line over the cooker to hang and dry socks and gloves.

Ricardo had composed a piece for the website, which I only saw later. In it he'd written, '*…not that far west of the legendary island of Cape Horn there is a patch of Pacific Ocean with no wind at all. The patch is as wide as London to Moscow! But a low-pressure system is already affecting the area and Sunday will see gale-force winds and large seas blasting through the small gap between the South American and Antarctic continents. Cape Horn is not going to be friendly and Adrian will be right in the middle of it…*'

Staten Island was now just 74 miles south of my position. Past the island, the Cape Horn current ripped along, sometimes reaching 9 knots close inshore, sufficient to overpower a small engine. Only by venturing deep into the Southern Ocean could we avoid it and create a better angle to climb north towards the Pacific.

Ricardo and I communicated frequently, sometimes exchanging several emails a day. I could have no definitive plan to get round Cape Horn. Conditions were too unpredictable. I decided my best strategy would be to heave-to in the westerlies and play the veering winds to our advantage as the depressions tracked eastwards.

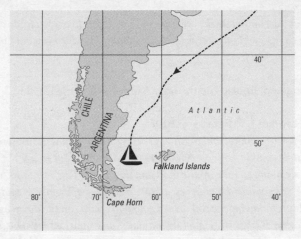

The depression was deepening. Winds to Storm Force 10 (48–55 knots) were imminent and expected to last for three days! I decided to back off and wait in deep water, protected by the continental land mass, avoiding Burdwood Bank east of my position over which the shallower water might gather into monstrous seas.

The vicious low cell tore through Cape Horn on Sunday 12th February while I held station, hove-to 100 miles north in lighter winds. I ordered up a five-day GRIB of the Cape Horn area, studied the data intently, then went on deck to make checks – running rigging, standing rigging, cuddy, emergency tiller, guardrail wire tension, life raft, dinghy lashings, hatch storm covers. The Hydrovane was vibrating – the bolts securing the gear to the transom needed tightening – all other checks were clear.

In the murky twilight, I saw the distant lights of a ship on my forward horizon. I absently watched the lights migrating west, towards Argentina. Was it a fishing boat or a cruise ship? The relative safety of a larger vessel compared to my small yacht seemed to compound my vulnerability and with that, my tension ratcheted up a notch at the prospect of facing Cape Horn alone.

Adrian: Monday 13th February 2006

I have looked at the weather for the next week for the Horn and whilst not ideal, I'm going for it now! I could wait a week or two and find that no good window materialises. Cape Horn is not going to lie down for me. There is nothing

hysterical in the coming week's weather but the situation is so volatile down here things can change without warning. I know that if I delayed it would be because of my psychological fear.

Back in England, Louise and the boys had come down with 'flu.

Louise: Monday 13th February 2006

As long as you are comfortable with your decision then that is the most important thing. I will be thinking of you. Shouldn't have ventured out today but I did. We went to your house to pick up the mail and then on to Tesco to shop (cupboard bare). As I was coming down the escalators from the café, Gabriel had a change of heart about following me so I turned round to go up (on the down escalator!), lost my footing, bashed my leg on the escalator and smacked my temple and eye on the Perspex side panel. Very nice couple picked me up and the man went to the top to retrieve Gabriel. I have a black eye! I have cursed you a few times this week for not being here to share the load while we all feel so shitty. Hopefully by the end of this week we'll all be feeling better. Hope you're feeling strong about tomorrow…

Ricardo: Monday 13th February 2006

I would back a decision to go for it if you feel comfortable with that. Josh Hall has sailed alone around the world three times. He is a good friend and a guru of the sailing world. He says what you are doing is very special, he admires you and sends you best wishes. He also said that to get around the Horn will be life-changing and that the good modern solo sailor has "…good movies, good porn, good wine and a sense of humour…" So there you have it!

There was no wine on board, no movies and no porn (how did that happen?) and as for a sense of humour, mine was still intact.

Louise forwarded a message from Bernard de Castro. *'Je suis la route de Adrian jour après jour, le Cap Horne n'est pas loin! Je lui souhaite courage et détermination pour la suite.'* ('I am following Adrian's route day by day, Cape Horn is not far away! I wish him courage and determination for what lies ahead.')

Strip all else away and the essential heart of adventure becomes clear – the unknown. Take that final step into the unknown and a traveller becomes an adventurer. *Barrabas* and I had travelled from England to this place, the

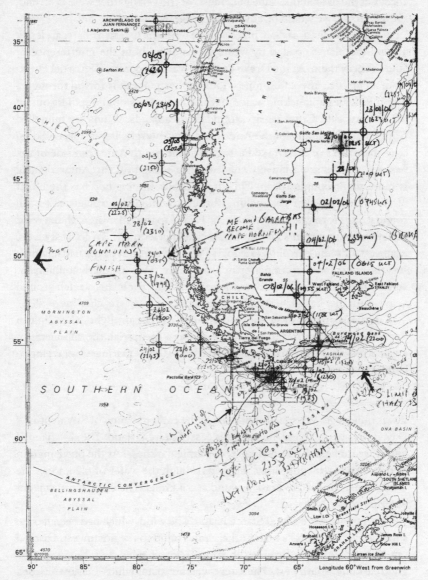

Barrabas's *route around Cape Horn.*

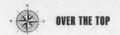

coccyx at the base of the Andean spine. Our travels together were at an end. From here on, we would be adventurers together.

Cape Horn is a savage place. The Southern Ocean rolls ceaselessly around the planet goaded by westerly winds without the interference of land to decay them. At the Drake Passage, which separates Tierra del Fuego from Antarctica, the 2,000-mile wide Southern Ocean is forced through a 600-mile wide gap, sucking water in from the Pacific side and spilling out on the Atlantic side. Currents rip around the headlands. Winds are funnelled by the high mountains of the Andes and the Antarctic Peninsula, colliding over the waters of the Drake Passage. On the South American side of the passage, depths are relatively shallow. The seabed on the Antarctic side is more than six miles deep. This dramatically sloping bed has the effect of spinning the water channelling through, adding to turbulence. To sail round Cape Horn eastwards, from the Pacific to the Atlantic, with the wind behind and the currents favourable, is challenge enough. To go westwards, against winds and currents, effectively against the spin of the earth, which sets the wind and current patterns, is arguably crazy. Of all the millions of square miles of water that cover the earth's surface it is this stretch around Cape Horn that has earned the reputation as the most treacherous of all.

On the island of Cape Horn there is a navigation light. The Chilean navy maintain a station there. There is also a memorial, the silhouette of an albatross. It is there to commemorate the 10,000 mariners lost trying to better the Horn.

* * *

It was time to go. We sailed southeast in the early morning of St Valentine's Day, on a course to clear the overfalls east of Staten Island. The sky changed quickly from light, broken cloud to a purple darkness. At the outer margin of the overfalls, the log showed speed through the water of 6.2 knots. The GPS displayed speed over the ground at 3.4 knots. The Cape Horn current was running at 2.8 knots.

By 7pm, we were round Staten Island. The wind, which had been flukey, shredded by the island's high peaks, came round to the northwest. I picked out Vancouver peak, shrouded in snow. Close-hauled, *Barrabas* was on a good heading, southwest. The latest weather data, which I'd downloaded at 4pm, indicated the northwest winds holding, the perfect wind to get me towards the Diego Ramirez islands.

During the night the wind shifted to the west. I hove-to and monitored our drift. Too fast! We were moving east at 2 knots borne along on the Antarctic current that drives the Southern Ocean ever eastwards. The strategy that I had deliberated over was not going to work. I gybed *Barrabas* and headed south to take us towards the latitude of the Diego Ramirez islands, still 150 miles away to the southwest. Through the night of 15th February, the winds then moved to the north as I slept for a few hours. I woke, sensing a difference in the attitude of the boat. Something about her motion through the water generated an excitement in me. I stumbled from my bunk and peered at the GPS. I wanted and needed our course to be 260°, just south of west to put us on a line directly towards the Diego Ramirez islands. I blinked. I could scarcely believe the figures on the small screen. COG 2-6-0 (Course Over Ground 260). Bloody fantastic!

I trimmed and re-trimmed the rig for three hours – alternately bending in reefs then shaking them out, altering the sail combinations until I was squeezing every drop of speed out of the elements. The forecast suggested the northwest wind holding until midday Sunday. If not, I faced the prospect of being beaten back, unable to match the onslaught of wind and current from the west. For the moment though, we were heading west and eating the miles. Incredible surges of emotion swept through me, from the rock-bottom despair of drifting east to the euphoria of sailing due west… to sail Cape Horn solo, against wind and current, what a dream that would be…

At 9pm, a squall front came over. Our northwest winds disappeared replaced with headwinds. I hove-to, drifting north and east at 3 knots. Was this a permanent wind change or a temporary consequence? The precious westing we had made began to erode away.

Two hours later, another squall passed over, flipping the winds back over to the northeast. We were sailing again, due west! I tended *Barrabas* constantly, steering either side of due west to wring out every yard – it was grinding work. Every yard westward was like a small nugget of gold in the pan.

Reality defied the forecasts. Through Thursday 17th February, the wind huffed then stilled, speeding us on, then teasingly slowing *Barrabas*. Sometimes we stalled, drifting back. By late evening, *Barrabas* sat becalmed, the rigging flogging and groaning. I switched the computer on.

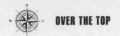

Louise: Friday 17ᵗʰ February 2006
*UK won silver in the Winter Olympics yesterday, a girl called Shelley Rudman
from Wiltshire in the bob. She only took it up four years ago! I am keeping
everything crossed that luck with the wind stays with you. Took the boys to see
Narnia yesterday, although Gabriel fell asleep in the best bit – the battle scene
at the end. Sun is shining today and I think spring is on its way… slowly – birds
pulling worms out of the lawn, a few crocuses and snowdrops here and there.
Cheers me up no end. Can't say I have been very happy for some time. I have
found this all much, much harder than I thought. Looking forward to sitting in a
warm pub with you when this is all over and dissecting it all. A good long chat face
to face would be great now.*

Barometric pressure was falling. I set *Barrabas* to a close-haul with the
headsail deep-reefed but the mainsail full to keep her bows pointing up on
our preferred course just south of west. As night settled in, the solitary rock
of Cape Horn lay 50 miles northwest. I didn't want to risk being caught
over-canvassed in the dark so I reefed down and then went to my bunk.
Sleep came easily. When I woke at 1am, we were sailing southeast on 142°.
The wind had spun round through the hours of darkness. I raced on deck,
gybed the boat, set full sail and eased the boom wide. We were running
downwind!

In the three days since coming round Staten Island, we had sailed close-
hauled tight to the wind, reached with the wind abeam and run with the
wind behind. We had braced squalls with 40-knot gusts and been set adrift
to ride the Antarctic current in despair without enough breeze to ruffle
smoke. I wrote caustically in the log:

> *Log: Saturday 18ᵗʰ February 2006, 1.43 am local time.*
> *56.38 south, 66.19 west, COG 270, SOG 4.2, Wind E 12, BP 997(↓)*
> *The only scenario left to complete the set is a real blow…*

To the west, a storm was gathering strength. *Barrabas* was delicately poised,
a soft wind from the east pushing her gently towards the Pacific. Ahead, a
low grey cloud pregnant with rain and incongruous among its fluffy white
neighbours headed towards us, propelled by an opposing wind at higher
altitude. Suddenly, the air exploded. The wind-speed indicator cycled
through numbers, 42 knots, 45 knots. I started the drill to reduce sail, hair

whipping around my face. I eased the vang (a line from the underside of the boom to the bottom of the mast) and tensioned the topping lift (a line from the after end of the boom to the mast top) to lift the boom and make it easier to get the mainsail down. Just then, the shackle connecting the halyard to the head of the mainsail failed. The sail, without tension, thrashed wildly. I tore at the sailcloth, pulling it down onto the boom. The halyard had dropped down inside the mast, only stopping at the masthead because of the knot in its end.

I furled the headsail. *Barrabas* settled beam onto the seas under bare mast (lying ahull). The pendulum motion of the boat was too great for me to climb to the top of the mast to retrieve the halyard. My immediate thought was to use the topping lift as a substitute halyard, but that would mean lowering the heavy boom onto the cuddy, then bracing it somehow to stop it sliding off and crashing down to the side deck. In those winds, the main shortened to fourth reef would suffice. I decided on a makeshift rig. The seas would build quickly. The main halyard would have to wait. The spare halyards were stowed in the aftcabin. I fetched a block, grabbed a spare halyard, then went back to the mast. I let the rope spill from my hands, then with one end between my teeth, I climbed the mast steps to the level of the lower spreaders, about halfway up. Wrapping one leg around the mast to hold myself, I shackled the block to a mast step, ran the halyard through the block and climbed back down to the deck. *Barrabas* bucked wildly – with no mainsail up she was unstable. I tied the end of the halyard to the head of the mainsail then pulled down on the other limb of the halyard for the hoist. *Barrabas* immediately settled. The wind had shifted. It was now screaming out of the west.

What were my options? Gybe and go north – not enough sea room. Run before the storm going east towards the Atlantic and lose ground – what then? Could I make up the lost ground? Would I? West, straight into wind, was impossible. I had to go south.

The storm raged all day and into the evening. The seas had built to 25 feet. A general rule of thumb: a breaking wave, equivalent in height to the beam of a vessel, has the power to roll that vessel over. *Barrabas*'s beam was 11 feet. I set the Hydrovane and lashed the wheel hard over to windward to create some angle between the side of the boat and the oncoming waves. This attitude would avoid direct beam-on wave strikes and keep *Barrabas* on her fastest point of sail as a defence to save our precious westing. The seas developed into cresting walls of water over 300 feet long. The question was no longer *if* we would take a dangerous wave strike, but *when*.

It was then that the head blocked, regurgitating effluent into the bilges. The manual bilge pump was out of action. The outlet for the electric pumps on the port side was underwater with the heel of the boat. I stood below decks, clinging to the companionway. 'Great,' I thought. 'I'm in a bloody washing machine with four gallons of sewage!' Braced below decks, I could hear the fuses of the bombs – the sizzling rush of breaking water, then the massive impact of the strike. Each time a wave hit, the boat stopped dead, her rigging shaking, bulkheads groaning as the hull twisted.

The capsize came at 4pm just as I was throwing some food waste over the side. The storm boiled around us. I pulled the companionway hatch open and took two steps up the companionway, poking my head and shoulders into the maelstrom. Bracing against the extreme heel of the boat, I readied myself to chuck the waste downwind, over the port side. Long, breaking crests raked the ocean, leaving great, flattened swathes of white. The boiling foam of spent waves crashed and tumbled. Then I heard a sizzling sound behind me, menacingly low at first, but amplifying quickly. I yanked myself round, protected from the wind by the side of the cuddy, but all I could see was a wall of crushed, white water. The wave covered the deck, filling the cockpit. It was slow enough for me to know what was happening, but too quick for me to move. *Barrabas* heeled, and then kept going, further and further with a heart-stopping momentum. My chest compressed against the side of the companionway hatch. The tip of the lower spreader touched the surface of the sea. *Barrabas* was neither floating nor sinking but suspended sideways on the ocean's surface. Below my feet, the instrument panel above the chart table on the ship's port side had become the new floor directly beneath my feet. Icy water cascaded off my shoulders, around my waist, between my legs and poured onto the panel. It's difficult to say how much water hit the chart table but half the panel was submerged – at least 20 gallons. I looked down in horror. If we recovered from this, I thought for sure I'd lose most of the electrics – cabin lights, bilge pumps, watermaker, deck and running lights, and maybe even the radar and GPS as the seawater went to work corroding the terminals behind the switch panel. Already, I could hear the sizzle and pop of electrical circuits shorting out. The boat kept going over – now her mast was submerged below the surface.

Barrabas's keel, filled with four tons of ballast, pulled her slowly back upright. The spreader lifted from the water, the wind caught the sail and smacked it taut, creamed water gushed from the deck, running through the scuppers like a hundred open taps.

I slammed the companionway hatch shut. The seawater inside had mixed with spilled sewage and was sloshing over the cabin floor. Acrid white smoke from an electrical fire began spilling from the chart table drawers. I used a cloth to douse the flames. The storm was building. Sleep was impossible. I was too on edge, too scared. Every bone-jarring impact seemed to sound the boat's death knell. Through the long, dark night, I braced myself below decks. Occasionally, I poked my head up above the companionway but all I could see was blackness streaked with the dull grey spume of broken waves. The noise was deafening. The rolling seas groaned a deep bass. The wind shrieked a high-pitched whine. This was the sound of fury and it terrified me.

The mess on the floor had mostly seeped back into the bilges. It was Saturday evening. I hadn't slept for 20 hours. Sunday was another country.

The storm raged through the night, driving us further south. Even with minimal sail, *Barrabas* heeled so far over that her port side deck skimmed beneath the surface. I stayed below decks – to keep warm, to stay safe. The latest forecasts indicated that conditions would continue like this for at least another 24 hours. I was exhausted and battered. Could I cope with more of this?

'Get a bloody grip!' I said out loud. 'Of course you bloody can!'

The further south we went, the longer we would remain in the path of the depressions. Drifting ice was another danger, more so the further south we went, but heaving-to in those big, steep, breaking seas presented an even greater risk than moving.

The seas continued to pummel *Barrabas*, hurling more big hits against her starboard side, but she absorbed the blows. Like a sparring boxer, she ducked and weaved, presenting her side obliquely to draw power from the waves.

Ricardo: Saturday 18th February 2006

You are in the top half of a low but Sunday/Monday as she moves east you will get southerlies, south westerlies, south easterlies. Make the most of them. It will all go quite light as you progress NW and into the eye of a high pressure. You will be on the east side of the system so will enjoy glorious conditions. All is clear at least

1,000 miles to the west of you so you will be OK and get around just fine now. Monday afternoon you will have a red carpet from Horn to trade winds. Get all sail up and just fly out of there and north as fast as you can.

At dawn on Sunday, I spent three hours pumping the bilges by hand – a mix of oil, petrol, seawater and sewage – into an empty fuel can. The joint of the flexible hose on the manual pump leaked so I clamped that with one hand while pumping with the other, eventually removing over 100 litres, which I tipped down the galley sink. The spill had turned the cabin floor into an ice rink. In the pitching seas, every movement needed planning. The consequences of a slip or fall, a broken leg or worse and my chances of getting through this would evaporate.

I talked aloud, for hour after hour. I had to control the panic chasing around my guts like some mad, cornered animal desperately seeking any means of escape. I went up on deck and clipped my lifeline to a strong point in the cockpit while the wind and the spume flogged my face. If the worst happened and *Barrabas* capsized and sank, I was out of rescue range. Death was close.

The realisation when it came was startling in its clarity. I was afraid of fear itself. I started to laugh.

'Is that it?' I yelled at the sky. 'Is that all?' Maybe fear had loosened my grip on sanity. Or maybe my fear, like smoke in the wind, had been shredded and was gone. I realised with a deep sense of shock that I was actually *enjoying* this. I went below, still grinning like an idiot. My focus stayed on the glass – just as Ric had predicted, barometric pressure was slowly creeping up: 1003, 1004, 1005... the wind still tore through the rigging, but without the intensity of earlier, as though the heart had gone from nature's fight. Even from below deck, I sensed the depletion.

That great British morale-booster, a cup of hot (and in my case, very sweet) tea was not available. The gas cylinder, housed beneath the cockpit seat, was empty and too inaccessible to change over in these conditions.

Barrabas had managed to stay west of south, but only by the narrowest margin. Now, with the air pressure rising, the wind began backing round from northwest to west, forcing our course off to 180°, due south and then progressively to east of south.

I gybed *Barrabas* several times during the afternoon to see if we could make a course west of north with the wind coming over the boat's port side but each time, the compass slid away to the east, forcing me to gybe back.

▲ Bernard de Castro lays *Barrabas*'s Frames.

▲ *Barrabas*'s refit gets underway at the Medina Yard, Isle of Wight. May 2005.

▼ Louise and I with Christian and Tracey Foures in February 2004. It would be the last time we saw them.

▲ Expedition funds from Timberland came just in time in August 2005, only two months before departure.

▼ A final hug with Louise.

▲ Louise, Benji and Gabriel.

▼ Ricardo Diniz provided invaluable routing advice from his base in Lisbon.

▲ Armed and ready. A suspected pirate boat was tracking *Barrabas* off the Brazilian coast.

▼ The first fish I caught with the spear gun.

▲ The approach to Oahu, May 2006.

▼ An ice-cold Guinness from Ernie Woodruff and Michael Roth, Rear Commodore for Sail at the Waikiki Yacht Club, Honolulu.

▲ My first step ashore after 193 days at sea.

▼ *Barrabas* is hauled out in Nome, Alaska, looking very tired after ten months in the water.

▲ *Barrabas* settles into her 'pit' in Nome, September 2006.

▼ Me with Rick – a remarkable man, and the kind of guy that makes the world turn.

▲ Saying goodbye to Cam.

▲ John Mann worked tirelessly to get the permissions I needed from the Russian government.

▼ My guard and I in Provideniya, Siberia, July 2007.

▲ The Port Captain of Provideniya, O.N. Yanenko came to stamp my logbook and wish me luck.

▼ The first ice I encountered heading west along the Northern Sea Route, August 2007.

▲ A polar bear checks our progress through a dense ice field.

▼ My calorie intake soared in the cold Arctic conditions.

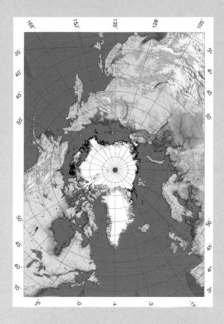 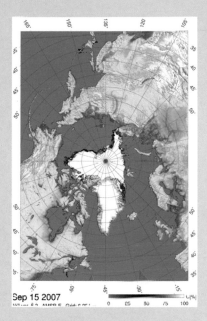

▲ The North Polar icecap on 15th September 2006.

▲ And on 15th September 2007.

▼ Vissarion, my interpreter in Tiksi, September 2007.

▲ *Barrabas* loaded on the deck of the Russian cargo vessel, *Kapitan Danilkin*, in Tiksi, September 2007.

▼ A toast on my 47th birthday with Captain Zagorsky aboard the *Kapitan Danilkin*.

▲ Captain Zagorsky, ice expert Nikolay Babych and myself in Murmansk, October 2007.

▼ Kare Karlstad and me, May 2008, on the day of my departure from Mehamn. An accomplished yachtsman himself, Kare was a tremendous help.

▲ HMS *Mersey* welcomes *Barrabas* back to UK territorial waters.

▼ A welcome cup of tea from the Royal Navy on my arrival home.

▲ Benji and Gabriel watch my final few miles home with HMS *Trumpeter* in escort.

▼ Cracking open the Champagne.

▲ Benji and I take a rest on the pontoon after the media scrum has dissipated.

▼ Gabriel, Benji, Louise and I celebrating her birthday, May 2017.

Barrabas battled on, shaking and vibrating. Wind-churned water found every weakness to penetrate the inside. Everything was wet: my bunk, sleeping bag, clothes and, once wet, they stayed wet. I glanced at the glass – 1008.

Finally, at 11.30pm, the wind went to the southwest – this had to be it! I gybed round, bringing the wind over the port side once again, setting *Barrabas* as close to the wind as she could go. The storm had forced us 200 miles south, deep into iceberg territory and serious danger. We had to get back north but our heading had to be the right side of north, west *not* east. Then the compass began to slide towards north – 350°, 351°. My eyes were riveted to the display. 352°, 353°. I could barely breathe. I murmured, 'Please hold! Don't go anymore! Stay west!'

The GPS compass heading stopped its slide at 354°, six degrees west of north. I stayed watching the compass and periodically checked topside until 3am on Monday 20th February. With little more to do but wait for the winds to back round more and improve our heading, I collapsed, fully clothed, into my damp sleeping bag. I had gone without sleep for 50 hours.

As I slipped quickly into the oblivion, I could not know that one of the greatest physical challenges of my life awaited me at dawn and that the red carpet Ricardo had promised would unroll before me in a way that I would never have dared dream.

* * *

At daybreak, with the storm spent, I stood on deck in the cold early light. To take advantage of the favourable weather window that had emerged in the night, *Barrabas* needed to fly full sail to make north and out of the path of the storm-stuffed low-pressure systems flooding in from the west. To do that, I had to go to the mast-top to retrieve the halyard. The wind was gusting at 30 knots. The sea was running with a 20-foot swell, the aftermath of the storm. As I stood on the pitching deck and watched the horrific pendulum motion of the mast, I realised I had another mountain to climb.

I attached two straps to the D-ring of my safety harness, each strap fitted with a carabiner at its other end to clip to the mast steps as I ascended. Clutching the mast, I stared up. Although not particularly high as masts go, it seemed to tower above me to an impossible height. It was a psychological game.

Speaking aloud, I said, 'Just climb, don't look down, don't think about the movement of the ship, just hold on, don't think about the consequences of a fall.'

I raised myself up, standing on the granny bars, then reached up and gripped the steps at full stretch. Right foot on the mast winch, left foot in the lowest step, leg bent at the knee. I breathed deeply then heaved myself up, half a metre with each step.

The physical effort of just holding on was exhausting and, the higher I climbed, the greater the arc of the mast's pendulum motion. Finally, above the upper spreaders, I heaved myself up 10 more steps, resting between each. When I judged the knotted end of the halyard within reach, I grabbed it with one hand, clamped it between my teeth then clung to the mast with both arms.

Thirty minutes later, bruised and drenched in sweat, I stepped back onto the deck. My knees buckled and I fell forward among the rigging, feeling the reassuring strength of *Barrabas* waiting patiently for me to get up.

Log: Monday 20ᵗʰ February 2006, 7.40am local time
57.05 south, 66.13 west, COG 344, SOG 3.2, Wind W 18, BP 1014(↑)
Barrabas *has been utterly magnificent. She has taken the punishment. Time and again she has been dealt keel-shuddering blows. Most times they stop her dead in her tracks. But she brings her bow round and surges on. She is so brave, so courageous. She has spared nothing to keep me safe. I weep in gratitude to her as I write this. I could not have asked more of her. She has the heart of a lioness. And still she fights on.*

Through the day, the wind continued to lighten and the glass kept rising. At long, long last, *Barrabas* was flying. At 5.53pm, she crossed westwards over longitude 67°.15′ west, the longitude of Cape Horn. We were on the Pacific side.

The Diego Ramirez islands, my target when I had entered the Cape Horn area, now lay 45 miles northwest. At 4.30am on Tuesday 21ˢᵗ February, I came on deck and sighted the islands – black, jagged teeth in the steely maw of the ocean. A single whitewashed house, a weather station, was perched precariously on the largest island of the group, San Bartolome. I called on Channel 16 and spoke briefly with the weatherman.

The high-pressure system over Cape Horn was blocking the depression to the west, giving me fair conditions until Saturday! If the high pressure stayed static, as Ricardo reckoned, then *Barrabas* would be pushed downwind all the way to latitude 50° south on the Pacific side, the official finish of our Cape Horn rounding.

After my brief conversation with the weather station, I slept again for four hours. By evening, the winds were in the east. *Barrabas*, her sails full, sped along at 7 knots, her boom splayed out on one side, her headsail poled out on the other. We sailed on over the following two days, the air temperature becoming noticeably warmer, my breath no longer clouding and my feet no longer like blocks of ice. For now, Cape Horn smiled as we sailed beneath blue skies. Albatrosses wheeled in fanciful free flight. On my northern horizon, sun-polished ice peaks towered heavenwards and the sea was a mauve cushion laced with white. It was a scene of staggering beauty.

With the prospect of running almost literally downhill out of Cape Horn, I had time to think of other things. The Russian government had acknowledged my application to sail the NSR but, as expected, Northern Sea Route Administration, Nikolai Monko's department, was insisting that I have an ice pilot on board.

As we rolled along the red carpet, the Hydrovane threw up a problem. With the main shortened to second reef, *Barrabas* was still turning into the wind, the sails flogging as they depowered. At first light on Saturday 25th February, I put a third reef in the main, then a fourth.

By this time, I had personified some of the gear on board and the strongest character to emerge, essentially a helmsman who didn't need food or sleep, was Harry (the Hydrovane). I spoke to him whenever I was on deck and occasionally yelled up from below, 'What the hell are you doing, Harry?' 'Well done, Harry!' Now I was talking to him again. 'What's up, Harry? You're not holding course. Look, I've even reduced sail to help you out!'

Still *Barrabas* turned her bows into the wind.

'Alright, Harry, let's have a look at you,' I muttered going aft to check the Hydrovane. The screw linking the vane to the pendulum that moves the rudder shaft had sheared, effectively disengaging the vane from the rudder.

'I'm so sorry, Harry. And there I was thinking you were being bloody lazy.'

I tried to get the sheared bolt out, but it was jammed in too tightly. I removed the linkage piece, clamped it in the vice (a bit of good thinking buying that vice!) and got it out. Then I put the whole thing back together with a new screw. Harry was back to his old, reliable ways again.

I charted our position – 279 miles south of latitude 50°. I rewarded myself with a hot-water footbath in the cockpit. Meanwhile, my socks were drying out in the oven – baking on low heat. That worked very well and raised my morale for the rest of the day.

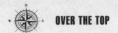
At 3.18am local time on Tuesday 28th February (2218 UTC, Monday 27th February) *Barrabas* breached latitude 50° south in the Pacific Ocean. We had officially completed our west-about rounding of Cape Horn!

I came to this place with hope and fear. Now I was leaving exhilarated and with memories of an experience that would endure for my lifetime.

I quickly sent an email to Louise, asleep in her bed, and then collapsed into my own bunk. The next morning Louise called, in tears.

My friend from school days had also written an entry in the website's Guest Book.

Guest Book: Tuesday 28th February 2006
Adrian, WELL DONE! Huge congratulations. I am delighted for you achieving this lifetime ambition. I remember you talking about this at school. All the best, Roger.

CHAPTER 15

THE RUSSIAN FRONT

COULD I REALLY GET PERMISSION from the Russian government to sail their Arctic waters? This question came to dominate my passage across the Pacific Ocean.

More immediately, sleep became imperative. Although the Chilean coast was close, 200 miles to the east, I had enough sea room to manoeuvre even closer in as we sailed on, putting distance between Cape Horn and myself. The air, still heavy with moisture, kept the inside of the boat damp. I didn't mind. *Barrabas* could ride the Humboldt Current running along the coast to speed us northwards towards the southeast trade winds, which would sweep us on into the tropics. The thought of warmth and light after the long weeks of greyness added to my relief.

I got to thinking about solitude. Since childhood, being alone had never bothered me. I was happy in my own company. Four months of solitude with *Barrabas* did not pose the difficulties for me that it might to others. Through the isolation, I felt the closeness of the people following the expedition's progress, especially Louise, who had lived almost each moment. I felt responsible to her and that sense of responsibility created the illusion of our being together. I had the advantage of satellite communications. I only had to pick up the phone and within seconds I could be talking to anyone I chose. That simple knowledge was sufficient to dispel any feelings of loneliness.

Louise, whose jubilation at the successful rounding of Cape Horn was greater than mine, had slipped into despondency. I called her on 1st March. She and Ricardo had fallen out. I felt that Ricardo's most important role was in his support of Louise, not me. If that crumbled away, she would feel more isolated than I did. The problem was Louise's concept of herself. Her lack of self-belief generated a tendency for over-reliance on other people, yet she had huge resilience. Louise was, in many ways, a conundrum. I knew she would bounce back. Management of the expedition would, I hoped, peel away the doubts she harboured about her own abilities and, from there, the confident and able woman that I knew was hidden beneath would emerge.

I spoke to Louise the next afternoon. Thankfully she and Ricardo had patched up their rift. Benji was poorly again. Maybe he was like me – a warm weather person (why the hell was I going to the Arctic?). The news reinforced the one negative aspect about the voyage: missing my boys.

* * *

Now that I was past Cape Horn, I looked in more detail at making an antipodal point. I studied the charts. Any point I selected had to be antipodal to one I'd already passed in the Atlantic. Because of my proposed route through the Arctic, points antipodal to that part of the route were not available (they all fell on the Antarctic continental landmass). The selected point would have to be somewhere in the Pacific. I settled on one southwest of Japan (at 24°11′ north, 143°22′ east) diametrically opposed on the earth's surface to a position I'd passed off the coast of Brazil (24°11' south, 36°38' west). The problem was that my selected point was in typhoon country. The hurricane (or typhoon, which derives from the Chinese *tai fung* or *tai feng* meaning *great wind*) season in the northwest Pacific ran from May/June to September/October and, if my assumed timings were anywhere near accurate, I would be there in June! But my other options were worse. To go to a point south of the equator would mean navigating the labyrinth of the South Sea Islands and risk getting caught in the hurricane season around New Zealand and the eastern coast of Australia.

As *Barrabas* sailed further from Cape Horn, I set about compiling a 'wish list' of spares and replacement parts. To my amazement (and great relief), none of the electrical circuits had been damaged following the switch panel's dousing with seawater during the capsize at Cape Horn. The computer-voltage converter and the electronic control head for the heating system were the only casualties. I hadn't decided whether to take a supply drop, but Louise could begin to get the items together just in case. Aside from the converter and the heating-control unit, I also needed a new dynamo for the wind generator as an auxiliary battery charger. A resupply would mean sacrificing the 'unsupported' status of the voyage, but this consequence no longer held much significance for me.

The high-pressure system over the southern Pacific had shifted east. Depressions queuing up behind were now rampaging though Drake's Passage to Cape Horn where I'd been only a few days before.

Colonel Mario Montejo, Commander of the Chilean Coastguard, who had been in regular contact with me, apologised for a late response to one of my position reports. He'd been dealing with an incident involving one of the boats in the Volvo race, which had entered Cape Horn eastwards just as I made my exit. This, and my lucky escape, were soon confirmed by Ric.

Ricardo: Thursday 2nd March 2006

The mother of all lows is about to blast Cape Horn with 10m waves and 70 knots of wind. The Volvo Ocean Race boats are in trouble…

Boy, was I pleased to be out of there!

Then came Friday 3rd March. I climbed onto the aft deck frame to get the serial number of the wind generator so Ampair, the manufacturer, would know exactly the model I needed. *Barrabas* lurched. I slipped. As I fell back, I grabbed the frame with my right arm fully extended. My right wrist separated. Perhaps not quite a full dislocation but the bones 'stepped up'. My wrist looked horribly deformed. I knew from repeated previous dislocations of my shoulder that I only had a very short time before muscle spasms would make it difficult to get the bones back in place. I stepped down onto the deck, leant forwards and closed the fingers of my right hand around the grab rail running along the top of the aftcabin coach-house. I then leaned back, arm straight, tractioning the wrist. A low *clunk* sounded as the bones realigned themselves. Any pressure through the palm caused excruciating pain. Soft tissue injuries often take longer to mend than broken bones. For a lone sailor, the problem of injury or illness compounds because there is no one else to keep the boat tramping along. For most of the remainder of the voyage, both wrists had to be tightly strapped for support.

Barrabas was slamming badly as the wind built from the northwest, but making 5 to 6 knots with the help of the Humboldt Current. Being inside a boat bashing into headwinds is like being in a series of minor car crashes. The boat shudders and vibrates. Anything not lashed down or properly stowed gets thrown about the cabin (including me if I'm not holding on). I reefed the sails to give her a more comfortable, slam-free ride at the cost of having to bear away and reduce speed. The Chilean coast loomed 100 miles off my starboard side. The wind shifted in the nick of time so I could head away from the coast. I set full sail and went to bed. I woke 10 hours later to a beautiful 'blue' morning – blue sky, blue sea. *Barrabas* had done well during the night. We were now only 53 miles from latitude 40° south and pulling steadily westwards and away from land. I plotted a course for our next target – Hawaii. If I did decide to take a resupply, Hawaii was the logical option. From there, my antipodal point was a downwind sail westwards of 3,000 miles in the trade winds. That evening *Barrabas* crossed northwards over latitude 40° south and out of the Roaring Forties. I recorded the moment:

> *Log: Monday 6ᵗʰ March 2006, 7.45 pm local time*
> *39.59 south, 76.18 west, COG 340, SOG 5.0, Wind WNW 22, BP 1022 (↓)*
> *Yippee! I am officially out of the shit zone!!!*

The weather settled into a more predictable, stable pattern, a forerunner to the southeast trade winds. I set the sails and the Hydrovane, then busied myself tidying the boat. I fixed the manual bilge pump, a difficult job because of the awkward access. I found myself wandering about in flip-flops and sleeping without the washboard in place at the head of the companionway. T-shirts and shorts replaced base layers and mid-layers.

Drawing level with the Chilean capital city, Santiago, I rewarded myself by stripping down the sink drainage in the galley, clearing handfuls of stinking, black sludge – the legacy of dumping effluent down the sink after the Cape Horn capsize. The work was cleansing in a metaphorical sense, wiping away the residues of fear that had shadowed me for weeks.

A whale (type unknown) came alongside, then dived under the boat, nudging the keel, causing the boat to heel over. I didn't believe it was aggressive behaviour; nice to think *Barrabas* had a new friend. I was more concerned that the whale might damage the self-steering rudder.

Heading north on 10th March and gradually widening the gap between *Barrabas* and Chile turned into the best day of the voyage so far: a perfect temperature, a warm 12-knot breeze coming over the port quarter, blue skies studded with high cloud, sparkling indigo water. *Barrabas* was reaching at 6 knots, but hardly heeling. The serenity, the space, the singsong of the sea, made it a day to savour.

The Pacific Ocean had a very different character to the Atlantic. It felt somehow fresher and the ride of the swell was smoother, less short and choppy. For the moment, I was happy and so was *Barrabas*.

On Saturday 11th March, I sat at the chart table plotting our position. I glanced across the South American continent to the Atlantic side. At the same latitude, the date read 13th January. I arrived at Staten Island on February 14th, one whole month later. We had made it here from the same latitude as Staten Island on the western side in 15 days – twice as fast!

The wind shifted more deeply to the southwest, bringing our course round to 295°, aiming us at the islands of the Juan Fernandez archipelago. I trimmed Harry, altering course to 310°, and eased the boom. High above, the Milky Way dazzled so brightly it looked like a stage set.

The following day I cooked a wonderful meal of sardines, tomato sauce and spaghetti (ironic that my favourite meal should be tinned fish) and then slept. My charts of the area were small scale. The thickness of a pencil line equated to 10 miles. I knew we had to be getting close to the archipelago. In the early evening, I went up on deck. There, looming on the western horizon was the mountainous silhouette of Juan Fernandez Island. This was the island where in 1704 Alexander Selkirk, a crew member on the privateer *Cinque Porter*, marooned himself following a violent confrontation with the ship's master (he actually asked to get off the ship). Four years later, Woodes Rogers, circumnavigating on an expedition of plunder, picked him up. Quickly recognising Selkirk as an outstanding seaman, Woodes Rogers awarded him command of the ship. In England, Daniel Defoe heard the story and based his novel *Robinson Crusoe* on Selkirk's adventures.

Unlike Selkirk, I had clothes, although most of my stock, save for a pair of underpants and two T-shirts, festered in a bin lashed in the aft cabin. To save water and tedium, I decided to wash one item a day. The heated drying cupboard no longer worked. The oven proved a good alternative. I cooked less in the rising heat and the savings in gas went on 'baking' my laundry to bone dryness.

We discussed the Russian question. Time was becoming an issue. Louise immediately wrote a letter to Prime Minister Tony Blair at 10 Downing Street and then called John Bercow, our local MP, at the House of Commons. He could get an inside track to the higher echelons within the Foreign Office.

I don't believe in coincidence as some kind of arbitrary occurrence. Cause and effect can transpose to the metaphysical – that's my belief. Many proverbs testify to some ill-understood machination that contrives to bring about some wished-for event – for example, *'Where's there's a will, there's a way'*, *'Be careful what you wish for'*.

In fulfilment of this bizarre effect, Louise received a call from Ian Johnstone-Bryden on 13th March. Fully versed with my progress via the expedition website, Ian planned to write articles for his own boating and shipping news website. He wanted additional information. During their conversation, Louise outlined the difficulties in penetrating the Russian administration. A one-time computer 'researcher' and former government employee with a web of contacts within the military and intelligence communities, Ian offered to help. Two days later, Louise received an email:

Ian Johnstone-Bryden: Wednesday 15th March 2006

I have spoken with the Russian IMO (International Maritime Organisation) representative. Nice chap, enthusiastic and prepared to take your case forward, although how fast or how successful he will be we have yet to see. His name is Igor Ponomarev. He is expecting an email from you following my conversation with him 20 minutes ago. He is in the right part of government, if not the same department. I did check and he is not FSB (at least as far as SIS is aware).

I am also due to speak with William Hague later today. He is a very nice chap and has lots of vigour. As Shadow Foreign Sec it's in his brief but he also has some personal contacts in Russia that may be useful.

On the same day as Louise achieved her breakthrough on the Russian front, *Barrabas* hooked onto the Pacific trades.

After long consideration, I decided to take a supply drop off Honolulu – principally for spare parts for the wind generator, computer and heating system.

For the next few weeks, my daily position plots would describe a more or less straight line to the Hawaiian Islands. The plan at this stage was straightforward. I would sail past Honolulu. A boat ferrying the items shipped out from England by DHL would come alongside, transfer the items and on I would go, without stopping.

The next day at 4.32pm, the log tripped over to 12,500 nautical miles. We had sailed more than half the distance around the circumference of the earth and, for the moment, it seemed that everything was going well.

Louise: Thursday 16th March 2006

I have now spoken to the Russian Gov Rep for the IMO in London, he sounds great and is going to try and help. Ian has spoken to William Hague and written to Prince Philip's office. I have contacted Blair and John Bercow... so let's see what happens.

Tim Thornton, always available at the end of a phone to give me technical advice (to deal with my temperamental back-up laptops), emailed me with another piece of great news. We had been discussing the best way to get ice maps for the Arctic transit, assuming of course I ever received the requisite permissions from the Russian government. Tim's contacts through his work on the Galileo project, the European rival to America's Global Positioning Satellite network, had come through with a means of providing me with near real-time satellite imagery of the Arctic ice. Unless the ice cleared completely (unlikely), ice maps as an aid to navigation were, in my opinion, essential. Tim had spoken to Richard Proud, who was also subcontracted to the Galileo project. He, in turn, had contacted Simon Chesworth at MDA Geospatial Services, a Canadian company operating the Radarsat I and Radarsat II earth orbiting (EO) satellites.

Tim to Richard: Thursday 16ᵗʰ March 2006
A friend of mine is heading up the Pacific to go across the top of Russia or Canada in a sailing boat (preferably Russia, but he is still trying to get permission). Can you think of any good high-res EO imagery that will help him with icing? We can download here and give him the info he needs. Obviously a short time from satellite pass to image availability is pretty important.

Richard to Simon: Thursday 16ᵗʰ March 2006
If you guys happen to be making routine acquisitions in the above area of interest, would you be interested in sponsoring him and supplying some imagery or ice maps?

Simon to Richard: Thursday 16ᵗʰ March 2006
We are not making routine acquisitions over Russia – only Canada. However, if we can get some publicity out of this, then I think I can persuade a few people that we can help provide imagery.

Great news for two reasons – satellite imagery would give me 'eyes' on the ground and if the Russians knew this facility was available to me, the impression of a well-organised expedition could only be reinforced. Taken together with the enhanced safety of having detailed ice maps to aid navigation, the argument for a solo transit became, I felt, more persuasive.

Up until mid-March, I was quietly satisfied with my emotional and psychological resilience, surprised even. Now, like a sandcastle, I felt myself slowly crumbling. I missed my sons. The prospect of enduring a similar period, five months, perhaps longer, before I saw them again became harder to bear. My conviction was great, but I felt vulnerable in the underbelly to morbid introspection. Benji, a strong, healthy, happy boy, had frequently been ill since my departure. Was he pining? Was I? Gabriel, younger, less aware and less emotionally developed, seemed fine. My guilt at leaving the boys never really left me at any time during the entire voyage. Guilt, like jealousy, is a canker, which can grow, corrupt and eventually crush. I realised too that I felt guilty about something else, something to do with Louise. I had to think hard to understand it.

Our telephone exchanges had become increasingly technical, impersonal. Louise did her thing, I did mine and somewhere in between, the umbilical link carried only data – weather, position, conditions, updates – and always short and sharp because of cost. The emotional support we sought from one another had vanished.

I telephoned Louise. We had a long chat, nothing technical, just stopping and spending time with each other.

Louise: Monday 20th March 2006

It was great to chat 'normally' last night. I know it was expensive but I think once a month or so we need to have a good chat like that. Good for both of us!

Got a call from Tony Blair's office this morning to say they are looking at my correspondence and will get back to me.

Igor Ponomarev, the permanent representative of the Russian Federation to the International Maritime Organization and chairman of the Maritime Safety Committee had been as good as his word. Louise called me.

'You're not going to believe this!'

'Try me.'

'I've just put the phone down to Igor. He's had a long talk with Nikolai Monko…'

'Does Monko know about the AGX?'

'110 per cent. He said it was uppermost in his mind!'

I sat stunned. It had taken so long to get through to the right person and now that we had, it seemed scarcely believable.

'That's great,' I said. 'Look, you'd better send a note to Sam filling him in.'

'Already done. I did it straight away. There's more.'

'What?'

'Monko told Igor he would do everything in his power to get you through the Russian Arctic!'

'Wow.'

'And Monko said he can see that potentially there's some very good publicity for them, positive British Russian relations, co-operation, all that.'

'What about the idea of the escort vessel?' This was something I had suggested to get round having an ice-pilot on board.

'Yep. Monko's prepared to talk about it, but this bit's a little confusing.'

'How?'

'Well, unless I misunderstood Igor, Monko's insisting on at least a Russian speaker on board and an inspection. An inspection would mean

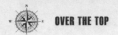

stopping in port. I asked Igor if he could go back to Monko and ask whether it'd be possible to have the inspection at sea and for a costing on an escort rather than an ice pilot.'

'That's bloody fantastic.'

'Good, eh!'

'I knew you were the right girl for the job!'

I went on deck. A mauve wash coloured the skyscape. The clouds seemed oversized. Through squinted eyes, I looked at the vastness of the space and the clouds scattered about the horizon and I could imagine a futuristic city silhouette of close-knit tower blocks and domes. I hoped the Russian developments were more concrete.

An email from Sam the following day confirmed the solid progress.

Sam: Wednesday 22nd March 2006
Louise

I hesitate to mention this but Sergey Frank, CEO of Sovcomflot, says he is 90 per cent certain that he will be successful in securing the necessary permissions. It is not clear yet whether this is with or without a pilot but Sergey is a keen sailor and understands the point and the promotional possibilities.

This was movement! The combined approaches from within both British and Russian government circles and Russian commerce now seemed almost certain to yield results. To allow *Barrabas* to go through short-handed would not be new, given that in 2003 and 2004, *Campina*, Henk's boat, had entered the Northern Sea Route with a two-man crew – himself and Boris, his ice pilot. Could Nikolai Monko be persuaded to go one further and let me try it on my own?

Henk de Velde: Friday 24th March 2006
Great news. As long as you don't have a Russian NO there is a YES.

CHAPTER 16

TUNING IN

I HAD ALWAYS WANTED TO SEE Hawaii but it looked as though I would only get a glimpse of Honolulu from the sea. DHL had agreed to airfreight the re-supply package to Honolulu. To take the plan forward, Louise had contacted a few yacht clubs on Oahu. Ivan Chan Wa, Commodore of the Waikiki Yacht Club, had responded immediately – no problem bringing the stuff out to me and for good measure, they would chuck in fresh fruit or 'whatever Adrian may need'.

I wanted to show Louise my appreciation. I called Nikki (incredible that from the middle of the Pacific Ocean, I could talk to Nikki in rural Suffolk by dialling a few numbers!). Could she arrange a delivery of flowers for Louise on Sunday, Mother's Day?

As in the Atlantic, the constancy of the trade winds meant I had little to do to sail *Barrabas*. She happily ploughed on, recording daily mileages from 100 to 120. Occasional variations in the weather might involve bending in a reef or shaking one out but otherwise I could relax, giving my damaged right wrist a chance to mend.

I made twice-daily tours around deck at dawn and dusk, armed with my spear gun, peering over the sides for any fish that believed they had found the protection of the mother ship but which to me might look good in a curry.

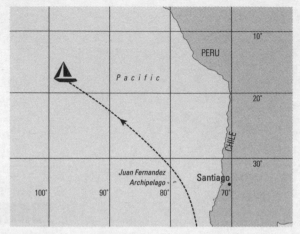

I saw no sign of human life – not a single aircraft or the lights of a faraway ship. My total isolation emphasised the enormity of the Pacific Ocean and whereas I'd previously felt the world to be small, its size now ballooned in my imagination. This place was vast, limited only by the horizon, beyond which the enormity of the ocean fell away and continued on, out of sight.

I was back to glorious nakedness, like a character from *Lord of the Flies* who'd escaped the book, grown to adulthood in the intervening years and materialised on a boat somewhere in the South Pacific.

Monotony crept into my diet and, although eating generally disinterested me in the heat, I developed a craving for sweet, stodgy food, so my breakfast now consisted of coffee and '*Barrabas* Pancake' – oil, flour, oats, sugar (lots) and evaporated milk blended together and deep-fried. I ate it with a coating of condensed milk.

On the chart table, an ever-evolving list of jobs rolled, like the Pacific swell, from one page to another. Each time I struck one job off, I added another to the bottom.

The stench of diesel seeped from the lazarette. This large stowage compartment at the back of the boat, measuring the width of the ship, 3 feet long and 4 feet deep was filled with 20-litre jerry cans. Two of them had leaked, punctured by constant agitation against the end threads of bolts securing the Hydrovane to the transom. All 17 cans had to come out. I cleaned out the lazarette and fixed rubber pads over the ends of the bolts before re-stowing the fuel.

The port main winch seized. I took my time servicing it, sitting in the sunshine, enjoying the breeze, naked and nut brown. I had no spare parts for the winches and worried that a spring might have failed. I discovered that solidified dirt and hardened grease were stopping the free rotation of the gear cogs. I cleaned every part and put the whole thing back together but no dice – it remained stubbornly seized. I stripped the starboard winch to check rotation, cleaning and re-greasing it in the process, then repeated the procedure on the port side winch. The parts were small and intricate so, to remember the sequence, I put each part into a numbered plastic bag as I took it off, beginning with 1 and ending with 17. Reassembly was by components in each bag in the reverse order. This time round, the winch worked perfectly – one of those peculiar mysteries.

The gaps between jobs (or during jobs – the winches were broken into several 'shifts') I filled with reading or napping, more usually both. For the moment, Yann Martell's *Life of Pi* was on the reading menu.

Health-wise, I was in good shape. My loss of appetite resulted in an almost visible shedding of surplus flesh put on in the colder climate of the high southern latitudes, although a nasty mouth ulcer developed at the front of my lower gum – not much to see but it hurt like hell. Vitamin depletion, perhaps. I started taking a range of Viridian supplements.

Nikki had arranged for a single orchid. I said to Nikki not to get a big bunch of flowers because Louise and the boys were off to Dubai to visit an old school friend, and she would not get the opportunity to enjoy them. The orchid was a great idea. Louise was thrilled. She called to tell me. Benji said he wished I was going with them, and so did I! After the miserable English winter, the sun would be good for the children and would revitalise Louise.

I had a nightmare session with the laptop, not for the first time. The email programme kept tying itself in knots. I was starting to develop a Pavlovian-type reaction to the sight and thought of using the laptop but, instead of salivating, I felt my blood pressure rising. Very few people had direct access to me via email, mainly to prevent viral contamination. Asking people not to send large emails seemed to get the same response as asking them, please, to bite their hands off! Someone (better to remain nameless) had dumped a 480kb message. Fifty dollars later, because the line kept dropping part way through transmission, the computer got itself tangled up again. The only remedy – a rushed call back to Louise before they set off for the airport to ask her to access the server on the internet and get rid of the message.

Two jobs remained outstanding before I could get down to some serious lounging about. The first was a slow leak from the fuel day tank that was staining the hot air inside the cabin with the sickly smell of diesel. I repaired it by draining the tank then applying a two-part epoxy. The second involved the watermaker holding tank. To avoid a vacuum inside the tank preventing the flow of seawater to the watermaker, air had to get in. I sealed the water-in and water-out hoses in the tank with a quickset two-part epoxy and introduced an air bleed pipe, 4 feet of narrow bore tubing, sealed at its point of entry into the tank. I tied the end of the air tube to the bulkhead, high above the waterline.

The next day, after the epoxy had fully cured, I checked my work while the watermaker was running. No leaks!

Small improvements like that made an enormous difference to my life on board as did a sense of personal cleanliness. I gave myself a haircut on deck in case hair in the bilges clogged the pumps. The result was not bad, at least from the front.

Twitching, I fired up the laptop. It worked. A message arrived from Louise:

Louise: Friday 31ˢᵗ March 2006
Having a lovely time. Spending mornings by the pool after a hearty buffet breakfast then out with Karen in the afternoon to a mall where they have huge kids' play zones more like funfairs. Karen and I went to a BBQ last night and Rosie her house-cleaner came and babysat at Karen's new lovely flat and we all spent the night here. Off to the hotel for big brunch this morning. Boys' behaviour not great! Maybe it's because they are acting up for Karen, but hopefully it will pass when they get used to it here. Ric says you have fab sailing conditions for at least the next 30 days!

Sliding the laptop to one side, I glanced at the GPS. 3,300 miles to Hawaii. I looked at the chart. The Galapagos Islands were presently the closest land to me at just over 1,200 miles to the northeast. I was about as far from land as it was possible to be anywhere on the planet.

* * *

Louise and I had reconnected and that equilibrium fed through to other areas. I slept more deeply and met jobs with greater enthusiasm. I took greater pleasure in the seascape around me and enjoyed my time more fully.

The idea of supermarkets, cars, television and the threads of ordinary life had receded. Looking out over the vast expanses of the ocean, my solitude, living on *Barrabas* – these things seemed normal, natural. Roof tiles, shops, Wellington boots, mud, crowds – these things seemed no more than the memories of a long-ago visit to a strange place.

Was this just a trick of time? Of course. When I stepped on land again, everything would be as familiar as though I had never been away. And yet, out there on the ocean I had a keen sense of something else, something elemental. I no longer sailed *Barrabas* with constant reference to instruments. She spoke to me in her soft voice. I often woke at night and went on deck to trim the sails or adjust the Hydrovane without any tangible reason to do so – no wind fluctuations, no alteration in the sea state. I began to know by instinct what was coming. I was fusing and merging with the natural world around me. My rhythm no longer beat to a different drum. I was beginning to breathe with the sea.

That night I drifted off to sleep while the earpieces of the MP3 player delivered Robbie Williams to somewhere inside my auditory cortex. A small vibration brought me awake. *Barrabas* seemed to be 'tugging'. I stared through the open hatch. Against the stars, the spinnaker pole's up-haul twanged like the strummed string of a guitar. On deck, the night air plucked at me with cool, refreshing fingers. I tightened the up-haul. The headsail ceased its luffing and *Barrabas* settled back to an even pull through the water. I went below and slept, dreaming of cucumber and tomato sandwiches and ice-cold Coke.

Bright sunshine was streaming into the cabin when I woke. I sensed the boat was fine. She had kept on while I slept. I looked around my small living space. It would be a photo finish as to which was the bigger – my space or a prison cell. The fore and aft cabins were full of fuel, stores, sails and accumulating garbage in white bin sacks. I lived in the central section, comprising the saloon and chart table, with the head on the port side and the galley on the starboard side. For the moment, I was on the port side, the low side of the boat. Either way, my bed measured 21" wide and 78" long. Two layers of 3" deep foam cushions laid end-to-end provided mattressing. The saloon table stood between the banquettes, its leaves folded to give me access to the fore cabin. The companionway steps, between the chart table and the galley, led up to the cockpit.

The inside of the boat was by now crisply dry. Below deck, the temperature climbed to 40°C under the tropical sun. To escape the heat,

I constructed a crude sunshade from the ruined cruising chute which had blown out somewhere off the Argentine coast. Beneath this turquoise tent, the whole of the cockpit area was in shade. I furnished it with cushions taken from the saloon, laid them out on the cockpit seating, providing myself an alternative place to read or eat.

Slowly, the winds moved east, tentative flicks at first as the southeast trades gave way to their northeast counterparts. To get a better angle, I gybed the sails, re-rigging the spinnaker pole on the starboard side. Both my wrists still ached. Planning tasks became essential to avoid further injury. I was only halfway through the voyage, at best. How were my wrists going to hold out until the end?

From deliberation and long habit, routine divided up my days: breakfast, morning chores (two hours), coffee, reading, lunch (occasionally), studying astro-navigation, nap, practice with the sextant, reading, bed. Like a child, I needed the structure and predictability of a set timetable. During the afternoons, I was usually in the 'tent'.

Years before, while I was a bachelor living in London, I'd taken myself off to night school to study the theoretical side of astro-navigation. Now I had the opportunity to put it into practice. The challenge to master the art (and science) of astro-navigation provided me with mental stimulation in addition to reading.

Once I'd refreshed myself on the academic principles, I moved onto to familiarising myself with the Almanac and reduction tables (computations used to interpret sextant readings and extrapolate meaningful positions). I then had to adjust the sextant, using the moon for side and index errors (a sextant measures angles of planetary bodies relative to the earth – a sextant's mirrors need to be correctly calibrated). I was then ready to practise 'pulling down' planets, the sun, the moon and stars.

A school of dolphin appeared one afternoon. I tapped out a simple numerical sequence on the side of the boat with a winch handle. They stayed for what seemed the mandatory 10 minutes, splashing around the bows, looking at me as if I was as simple-minded as the elementary language echoing through the water. One dolphin did seem intrigued, staying on for a further few minutes, chippering and squealing.

Louise: Wednesday 5th April 2006
We are all really brown. We went to Wild Wadi, a water park which was great and of course, the boys loved it.

Had an email today from Douglas Alexander, the Overseas Minister from the Foreign and Commonwealth Office! He is talking to the Russians too!

I took my first-ever noon sun sight and calculated my latitude at 04°.55.2′ south. By comparison, the GPS showed 05°.14′, so fair to say then that I was out 'by a mile' – 18.8 nautical miles to be exact. However, for a first, self-taught effort, I was reasonably pleased. The next day, I plotted my first sun-run-sun. The sun sight gave me a decent fix but the noon sight was wrong, 40 nautical miles out. Practice with the sextant would put that right!

A big bank of nimbostratus brought northeast winds, the first sustained northeasterlies since Cape Horn. We were closing on the equator, now just 240 miles away.

Louise: Sunday 9th April 2006

Tomorrow is our last day and then back to cold and reality. Two weeks more of school holidays so I will have to think of things to do to occupy the boys. One sure-fire appointment is at the cinema as Ice Age 2 has come out at home. I am going to have to spend quite a bit of time getting your shipment together. I take it all to DHL on the 21st. I have managed to really switch off from the AGX on this holiday, but I will be ready to do battle when I get home.

We crossed the equator for the second time at 1.57am local time on Tuesday 11th April (0957 UTC) and, as though to mark our completion of the southern hemisphere phase of the voyage, the equator manifested itself as a white line! The line, two feet wide, ran arrow-straight across the ocean, east to west as far as I could see in either direction, like a freshly painted road marking or an aircraft's vapour trail blazed across an azure sky. Was this the convergence between the equatorial and counter-equatorial currents? I doubted it. Algae of some kind? Unlikely. Spillage or discharge from a ship? I never did figure it out.

One spike pierced the benign constancy that had come to mark the passage of my days – the fragility of the email system. Aside from communicating with Louise, I requested and received weather information by email. What should have been a simple procedure for sending and retrieving emails usually became an hour-long battle, reprogramming and rebooting and, more often than not, long (and expensive) conversations with Tim on the satellite phone.

To make myself feel better, I called Louise.

'My sitting room looks like a bloody warehouse!'

I asked, 'How big is this package going to be?'

'A pallet.'

'A pallet?' I wondered where I would stow everything.

'You've got the new cruising chute in there from Kemp.'

'Great. I'm using the old one as a tent on deck.' I explained what I meant.

'I've just had a conversation with Michael Roth.'

Michael, Rear-Commodore for Sail at the Waikiki Yacht Club, seemed to have taken personal responsibility for me.

'And?'

Louise was giggling. 'I asked him, "Will you be able to get a boat to take this stuff out to Adrian?" "Yes," he said, "No problem and I'll put on a couple of lays." I was shocked, so I told him, "Michael, what you do is your business, but I don't really think it's appropriate that you tell me that. I may not be Adrian's wife, but I am his ex-wife. And furthermore, I said, anybody else on *Barrabas* will cancel out the single-handed nature of his voyage!"'

'What did he say?'

'He told me I was his kind of woman! Anyway, what he meant by lays was L E I S – you know, the traditional Hawaiian flower garlands.'

I couldn't help but laugh.

I was approaching the central Pacific shipping lanes. At 4.38am (local time) on 18th April, I went on deck to check my horizons. There, on my starboard bow, were the lights of a passing ship – the first sign of human life I'd seen for 65 days! I sat watching the lights until they disappeared, feeling a peculiar mix of emotions. My complete isolation had brought me to the point where I existed in my own realm of the ocean – just me, the dolphins, the wahoo, the seabirds.

The Hawaiian Islands were now 2,000 miles away. On such a long voyage 2,000 miles seems like nothing at all. If I could hold a 100 mile-a-day average, I would see Hawaii in early May. But 2,000 miles is the same distance as London to Nova Scotia on the other side of the Atlantic Ocean! Or as far as Lisbon to the Azores and back!

Michael Roth had given Louise co-ordinates, which she passed onto me: a waypoint at Diamond Head buoy offshore from Honolulu, where I was to make the rendezvous with the supply boat from the Waikiki Yacht Club.

I woke at daybreak. I could tell by the boat's motion and the rush of water past the hull that the wind was 16–18 knots and we were making 5 knots through the water. The sky through the battened Perspex was blue.

Suddenly, an almighty bang reverberated around the starboard side. Green water cascaded over the deck, obliterating the blue sky. I had closed all the hatches and the companionway as a precaution against spray strafing the deck. *Barrabas* lurched. An organisation tray containing nuts, bolts, screws, torch, knife, MP3 and a collection of other odds and ends flew off the saloon table, over my head and hit the ceiling, which was now horizontal. *Barrabas* had just taken her second capsize.

Then she screamed.

A year before, Benji had run into the path of a car. The car swerved, missing him by inches. In that instant, everything stopped – breathing, heart, movement. Life, for the brief time it took for the car to go past, floated in a kind of adrenalin-soaked animation. So it was when *Barrabas* screamed. All other sound muted, just the solo high-pitched, grinding, tearing of steel as *Barrabas* slowly righted herself. I rushed on deck. The sails remained tautly shaped by the wind – no telltale chinks of daylight coming through rents or tears. The shrouds, I counted all twelve, were rigid. The mast stood proud, erect. I could not see any damage. I searched, but could find nothing.

* * *

As I broiled on deck, a school of wahoo sought shelter beneath *Barrabas*'s hull. I spotted them by chance five or six feet below the surface, the sun's rays glinting turquoise and green off their backs. Bits of stale pumpernickel excited their cursory interest, then they disappeared forward into shadow. The abundant gooseneck barnacles seemed much more appetising. I found an out-of-date can of fruit, spilled the peach segments into the sea and polished the ring-pull top. Four feet of fishing twine knotted through the ring-pull and my lure was ready. Beside me, the spear gun was armed. The ring-pull skimmed and twisted in the roughened wake, catching and reflecting sunlight. This proved a greater temptation than stale pumpernickel and slowly the wahoo emerged from beneath the stern, expertly slowing to let *Barrabus* pass over. They surfaced like miniature, iridescent submarines, nosing the can top. I reeled the ring-pull in until the fish were only inches from the back of the boat. Spear gun in hand and standing on the sugar scoop, I fired and missed. Their patience exhausted, the wahoo dived to their cruising altitude, accelerated and disappeared once more into their shadowed sanctuary.

On the same day I was harmlessly firing at fish, Louise turned forty-six. I dialled her number.

'*Barrabas* calling,' I said in the manner of a Eurovision Song Contest judge when Louise picked up.

'They're wonderful…'

Nikki had come to the rescue once again. A huge bouquet had just arrived on Louise's doorstep.

'Picked 'em myself, swam across two oceans…'

'Seriously, thank you. I've just put them in water. How are you doing?'

'Okay. I spoke to Ricardo. I'll go over the top of Hawaii and approach Oahu from the north. That way I won't have to beat into wind. Ric reckons the northeast trades will funnel between the islands so if I go over the top I can approach Oahu downwind.'

'Well, everything's ready for you.'

'Thanks. I do have one problem.'

'What?'

'I've got no charts for the islands.'

'You'll manage.'

Louise's belief in my ability to get *Barrabas* to where I wanted to go – reinforced by my successful passage round Cape Horn – was heartening.

'Well, I'll call Michael and get his view – local knowledge and all that. You doing anything this evening?'

'Some of the girls are coming round.'

The idea of people 'coming round' seemed odd to me. Today, 1st May, was my 186th day at sea. I had not seen another person in all that time. The prospect of talking to people on the resupply boat made me apprehensive.

My advance towards Hawaii had come to be dogged by stalling wind, a legacy from the bizarre weather patterns since crossing north over the equator. The following day I was on deck. Beneath a steely sky heavy with the promise of rain, *Barrabas* bobbed on a mirror flat sea. In the thinning light of evening, occasional zephyrs stroked the surface and ruffled the hot air. Mug of tea in hand, I stood on the aft deck looking sternwards to the south. Some inexplicable sixth sense compelled me to continue staring in that direction. The horizon showed only the gentle curvature of the earth, but I was convinced a wave was coming – I simply had a sense of it. For 20 minutes, I maintained my vigil. Nothing happened. I did not feel alarm. This was not an area noted for rogue waves. I was far from land and in deep water. A tsunami only presents danger when the massive energy of the surge strikes the continental shelf.

I called Ricardo. There was no answer so I left a message and then called Michael.

'Aloha, Adrian,' Michael said. We talked for a short while then I asked him his advice about approaches to Oahu. 'The seas south of the big island are among the roughest in the world. Give that area a wide berth…'

'The big island?'

'Hawaii Island, we call it the "Big Island".'

'How far south?'

'Where are you at the moment?'

I gave him my position, about 270 miles from Hilo, the main town on Hawaii's east coast.

'Or pass east of the big island then come south through the Molokai channel between Molokai and Oahu. That's the general rule here, come in from the north, leave to the south.'

'Sounds good to me.'

'You got an ETA?'

I computed quickly.

'Monday 8th May.'

'Alrighty then.'

We said our goodbyes with the promise I would call as I neared Diamond Head.

The following day, on deck again, I heard a distant beep announcing the arrival of a text message on the satellite phone. The message was from Ric:

'Feel free to call now if you wish. Expect the same as today for the next 20 hours or so. Now wind will arrive from southeast and back east and north-east, max 15 kn. Tsunami warning false alarm.' (04/05 00:00 UTC).

I re-read the message several times, just to make sure I had understood it correctly. I immediately called Ricardo.

'I didn't know anything about a tsunami!'

'Your message said you thought a wave was coming?'

'That was just a feeling!'

There was a pause on the line filled with slight crackling.

'Wow, man – really? Hey, you're really tuned in!'

'When was the tsunami alert issued?'

Ricardo consulted notes and gave me a time in UTC. I converted the time difference. An earthquake in the region of Tonga 3,000 miles south

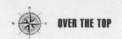

had initiated the alert at exactly the time I had sensed its presence the previous day.

Still feeling dazed at the idea of what I could only think of as some kind of heightened perception, I wandered around the deck making a casual inspection of the rigging and deck gear. Perhaps we are all linked to the natural world in some fundamental but indefinable way. Perhaps our abilities to 'tune in' are at a rudimentary stage of development and in our broader evolution, this ability will evolve over generations into some higher language. Or perhaps it was once more developed as a survival instinct in primitive man, an ability we've now lost and which is awakened only after long immersion in nature's rhythms. I fingered the starboard lower shrouds. They seemed loose. I kneeled to hand-tighten the bottle screws, but how could the shrouds be *this* loose?

I went aloft to inspect the rig and found a catastrophic rigging failure. The through-mast bolt holding the tangs supporting the fore and aft lower shrouds had pulled down, tearing a three-inch gash through the steel wall of the mast on the starboard side. In a big blow, the mast would almost certainly come down!

How could I have missed this? When did it happen? It must have been the capsize – the 'scream'.

I jumped back on deck, dropped the mainsail and reefed the headsail to ease the load on the mast, although I needed to strike a balance because reduced sail area increased the pendulum motion of the boat, creating a different type of stress on the rigging.

I flopped into the cockpit, my pulse racing as much from the shock and realisation that my world had changed as from the panicky rush to shorten sail. Hawaii was no longer a sail-by. I had to go into port.

'Shit!' I shouted. Two immediate problems: one of additional, unforeseen expense, and the other, a crucial delay in my schedule, upsetting my delicate equilibrium. Could the knock-on effects jeopardise my chances of getting to the Bering Strait in time?

To relieve the damaged area from excessive loading, I quickly rigged two halyards around the lower spreaders in figures of eight to avoid fouling the mainsail track, tensioning each line with a block and tackle fixed to the toe-rail. As if to test both my resolve and the makeshift repair, the wind escalated to 26 knots. An electrical storm moved in overhead. Lightning illuminated the sky like giant bombs detonating in the clouds. *Barrabas* began to pitch wildly. I put a call in to Louise to give her details of this development.

'There's a reason for everything,' Louise said calmly.

I had noticed a progressive change in her disposition and philosophy as the voyage had unfolded. Now she was deploying calm and rationality against my volatility, a shift in the more usual balance of our relationship.

'I'm worried about getting to the Bering Strait.'

'You know your own favourite saying?'

'It is what it is.'

'Exactly. Think of it this way, you can fix the mast but also get the batteries checked over, sort the computer properly, wash your clothes, have a rest, see a wonderful place and you know what…'

'What?' I said.

'Have a bloody great, beautiful steak, French fries and a crisp salad all washed down with a cold beer.'

'Um… beer,' I said. 'What I wouldn't give for an ice-cold Guinness!'

CHAPTER 17
HONOLULU

THE 'BIG ISLAND' LAY HIDDEN beneath mist as I passed round its eastern and northern flanks. In the northeast trades, I was now on a lee shore. As a precaution, I called the US Coastguard, explained the situation and agreed to maintain a four-hourly reporting schedule. If the mast (or engine) failed, I would need a tow into port.

The winds accelerated between the islands, kicking the waters of Molokai Channel into a moody, choppy confusion. Circular currents neutralised the Hydrovane's attempts to hold course so I hand-steered *Barrabas* through the night of Sunday 7th May. At dawn, the lights of Oahu's coastal settlements gave way to a raw and breathtaking landscape: a mountainous, volcanic spine drifting to a flattened coastal plain thickly covered with vegetation.

Diamond Head, a volcanic crater edging seawards from the southern shore, shimmered under a morning sun already suffusing the air with heat. Buildings nestling in the crooks of its limbs emerged as I neared the land. Houses set among palm-fringed gardens close to the beach began to reveal themselves in detail. Moving cars winked in the sunlight. As *Barrabas* rounded Diamond Head, the great sweep of Waikiki's crescent beach backed by ranks of skyscrapers stretched away towards Pearl Harbor. I stood on deck and marvelled. Approaching land from the air is exciting but from the sea, the

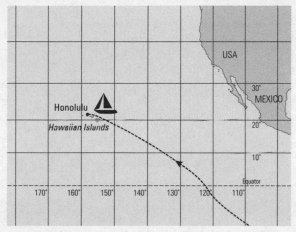

experience is more intense, smell and sound enriching the sight. Here, in the middle of the largest ocean on earth, stood a full-blown, money-fuelled city set in a lush, tropical landscape. I felt as though I had found Atlantis!

At 11am, I called Michael. Ten minutes later, while I steered *Barrabas* around the red-painted buoy at Diamond Head, a small cruiser bounced over the water towards us. Three men waved back: Ivan Chan Wa, Michael and a British member of the Waikiki Yacht Club, Ernie Woodruff, brought along as 'translator'.

I waved back.

'Aloha!' one of the men shouted.

I guessed by his voice that it was Michael.

'Good to be here!' I yelled back.

The boat buzzed around me for a few minutes taking pictures, then nosed closer in.

Michael was shouting across the gap. 'There're some reefs by the beach, so follow me in but stay right behind.'

'Okay,' I said. I had the headsail up but I dropped the mainsail and switched on the engine.

Michael cupped his hands around his mouth. 'What'd you like to drink when we get in?'

I didn't have to think for long. 'An ice-cold Guinness if you've got one!' I yelled back.

Michael waved, gunned his engine and moved ahead of me. As I entered the channel into the Ala Wai yacht basin, the Ala Moana Park slid by on my left: manicured lawns, trees, shrubs and flowers. I drank in the sight, the liquid green whetting my parched imagination. Even the name of the city was appropriate. In the Hawaiian language, Honolulu means *place of shelter*.

Sails furled and engine gently gurgling, I nosed *Barrabas* to her mooring on a hammerhead pontoon behind an American yacht, *Astor*. In the stillness of the basin, the heat pressed down. Sweat trickled down my back. I took off my heavy weather salopettes. People on the pontoon made off my lines. I cut the engine. After six and a half months (193 days) at sea, *Barrabas* was at rest.

The yacht club had contacted US Customs and two officers were on the pontoon to clear me in. Until the formalities were complete, I had to remain on board. As the two officers fired routine questions at me – last port of call, intended length of stay – a thought occurred to me.

'I have a weapon on board, a pump action shotgun, and fifty rounds of ammunition.' I fully expected the officers to demand its immediate handover and was already moving towards the cockpit in anticipation.

'Don't worry 'bout that,' one of the officers said.

'You sure?'

'No problem,' the second officer said, more intent on recording irrelevant information like my height and weight.

The escort launch had parked up elsewhere. I saw a tall, bearded figure amble along the pontoon carrying a tray.

'Aloha, Adrian,' Michael said when he reached *Barrabas*'s side. 'Welcome to Honolulu. Here's something to cool you down!' A can of ice-cold Guinness beaded with condensation sat on the tray. I began to salivate. The Hawaiian press had gathered on the quayside, notified and briefed by the club's PR manager, Bobbie Jennings, who had been in constant touch with Louise during the preceding weeks. Cameras rolled, shutters clicked, microphones pointed. I drank the Guinness and talked, my words tripping out in an unstoppable flood. The leis that had caused Louise so much confusion appeared from somewhere and were draped around my neck. Michael presented me with a special lei of woven tea leaves, a particular honour for *Barrabas*, which I hung over her bow as is the tradition.

Finally, the moment of setting foot on dry land arrived and with it a mixture of conflicting emotion: relief, satisfaction, pleasure, hesitancy. It was time for me to leave my ship, if only temporarily. The prospect of our separation was strangely daunting as if, by stepping ashore, the umbilical link between me and *Barrabas* would be severed, leaving me more alone on shore surrounded by people than I had been on my own for months at sea. I realised in that instant just how connected I had become to her, how much I cared for her, how much I loved her. I kissed *Barrabas* and stepped ashore surrounded by a brace of well-wishers and press.

The Waikiki Yacht Club is in the heart of the Waikiki downtown area. The clubhouse itself is an idyll of urban tropical splendour: a long, low building open to the marina and overlooked by towering sentinels of glass and steel with vanguards of gently swaying palms. Bobbie Jennings, in her sixties, clutched my arm as we made our way towards the clubhouse along the pontoons, fearing that I might pitch head-first into the water. Surprisingly, I was steady on my feet, but her arm through mine was comforting. We sat at a table. I was being garrulous and foolish, but I didn't care. They looked at me as if I was a space cadet but let me talk. Lunch arrived: New York steak, fries, chicken mayo, papaya salad and ice-cold beer! Food had never tasted so good.

That first evening ashore, Ernie drove me to a mountaintop lookout before descending to Kailua where the beach, fringed with fir and palm, would compete with any in the world. Dinner followed at a beachside restaurant. I couldn't resist a second steak washed down with cold Budweiser. To be there, seeing people, hearing the hubbub of conversation, smelling the scents of land and feeling the firmness of the ground beneath my feet instilled a fresh sense of pleasure and appreciation after the months of isolation.

The following day, Les Vasconelles, a diver specialising in scraping the undersides of boats visited *Barrabas* offering to clean off the hull. *Barrabas* was losing half a knot of boat speed caused by the drag from marine growth on her undersides. He refused payment saying he wanted to be part of the expedition and this was how he would like to be involved. Les surfaced to show me the size of the gooseneck barnacles. Some of them, growing in clusters, measured six inches.

'You got somethin' fouled on the prop,' he said, pushing his mask up onto his forehead.

'What d'you think it is?'

'Dunno. Could be fishing twine. I'll go take another look,' and with that, the mask came down and he disappeared. A few minutes later, he surfaced again. 'Seems solid.' He handed me a piece of material cut from around the shaft. I turned the piece over, shaking my head with incomprehension.

'I reckon it's twine, got wrapped round and melted with the friction,' Les offered.

That seemed like a plausible explanation. The material was grey and had been molten at one time; now it was set in rucks like a tiny piece of lava.

'Can you cut the rest of it off?' I asked.

'No problemo,' Les said and he was gone again.

I heard the scraping and cutting while I pottered about inside the boat. Eventually, I heard Les haul himself onto the pontoon and went to join him. He had a collection of bits of grey plastic. 'Got most of it off. Reckon your prop shaft's a bit loose, though.'

I thanked Les and thought no more about it.

The consignment of replacement parts and additional supplies was in Ernie's warehouse from which he ran his quilting company. Michael arrived in a pick-up and together we delivered the various packages to the yacht club. I spent the rest of the day opening and disseminating everything that Louise had put together – the target list had been filled 100 per cent, plus some additional cold-climate clothing items.

At lunchtime, Rick, a yacht club member who operated Blue Diamond Welding, inspected the mast damage. We could make repairs with *Barrabas* afloat. To get access to his equipment, *Barrabas* needed to move to the work dock where the hoist could lift Rick's equipment to the level of the lower spreaders. I cast off at 6pm with Ernie on hand to help.

I set to work wiring in the new wind generator and the new heating-control unit. A tricky piece of work involved replacing and rewiring the voltage-converter unit that powered the ship's computer which had caught fire and burnt out during the capsize at Cape Horn.

Articles appeared in Tuesday's press following the television news coverage of the evening before. The club secretary told me that a number of people had come down to the club wanting to see *Barrabas*, including visitors from England. Unfortunately, they were barred entry for security reasons. When I went to a local store to pick up copies of the *Honolulu Advertiser*, the checkout lady recognised me and became very excited!

Dan Toye, an itinerant marine electrician, charged up the boat's battery bank and put the batteries through a thorough health check, using a galvanic meter to test for currency leaks. The all-clear came as a relief.

I took the mainsail to North Sails Hawaii for minor repairs. There, Jim Maselli wasted no time in getting to work, immediately appreciating the need for urgency. Sailing via my chosen antipodal point southeast of Japan, *Barrabas* and I would have to travel more than 7,000 miles from Hawaii to reach the Arctic ice. Time was not on my side.

Rick's crew fixed the mast by welding two 3-inch square, ¼-inch thick stainless steel plates over the damaged areas and made a new through-bolt, slightly longer than the original to account for the additional thickness of the new plates. Despite the repair, I decided I had to modify my sailing strategy by reefing the sails at lower wind thresholds than previously. The consequence of slower boat speed would, I figured, be compensated by the reduced drag of the newly scraped hull.

I wondered around the sprawling shopping mall just across the road from the yacht club. Presents for the boys needed to be lightweight for airfreight. I settled on Hawaiian shirts and for Louise, a handmade necklace of delicate shells and a shoulder bag decorated with a Hawaiian palm print pattern.

Michael drove me to Costco to restock on vital commodities like tinned milk, then, together with Ernie, I had lunch with Ed Reinhart, another club member at his house at Koko Head. The setting was sublime, part way up the side of an extinct volcano with a pool terrace out front and a sweeping view of the bay and Honolulu beyond. The conversation centred largely on philosophy and self-knowledge – he was interested to know how long periods of isolation had affected me. I think I disappointed him.

The following evening after dark, while I was refitting the shrouds and putting on the repaired mainsail in the orange glow of the work dock floodlights, Ed arrived carrying two bags.

'Bought these for ya!' Ed hoisted the bags on deck. The bags were marked with the Borders bookstore logo. 'Thought after yesterday's talk you could do with some more reading material.'

I made coffee and we chatted for a short while in the cool of the evening. On Monday 15th May, I loaded all the fuel onto the boat then went out to dinner with Michael and his family at his mountaintop home. Being a sailor, Michael needed no explanation of antipodal points and when I explained my selected position was southeast of Japan, the information met with a pursing of the lips.

'They've just had a big hit.'

'Typhoon?' I asked.

'Yep.'

I felt dread. My ETA at the antipodal point, 3,200 miles due west, was 20th June – four weeks. Historical data suggested that the majority of typhoons spun away from Japan and tracked northeast over open water, exactly the course I would be following once I reached the antipodal point and made the turn for the Bering Strait. With the damage to the mast and the delay in Honolulu, the chances of meeting with a typhoon escalated dramatically.

On Wednesday 17th May, Elizabeth, DHL manager in Honolulu, came to the marina in the morning to collect the box of mini-DV tapes (I had shot 20 hours of video footage since leaving England) and the gifts I had bought to send back to Louise. Before packing the tapes, I recorded a video message for the children. At 1.30pm after a (healthy?) lunch of hamburger, fries and Coke on board with Ernie, I slipped my mooring. After the Honolulu bustle, it felt strange to find myself once again on the wide ocean with only *Barrabas* as company.

As the mountains of Oahu and the high-rises of the city faded into the mists of low cloud, sadness descended at leaving a group of new friends. Ivan's efforts to locate the right people to carry out the work on *Barrabas*, Michael's generosity with his time, Bobbie's enthusiasm and Ernie's inexhaustible good nature had all combined to enrich my adventure.

Through all the drama of discovering the damage to the mast, the last-minute change of plan to enter port and the excitement of seeing Honolulu, I had pushed the Russian dilemma to the back of my mind, helped along by the knowledge that Igor Ponomarev was on the case.

Just before I left Honolulu, Nikolai Monko wrote to Louise stressing again that an inspection of the yacht was necessary and quoting various rules and regulations suggesting that the presence of an ice pilot on board was mandatory to assist with communications, navigation and search and rescue, should that become necessary. Nonetheless, the guidelines for shipping through the Northern Sea Route constantly referred to ships over 300 tonnes. This apparent contradiction still left us with some room to manoeuvre. Louise decided to insinuate herself into this narrow gap by contacting Roman Abramovich in London.

While *Barrabas* headed west in the balmy trades, Louise sent me an update on the Volvo Ocean Race fleet, now crunching into 15-foot seas and 30-knot winds 1,300 miles from Land's End. A Dutch crewman on *ABN AMRO TWO* had been swept overboard. The yacht immediately launched a man overboard drill. Thirty-two-year-old Hans Horrevoets was located and lifted aboard. However, despite the efforts of fellow crewmembers to resuscitate him under the direction of medical advisors from Derriford Hospital in Plymouth, Horrevoets failed to regain consciousness and died. He was married with a young son. The tragedy brought home just how close I had come to death in the English Channel. Louise added a caveat to her message: *'KEEP YOUR SAFETY HARNESS ON PLEASE!'*

Ernie Woodruff: Honolulu, Thursday 18th May 2006
Hi Louise,

Well, it was sad to see Adrian leave. In a few short days, we had become good friends. However, it was also exciting to see him motoring out down the channel to the open sea. We raced around Magic Island to see him pass the last channel buoys and unfurl his jib. Barrabas was underway on a quiet sea with a steady breeze. You have done a sterling job in support of this challenge, and as ever, these things never work without the right team around you. Keep up the good work and stay in touch. Let Adrian know that we watched him out and he and the boat looked good.

I LOST MYSELF IN READING, beginning with Gerald Seymour's *Traitor's Kiss*. The reading helped time pass. I forgot the closeness of land and once again established my shipboard routine.

During my shopping foray in Honolulu, I had bought a comb-through haircutter in Walmart. I tried it out on deck. When I checked in the mirror, I had inadvertently given myself a 'flat-top' cut – not bad. Feeling pretty pleased with myself, I finished *Traitor's Kiss* and started on Michael Connelly's *Lincoln Lawyer*.

My usual habit when dealing with delicate situations is not to rush. Ever since receiving the communiqué from Nikolai Monko, I had been turning the problem of the Russian permissions over in my mind. I decided to write to him directly and to copy the letter to the various people who had become involved. These included the Russian ambassador in London, the British ambassador in Moscow, Margaret Beckett (then the British Foreign Secretary), Tony Blair, Igor Ponomarev, Sam Laidlaw and Sergey Frank, the purpose being to apply subtle pressure. It was important to give Monko options. I concluded the letter:

…I do not wish to take unnecessary risk in making a transit of the NSR and will only proceed if ice conditions are very favourable; the boat is strong and well equipped; if it is possible to lay on a Russian escort vessel then requirements for an ice pilot can be satisfied and safety measures ensured. I trust you will appreciate

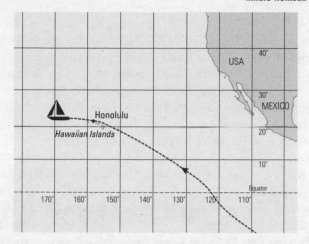

the unique nature of my endeavour and consider it worthy of making exceptions to the usual procedures governing vessels making a transit of the NSR…

While in Walmart, I made a second purchase, a small gold earring. On rounding the Horn, a sailor is entitled to wear a gold ring through the ear (or, if it's your preference, through the nipple). The direction round the Horn determines which ear. The ear (or nipple) closest to land gets the ring, in my case then, the right ear. The confusion with latter-day fashion trends is that a ring through the right ear signifies gayness in men, but since there was little prospect of my being propositioned, this did not concern me.

In her press release following my successful doubling of the Horn, Louise wrote, *'As for wearing an earring, I think Adrian will probably pass!'* She knows me well, but clearly not that well. I had my ear pierced in Honolulu. With difficulty, I fitted the ring, having worn a stud while the piercing healed (easier to rotate to keep the channel clear). Other privileges bestowed on Cape Horners are the right to piss to windward (presumably to avoid the streams of other pissers) and to rest one foot on the table while making the loyal toast (providing the table is in the wardroom of a British warship). So, hooped and bestowed, I drank a toast with one foot on the saloon table (seeing as *Barrabas* was flying a British ensign and carried a weapon and live ammunition, I decided she qualified for the occasion as a British warship) then went on deck to piss to windward.

The timing of my letter to Nikolai Monko coincided with the indefatigable efforts of Ian Johnstone-Bryden. He had spoken with Admiral Sir Jonathon

Band's PA. She asked for an email confirming the detail and promised to try to find a route to the Russian Navy at high level. Ian also spoke to an old friend of his on HMS *Warrior* who knew the personnel in the Royal Navy team which had rescued seven Russian sailors trapped for three days in an AS28 mini submarine off the coast of the Kamchatka Peninsula in August 2005, after fishing nets ensnared the sub 190 metres below the surface.

The British six-man team led by Commander Ian Riches flew to Petropavlovsk from Prestwick Airport and managed to free the submarine after a tense six-hour operation using a Scorpio 45 Remotely Operated Vehicle (ROV) to cut through the nets. The Russian crew only had a few hours of oxygen left.

An internal message would go from them to the Admiral's office with their Russian contacts' details.

On the same day, 23rd May, Louise received a phone call from John A Mann II, an American living and working in Moscow who handled public affairs for Millhouse, one of Roman Abramovich's companies. Roman Abramovich had tasked him with helping us out. A fluent Russian speaker, John promised to call Monko directly.

Ian Johnstone-Bryden: Tuesday 23rd May 2006
Hi Louise,

All of us, now thousands and maybe millions, following Adrian are immensely proud of his achievement. I am very pleased to have been a tiny help and pleased to see the threads coming together with the Russians.

The FCO lobbying from our embassy in Moscow will positively complement your direct communication with Monko and the very interesting approach from the Russian personalities. The latter will probably clinch things in the end because in Russia one hand washes the other and always has.

I am greatly encouraged that you will now have the help of the 1st Sea Lord. The Russian Navy owes the RN a favour or two for the rescue of the submariners. They are also in a position to provide an escort vessel. I do not know which part of the RN will make the approach but Sir Jonathon Band is as high as you can go in RN ranks.

When you next email Adrian, you should bring him up to speed because I doubt he appreciates just how many people are working to help him achieve his dream.

Ian was right. Louise was on the ground working through the daily correspondence and shaping developments while I received the occasional précis, once removed from the action. I was amazed at how Louise had managed to generate the momentum she had but not surprised. Her tremendous capacity to get on and do things without prevarication combined with her natural enthusiasm made her unstoppable.

During every moment at sea, I worried about the threats around me: would I collide with a submerged container and hole the hull; would I stray into a whale-breeding ground and excite an attack; would a storm bring breaking waves and knock the boat down or worse, roll her over? Now there was the additional concern about the rig – would it hold? Could it take the sustained pressure of another 12,000 miles? To live with fear is a grinding, exhausting business. I listened perpetually to *Barrabas* for any unfamiliar sound, even as I slept. I felt the movement of the boat, sensing impending change from myriad signals: the altered rush of water against her sides, her changed attitude, variation in her roll. If the worst happened, could I launch the life rafts in time, remember the grab bag, retrieve the emergency beacon and activate it properly? In Honolulu, I bought three sheathed hunting knives. I wore the biggest of the three on a belt. Another I lashed to the outside of the cockpit cuddy (starboard side) and the third to the stanchion bars at the mast. These blades had a single purpose – to cut the bindings of the inflatable lift raft stowed on deck amidships and the hard dinghy lashed to the foredeck. The knives gave me comfort – they would save precious seconds in the desperate panic of abandoning *Barrabas*.

Conditions since leaving Honolulu continued to be near perfect with the wind astern at 12 knots, the sea a deep and glittering blue, the sun warm on my back.

Admiral Sir Jon Band's Flag Captain had talked the Russian situation over with the naval attaché in Moscow who advised against a formal navy-to-navy approach. He believed this might encourage some searching questions about the Royal Navy's connections with the Alpha Global Expedition. This concern was in view of the very sensitive military installations along the Northern Sea Route and the deteriorating political situation between Washington, London and Moscow. However, the Flag Captain asked the commercial section at the embassy what they were doing to sort the situation, requesting that they keep him informed of progress so that he could report to the First Sea Lord.

Ian's opinion was that things had moved forward a notch. The combined efforts of the various threads in play might ultimately achieve a result.

Louise: Friday 26th May 2006
John (Mann) spoke to Monko who says he is simply not able to bend the rules for you even if he wanted to. They haven't had an accident since 1983 and are proud of that record! However, Monko did say that it might be possible to have an ice pilot on a separate boat at a cost. I have asked John to find out how much. He is getting back to me on Tuesday. He will also address the inspection issue with Monko although now that you are not going for non-stop it is a little hard to justify why an inspection would be a problem.

To me, this was a breakthrough. This concession towards an escort vessel implied a de facto agreement to let me try the NSR. Just as the breakthrough came, the wind died.

I called Louise to congratulate her on progress so far.

'And guess what,' she said after telling me first that Benjamin was losing all his milk teeth. 'Yesterday, I took the boys to a craft fair and afterwards to see an open garden in Brill and who should be there directing people in to the car park – Sam Laidlaw!'

'You're kidding.'

Brill was a hilltop village close to where we both lived.

'No kidding. Turns out it's his parents-in-law's place. Anyway, we had a good chat and he wants me to put him in touch with John Mann. Apparently, Sam knows Roman's two senior lieutenants and wants to chat it over with John.'

Our conversation returned to the children. I knew Benji had been getting occasional headaches. 'How's Benji? I know it's futile but I worry like hell about that sort of thing, makes me feel very guilty for being out here.'

'Benji's fine. The headaches have gone, but there's a new issue. Gabriel fell in the garden and hurt his arm. I did all the rotating and checking. I'm sure it isn't broken but I called David Skinner who said if he's complaining tomorrow I should take him in just in case it is a green stick fracture.'

'God! How's he now?'

'Dosed up with Calpol and he seems fine, just a bit sore.'

While I was at the chart table still angsting over the children, I logged my position – 2,400 miles to the antipodal point (AP). If I could cover 100 miles a day – eminently doable, but only with a sustained wind – I would reach the AP on 21st June, one day behind schedule. I could live with that but I still felt pressured, more so than at any other time during the voyage.

The thumbscrew was the clock – seconds dribbling inexorably into the void. The wind had disappeared five days before, a full 50 per cent of the time since leaving Honolulu and with each breathless minute, my window for making the Bering Strait and the Arctic shrank. I had anticipated a fast run towards the AP, flying a spinnaker most of the way with boat speeds of 5 to 6 knots pretty much a foregone conclusion. The routing charts indicated a less than one per cent chance of westerly winds, but that is what I was experiencing. It was frustrating. The slower the boat travelled through the water, the faster marine growth would colonise the hull in these tropical waters. Boat speed would erode, increasing time to target and closing my window even more. I tried to remain positive, cleaning the boat, checking the rig, servicing the engine, practising emergency evacuation procedures, planning ahead and corresponding. But mostly I read – escapism that ate time. I had just finished a book on psycho-cybernetics – first published in 1960, the year of my birth – by an American plastic surgeon, Maxwell Maltz MD. He died in 1975. Maltz was way ahead of his time in his evaluation of the self and what it means to be productive and happy as opposed to stressed. It was apposite reading. I reminded myself constantly that the lack of wind was not some celestial conspiracy to thwart my goal but nature working to nature's laws, in which a lone yachtsman on a small boat was an irrelevance. I accepted (grudgingly) that I was at the mercy of some greater power and my mind bent to the Taoist belief that I must be as water and flow around obstructions rather than try too hard to roll them aside. But flow as I tried, my eye was still drawn to the clock and the sweep of the hands around its face, leaking time.

I decided to head further south to find more stable wind. Perhaps I was floating too high on the top of the trade wind belt. Ricardo agreed in a text message: *'Go further south to 19° north. More wind there…'* (30/05 21.29 UTC)

Louise: Tuesday 30th May 2006

Gabriel was still in a certain amount of pain this morning so I took him to the hospital. He has a green stick fracture to the radial head. So it's a sling for a few days and then no contact sports (??!!) for three weeks. He will be fine for sports day at the end of term, though. I am taking him back tomorrow for a check. So that's how I've spent my morning. He is having a quiet time at home today and then back to school tomorrow.

Put Sam in touch with John Mann. Spoke to Damian at the Foreign Office. They are also going to write a formal letter requesting assistance for you to their counterparts in Russia and setting target dates for chasing if they haven't heard.

Damian Thwaites, a senior staffer at the Russia Desk of the Foreign Office, had spearheaded the dialogue with the Russian authorities in London, particularly with Andrey Chupin, First Minister at the Russian Embassy in London.

Adrian: Wednesday 31ˢᵗ May 2006
I'm very upset about Gabo's arm – I feel useless out here (I am useless out here!). Heavy guilt feelings going on now.

Louise: Wednesday 31ˢᵗ May 2006
Don't feel guilty, these things happen – they are boys after all! I took Gabe back to the JR and he is feeling much better. He doesn't even want to wear the sling but I am insisting that he does at school this week if for no other reason than the other children don't knock him. The doctor said it should be fully healed in 2–3 weeks.

So with that, I rummaged through my library with the 'stay positive' message from Max Maltz still ringing in my head. While *Barrabas* found her way south towards latitude 19° north, I lay in my bunk and got lost in Afghanistan reading Khaled Hosseini's *The Kite Runner*.

* * *

On a small boat, anxiety comes from either the brutish assault of heavy weather or the mind-numbing frustration of windless conditions. The pleasure is milked from somewhere between these extremes. The light winds continued through the first days of June. *Barrabas* crawled along at 2 knots. The sound of slatting sails grated on my nerves. I sat there, locked down in my still, oceanic prison with no means of escape.

I slept doused in sweat but woke at dawn. We had just passed 19° north. The wind, as though contained behind an invisible wall, began to blow. *Barrabas* skewered the water under full sail. At 6.25pm local time, we crossed the International Date Line – 24 hours disappeared. I would get them back when I re-crossed the date line sailing northeast towards the Bering Strait.

Louise: Friday 2ⁿᵈ June 2006

I love my presents – I am wearing my necklace as I type this. What a lovely treat. The boys were very excited when they got their letters and shirts.

I have been watching the tapes using my video camera on the TV. Boys and I watched your message to us. Yes… I cried. The boys thought you were actually talking to them and were kissing the screen. I am now working through and cataloguing each tape.

We hummed along at 7 knots. Dense banks of low cloud channelled the wind. Gradually, *Barrabas* clawed back some of the lost time. The trick was to strike the right balance between making the miles without stressing the rig. I loosened the lower shrouds so that the intermediates and cap (upper) shrouds took most of the strain.

If my problems with windless conditions were frustrating, a shocking reminder of the vagaries of life on land arrived in an email from Louise.

Louise: Monday 5ᵗʰ June 2006

Nikki just rang me and told me two weeks ago they were burgled while she was alone with the children at night. They came into her bedroom and took all her jewellery. She is devastated.

The idea of strangers poking around in the dark while the children slept was appalling, the more so to me cocooned in *Barrabas* with nobody else around for hundreds of miles. I went on deck savouring the peace and serenity of my environment. The message from Nikki reminded me that this time, this experience, was limited. I had to enjoy it.

The combined anxieties of deadlines, typhoons, the ongoing Russian saga and my imagined delicacy of the rig ganged up on me. For the first time on the voyage, I became ill. Simultaneously, a nasty sty developed on my eye, a huge boil erupted on my backside and on 6ᵗʰ June, just as the log tripped over to 20,000 miles, I went down with stomach cramps. Fever squeezed beads of sweat out of my skin, weakness pervaded my body, lethargy set in so that even raising a book required effort.

I figured the stomach bug had come from drinking the tank water. From now on, I would divert the watermaker output direct to clean 10-litre jerry cans and use the tank water only for washing, filling the kettle and as emergency reserve.

My days became long. Most of the time I lay naked on my bunk, a quick-dry towel spread beneath me to absorb the sweat running in rivulets down my face, neck and chest. With the steady trades bowling us along, we continued gaining back lost time. Clear of any shipping lanes and landmasses, *Barrabas* was free to sail on with little for me to do on deck. The title of the book I was reading pretty well summed up the state of my existence, *The Agony and the Ecstasy*, though of much greater interest was the story of Michelangelo it described.

As days passed, I rolled between moments of joy and incredulity that I had managed to come as far as I had on *Barrabas*. But, like a drug high, the euphoria dumped me down into the troughs of despair – had I bitten off more than I could chew?

I knew I was on a fever-fuelled rollercoaster made reckless in the absence of tempering advice from other people. I could have reached for the medical kit and dosed up on broad-spectrum antibiotics, but equally I knew that I would emerge stronger if I let the fever work itself out.

Louise, by some weird form of telepathy, seemed to sense my sudden zeal.

Louise: Wednesday 7th June 2006

I know you are apprehensive about the Arctic. Since you rounded the Horn west-about solo… YOU CAN DO ANYTHING. I believe in your ability 1,000 per cent whatever obstacles are thrown your way.

Boys really enjoyed the cricket last night so we will make that a regular thing. I will buy Benji his own bat as he shows a real interest. He says that cricket is his favourite followed by golf then footie then rugby.

Only four more tapes to watch. Your tapes are even better than Coronation Street *(boys hooked now!) or* Big Brother *(on again and addicted). I am loving every second and am not ever fast-forwarding.*

Sam Laidlaw had been in touch with Eugene Shvidler at Roman Abramovich's office to reinforce Louise's request for assistance. At the same time, Damian Thwaites asked the British Consul-General in Moscow to intercede with the Russian Ministry of Foreign Affairs. She in turn met with Sergey Krutikov, chief of UK-Russia bilateral relations. Krutikov promised to begin consultations immediately. Damian himself would follow up with Andrey Chupin at the Russian embassy in London.

While all this was going on, England beat Uruguay 1-0 in their opening game of the World Cup. I stayed horizontal, seeing off Michelangelo and racing through Campbell Armstrong's Jig trilogy, *Jig, Jigsaw* and *Heat*.

A cruise ship passed close by, two miles off my starboard side, presumably en route to Honolulu. It gave me quite a shock. I had gone on deck for some air to escape the stifling cabin and there it was, this oasis of bright lights. I thought about the passengers on board sitting down to three-course dinners, taking hot showers, sleeping in beds. The luxuries of everyday life had receded to distant figments. I was missing trees again and flowers and riding a bicycle and seeing the way the sun can glint off a woman's hair and the smell of cut grass and the hubbub of conversation in a crowded room…

David Skinner: Tuesday 13th June 2006
Sounds like a gastro problem from dodgy water together with rundown secondary to this and sty etc. Could take penicillin for eye but key is good water.

My reporting of the fever elicited a large response from various people around the world. One in particular came from Bob Kahn MD in Pacific Palisades, California. A yacht racer with over 100,000 sea miles, Bob had also been medical adviser to Brad van Lieu, a competitor in the 1998 and 2002 Around Alone races. Bob's advice was *'Re: eye sty… it is a bacterial infection… suggest if you have it, antibiotics and hot water soaks, do not squeeze! Re: abdominal symptoms… no solid food… liquids only till improves.'* I had not eaten solid food for four days.

Our friend Rose Dale took an alternative approach. She wrote to Louise, 'Has Adrian got any Marmite – sorts out a sty pretty quickly!'

Louise called to tell me that the Gabriel swept the board at his sports day! I wrote back.

Adrian: Sunday 16th June 2006
Hi… so pleased about Gabo… here's something you can read to him…

'My darling Gabo

Mummy telephoned me on my boat and told me that you did very well at sports day and that you won three races and came second in the other one. I am so proud of you, Gabriel. I wish I had been at school to see you, but next year I will be there shouting and cheering. You make me very happy. I love you, Daddy.'

The abdominal pain persisted. Every time I stood up, sweat erupted. I decided not to mention it any more to Louise. If it did not clear up on its own pretty soon, I would have to take antibiotics. Heavy cloud and squalls moved in all around us. When a shower came over, I went on deck and managed to wash my hair. It was pretty darn cold but at least I was clean.

I was somewhere in the northeastern Pacific, southeast of Japan – precisely where, I could not be certain because I was now navigating with the sextant. My GPS was alive and well (as were the three hand-held back-up units), but for want of some neural stimulation and to put theory into practice, I decided to navigate a 1,000-mile passage and then check my derived position against the GPS. Aside from the elemental enjoyment of navigating by means of the sun, there was the more serious consideration of acquiring a skill that might one day be crucial. Once, when I was crew on a yacht sailing the English Channel en route to France, the ship's GPS failed. Two of the crew were carrying personal hand-held GPS units. Both failed. Luckily, we were close enough to the French coast to identify landmarks against the chart and navigate to a safe harbour. But what if… no one on board (including me) knew which way up to hold a sextant!

Navigating by the sun, moon and stars compromises precision compared to GPS but that electronic sheath of insulation had kept me from fully appreciating the glorious contrivance of the universe to lead sailors across the featureless sea.

During the exercise, we reached another huge milestone. At 5am local time on 19th June, the log clicked to 21,600 nautical miles – a magic number. We had sailed a distance equivalent to the circumference of the earth!

That night as I turned in, the stomach pains were severe. I slept long and late. The next milestone followed that morning. At 8.40am local time, we reached the antipodal point at position 24°.11′ north 143°.22′ east (I used the GPS for confirmation). *Barrabas* had hauled back all the ground lost through the earlier calms. Down came the spinnaker pole and the goose-winged sail arrangement. I put *Barrabas* onto starboard tack (wind coming over the starboard side), course 027°, close-hauling for the first time since Cape Horn in a 12-knot east-northeast breeze. This singular event marked the end of one phase and the beginning of another. We were heading north towards the Arctic.

CHAPTER 19
BEARING UP

TYPHOONS CAN DEVELOP SUDDENLY and move with ferocious velocity. My immediate objective was to get to latitude 30° north. For the moment, only the warm zephyrs of the dragon's breath propelled us along.

The Jordan Series Drogue was my main defence against a typhoon – 300 feet of 1½ inch braided line stitched with 160 mini drogues each of 8-inch diameter. The drogue, deployed aft, would bring *Barrabas*'s stern to wind, reducing the risk of capsize. It would also slow the boat (carrying no sail or just a handkerchief of headsail). The multiple mini-drogues, variously deployed through all the phases of a moving wave, would create an elastic effect like a giant bungee.

Rogue waves and tsunamis posed other dangers. The spawning grounds for these monsters were the Izu-Ogasawara and Japan trenches, submarine cracks in the earth's crust running along Japan's eastern seaboard 10 miles beneath *Barrabas*'s keel.

Moving beyond the range of the northeast trades, the winds would become much more variable, particularly the 600-mile-wide band of the 'horse latitudes' between 30° and 40° north, so-called because horse-carrying ships, plagued by the frequent calms and soaring summer temperatures at these latitudes, often ran low on water, insufficient to sustain crew and livestock. The horses went over the side or into the pot.

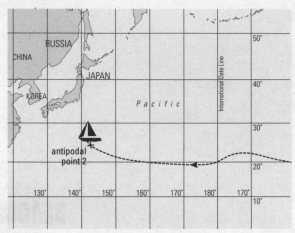

On the same day as I made my turn for the Arctic, Benji was watching England draw 2–2 with Sweden in the World Cup.

The high-pressure system shepherding us continued delivering very light winds at 4 to 7 knots. I was back to excruciatingly slow progress. I worked hard to keep *Barrabas* moving, constantly gybing the sails. After yet another gybe, I heard the ping of an Iridium text message alert.

Ricardo: Saturday 24ᵗʰ June 2006

TYPHOON WARNING!!!: something is brewing only 200 miles north-west of you. Not yet official, but it could cause unstable, unexpected wind shifts, and weird seas. Keep course over ground 060°.

Instead of dwelling on what might happen, I distracted myself by concentrating on my sextant navigation exercise. My final derived position after 1,048 nautical miles put me 2.8 miles north of actual and approximately 1.5 miles west of actual. So, all in all, not a bad result!

Aside from dealing with the damn fever and typhoon threats, I kept up a continual dialogue with Louise about developments with the Russians. The Alpha Global Expedition was hardly a priority in the greater scheme of Anglo–Russian bilateral relations, but to me, it was the centre of my universe and the lack of news made me think that nothing was happening.

I tapped Louise's number into the sat phone. After a quick chat checking that she was okay and asking about the boys, I said, 'I'll write to everyone. Well, to you and you can copy it out.'

'What'll you write?'

'Ask some questions, get Mr Monko to start thinking about the practicalities of my actually making the transit.'

'I'm onto everybody all the time, hammering away. They're probably all sick of me by now.'

'We'll keep bashing on.'

'The problem I'm going to have is raising money for the escort.'

'We can worry about that when everything's in place.'

'What are your questions?'

'First, has Monko definitively agreed to an ice pilot on an escort boat? Second, because time is tight, can we forego the inspection and third, from where to where along the NSR do I need to be escorted?'

'I think you'll have to go in for an inspection. You stopped in Honolulu, so it doesn't matter now.'

'True, but worth asking if only to save time.'

I also wanted to start moving forward with the question of where an escort vessel would come from: Russian Navy, Russian Coast Guard or more likely a charter of a commercial fishing boat or coastal trader. I wrote the letter, emailed it to Louise and she dispatched it onwards.

When it landed on John Mann's desk in Moscow, he called Nikolai Monko. The answer to the first question was a definitive 'yes'. The escort would accompany me from Chukotka in Siberia to the Straits of Novaya Zemlya. As for the nature of the escort, Nikolai Monko referred John to a Mr Zuev, an experienced mariner who he had instructed to put together a proposal for the escort. This latest development was encouraging. But John's take was, '*He (Zuev) is taking his time about it but I will call him again and try to speed him up…*'

In the meantime, Ian had followed up on his initiative with the Royal Navy.

Ian Johnstone-Bryden: Tuesday 27th June 2006

I have spoken with the RN today and agreed a form of email which I have sent this morning marked priority that can be forwarded to the Defence Team in Moscow by Jon Band's Flag Captain.

Reading the correspondence, I think you are very close to a breakthrough with the Russians. It is now a question of whether it will come through in time.

I have asked the Defence Team to come up with suitable Russian Navy and Coastguard contacts that FCO should be able to talk to or provide for you to pass on to your contacts in Moscow to follow through on.

It is always very frustrating trying to work out where things are going and where to apply pressure but the RN reps will either talk directly to the Russians or provide the Embassy commercials with the information and encourage them to follow through. As Monko appears to have warmed to the concept of an escort vessel etc, all approaches should prove complimentary. My feeling is that you are now pushing on a slowly opening door.

What we did not know and could not ask was whether Roman Abramovich or Sergey Frank had taken any direct action with their personal contacts within the Russian administration and particularly within the Politburo itself.

* * *

I had thought that music would be an indispensable part of my days and nights, but it turned out to be less so than I'd imagined. First, my concern about power consumption – the amplifier drank electricity – made me cautious. More than that, the sea sang its own song; its tempo, pitch and volume as varied and infinite as the potential for any composer with a handful of notes to arrange.

By the end of June, I began feeling chilly at night as we climbed north above the thirtieth parallel and east past 150° longitude. The threat from typhoons receded as *Barrabas* scampered away from danger. For the first time in weeks, I slept with the lightweight sleeping bag open as a cover. As I gazed through the open hatch at the stars pin-holing the black vault of the night sky, listening to Albinoni's Adagios, I was thinking about the ice. The Arctic ice mass would be beginning to break up at its coastal extremities. The Centre for Marine and Atmospheric Research at the University of Hamburg predicted the ice receding to an historic minimum during the oncoming summer of 2006.

Andrey Kechashin, one of Sergey Frank's subordinates at Sovcomflot in Moscow had also been in touch with Nikolai Monko. Northern Sea Route Administration was for the moment insisting that I put into port, probably Provideniya, for an inspection. Their ice forecast for the summer optimistically mirrored Hamburg's view. They reckoned the Vil'kitskiy Strait, the critical point of the transit, would clear of ice. It was early days, but we needed to sort out an escort boat and quickly. Now another difficulty loomed. If I got the green light, how would we pay for it? We would need as much time as possible to find funding.

On Friday 30th June, I started wearing clothes again, just a T-shirt and baggy, cotton trousers. A depression closed from the west, bringing 24-knot winds. I set *Barrabas* to run downwind along its eastern side. She bolted away, getting up to 9 knots, fast for her and good for me. I checked back through my log – 10 days since I had eaten solid food. The muscles of my stomach, chest and shoulder now stood out in sharp relief and my face was gaunt. I figured I had better force some food down so I made lunch of sardine spaghetti! When I'd eaten, I felt sick and a thunderous headache began rampaging around inside my head.

While England prepared to play Portugal in the World Cup quarter-finals, John Mann had been onto Mr Zuev. Early enquiries highlighted the difficulties of finding a suitable escort vessel. Zuev had reviewed several options, concluding that a tugboat offered the best solution. As for the cost, Zuev hoped to get back to John by the middle of the following week.

John Mann: Friday 30th June 2006
That's the latest information I have. I explained to Zuev that people are getting nervous, with just a few short weeks until Adrian's arrival. He asked me to pass along the message not to worry as he's confident everything can be resolved in time.

I sure hoped so!

During the night, running before the seas with the boom out wide and the mainsail tacked down at the fourth reef, akin to a storm trysail, the boat was still heading up into wind. I had to drop the mainsail. A preventer line stopped the boom from swinging inboard if the boat accidentally gybed. Attached to the aft end of the boom, the preventer ran to a block on the foredeck then back to the cockpit. To drop the main, I needed to centre the boom then heave-to. I had the boom halfway in when a wave crashed up behind in the pitch black. I could only see the luminescent froth as the crest broke a few feet astern. The rush of water beneath the hull gripped the keel and with a mighty flick spun the boat through 120°, putting the wind in front of the small area of mainsail. Then the preventer failed…

Time slowed to flow like molasses, sensations and awareness focused to sharp points, thought processes became magically lucid and accelerated. The boom was crashing inboard at alarming speed. I desperately worked the main sheet in the cockpit. I managed to duck as the boom flew across the cockpit – I sensed it more than saw it. Its flight caused the main sheet to slacken. On *Barrabas*, the main sheet controlling the boom relays up and down eight times through two blocks, the first attached to the traveller on deck and the second attached to the underside of the boom. This arrangement set up a ratio of forces so that I could haul the boom inboard, even with the full mainsail flying under tremendous load. The eight runs of line momentarily transformed from a regimented series into a viper's nest of tangled rope. I let go of the sheet, which then caught around my right shoulder. As the boom went over and the sheet began to tighten, I was bodily lifted and smashed against the cockpit coaming. My shoulder kept going, up, out and away. At the precise moment when my shoulder reached maximum stretch and where dislocation was the inevitable next stage, the boom stopped with a loud whipping crack as the main sheet became taut. If I had not taken the sheet in as much as I had, it might have ripped my shoulder clean out of its socket. It was a severe, excruciating wrench. For the next two days, I couldn't lift my right arm more than a few inches away from my body.

To make matters worse, I called Louise and discovered that England had lost their World Cup quarter-final to Portugal on penalties! (Ricardo was delighted.)

I collapsed into my bunk, cold, miserable and in pain. As ever, I found refuge in a book, this time *Shadow of the Wind* by Carlos Ruiz Zafón, and then finally slept until 5.30am.

In the dim, misty morning, I came on deck to adjust the Hydrovane. To my astonishment, a huge tanker lumbered past less than one mile astern! I called on the short range VHF radio.

'Did you see me on radar?'

'Yes, but only just. You were a very small contact.'

'Easy to miss?'

'Very easy to miss.'

The latest GRIB showed the west wind curling north and spiralling into a revolving low-pressure system, the centre passing directly overhead with wind speeds accelerating to 37 knots. From experience, I knew these wind speeds would be conservative. Another low-pressure system sat northeast of my position. A narrow high-pressure ridge ran between the two lows. If the depressions collided…

I telephoned Louise, gave my position and asked her to call the British Meteorological Office and get them to have a look. Weather bombs are the most severe of all winter storms, characterised as intense low-pressure systems coming together with a central pressure that falls 24 millibars or more in a 24-hour period. Something similar had caused the 1979 Fastnet disaster. The 1998 Sydney to Hobart race catastrophe came about by three low-pressure systems colliding. I didn't like the look of the forecast.

I checked the drogue. I hated to phone Louise with this kind of thing, but with Ricardo away competing in the tall ships race, I had little choice. Louise said she was going to call him also.

Ricardo Diniz: Monday 3rd July 2006

I am in Weymouth getting cleaned up and ready for the tall ships. All ok. Sorry to hear about your shoulder.

You should be in light airs now. That is because you are in between lows. 500 miles to the west of you there is a vicious little 997 brewing and she is heading directly for you. Expect variable wind directions since the centre of the system will be going over you. Max wind speed 40kn. I also think the seas will be really confused and quite large at times between now and Wednesday.

I comforted myself by baking a loaf of bread and eating two slices with my homemade anchovy paste (anchovies, mayonnaise and chilli sauce mixed).

Heavy rain pounded against the coach house, reducing visibility to half a mile. I switched on the radar. The grinding wind did not stop. The sky turned a low malevolent purple.

A ray of light in my otherwise dark world came in an email with the latest update from Northern Sea Route Administration.

Andrey Kechashin: Wednesday 5th July 2006

Reply received today from Mr Nikolai Monko:

'Dear Andrey Mikhailovich, good day.

The authorization for the yacht guiding through the seaways of NSR could be granted provided the following terms and conditions are fulfilled:

1. The yacht should be escorted. An ice pilot will be on board the escort vessel.

2. The inspection of the yacht could be carried out at sea by the ice pilot and the master of the escort vessel.

3. The agreement with Murmansk Shipping Company for yacht guiding through the seaways of NSR should be signed.

4. Navigation through the NSR to be carried out in ice-free waters.'

Had banging on about attempting the NSR *only* if the passage was clear of ice given Mr Monko assurance? I liked to think so. The Murmansk Shipping Company (MSCO) controlled the icebreaker fleet operating in the western part of the NSR where I would be most likely to encounter problems. I knew that an agreement with MSCO was mandatory. The idea of an inspection at sea would save time. Great news!

However, my immediate concern was still with the approaching depression. It had formed into a tightly packed ball of isobars. Ricardo's description of the system as a 'vicious little 997' was partially right: vicious, yes but little, no, this thing was 800 miles across, wider than the length of the UK, from John O'Groats to Land's End!

Winds climbed to 35 knots, heaping the sea into a lumpy, rucked carpet. I prepared the boat for the onslaught: storm covers over the hatches, deck inspected, repair on the mast checked, cabin stowed, bread made, JSD ready for deployment, storm jib rigged for a quick hoist.

During the night, I tried to relax (impossible) reading John Le Carre's *Absolute Friends*. The threatening storm dissipated and fractured before reaching *Barrabas* as we desperately scuttled northeastwards, but the winds continued blowing between 30 and 40 knots, piling the seas into hillocks of cresting water. Some kind of wave strike was inevitable, but I couldn't stand watch 24 hours.

It came at 5am on Saturday the 8th July, a massive strike on the starboard side. Everything on the saloon table flew off. *Barrabas* heeled to 70°. Water cascaded through the chinks and cracks at the edges of the closed companionway hatch and rained down onto the chart table. Not again! I tore out of my sleeping bag. Water sloshed as high as the radar screen, computer screen, radio, keyboard and switch panel.

I dried everything off quickly and inspected the computer compartment beneath the hinged chart table. It seemed to be dry. I needed a weather GRIB. The computer worked, dispatching my email request into the ether. I waited a few minutes, then went into email and dialled out to see if the new GRIB had arrived. An error-screen appeared. When I rebooted, a message popped up telling me there was no signal. The computer then went to sleep, and that's as far as I got. Water must have got into the machine somewhere. The computer never recovered. I went to the back-up laptop.

I reproached myself (harshly and loudly). After my experience at Cape Horn, I had organised a defence against just such an event but I hadn't put it into place. In Honolulu, I'd bought a transparent, plastic shower curtain

(Walmart \$5.99) and hooks that I'd screwed into the cabin headlining around the companionway hatch from which to hang the shower curtain. The arrangement of hooks created folds in the curtain to catch incoming water. I kicked myself for not hanging the curtain.

The Bering Strait beckoned, 1,523 miles to the north. I called Louise. She and the boys were off to a fête in the neighbouring village of Cuddington. We had all gone along the previous year. The thought of being at an English village fête in the summertime... I tried not to dwell on the weeks and months still ahead. Instead, I suspended myself in the present, moment by moment.

A combination of changing factors kept me pinned down in a black mood: the loss of the main computer, no word from Zuev despite his repeated promises of finding an escort vessel and now the Russians were insisting I had a valid visa (how the hell was I supposed to get a visa?). The effort to stay calm became increasingly challenging as the seconds turned to minutes turned to hours turned to days of lost time. As a 'treat', I put on the cabin heating.

Occasionally, just when I needed it most, some fillip would arrive through the post.

Campbell Armstrong: Sunday 9th July 2006

I read your reports and enjoy them enormously – I'm having a vicarious adventure, so it seems, and your descriptions of the sea, and your own fortitude, solitude and resolve are wonderful to read. The sea is sometimes cast as a demon, other times a benign but utterly unpredictable ally, or even a spiteful bully you need to beware of. I imagine the long nights, the emptiness of ocean, the vastness of sky – and you, sailing on and on. I wish you well and safe voyage, safe return.

To give myself a solid target to aim for, I set a deadline of 10th August, 31 days hence, to be on station in or near Provideniya, 1,800 miles away. That worked out at an average of 58 miles VMG (velocity made good) per day. Since turning at the antipodal point, the daily VMG averaged out at 63 miles. So, despite the seemingly slow speed and apparent abundance of time, the reality based on performance was touch and go as to whether I could make it.

From Provideniya, we would have to travel 2,300 nautical miles to Novaya Zemyla, across the length of Russia's Northern Sea Route. Sailing at an average speed of 3 knots for 20 hours per 24-hour period, with four hours stationary for sleep, we'd cover 60 miles a day. I needed 38 days, say

40 days with two days' grace, to cover the 2,300 miles. Forty days from 10th August took me to 19th September. The re-freeze would begin around 16th September. If I had any margin at all, it was the width of a cheesewire.

Barrabas had now slogged through 23,000 miles. Maintenance became more of a pressing necessity. I went to the top of the mast to string 'halyard preventers' between the mast steps and the shrouds to stop the main halyard from wrapping round the steps. I also inspected the rigging aloft and noticed severe chafing to the headsail halyard on its sheave. I dropped the headsail with *Barrabas* hove-to, cut off 18 inches, retied the halyard with a bowline and then re-hoisted the headsail.

Louise: Monday 10th July 2006
I am sure as every day passes you are feeling more and more apprehensive about your Arctic approach. Hopefully the issues can be resolved by the end of this week and we will know how to proceed. You have lots of people behind you now. You are not alone and as I keep saying…

We continued our slow crawl towards the ice zone. Already, two layers of thermals, gloves, woolly hat and thick socks insulated me from the cold. My lightweight sleeping bag would soon have to give way to the heavy-duty one. If temperatures got seriously unpleasant, I could always put one sleeping bag inside the other to create a 'mega' bag.

My right shoulder remained sore but serviceable. I had damaged the last surgical repair while showing off in France two years previously.

''Ave you ever been rolleur blading?' Christian had asked.

'Non.' Emphatic.

'Non! Mon Dieu! You must.'

Christian (an excellent all-round sportsman) decided now was the time. Down we trouped to the boardwalk along Deauville beach. The scene was classic: two pretty French girls, me overconfident. The next thing I knew, my legs were in the air, my backside on the deck, my fall broken (just) by my right elbow, the force of which had tried to push my shoulder joint up through my skull. I felt the surgical fix tear. All thoughts of pretty girls (French or otherwise) were washed away as waves of nausea swept through me. I never had the damage looked at and I realised at the outset of the Alpha Global that this weakness needed protecting. After going over the side and snagging the shoulder in the main sheet during the accidental gybe, I felt grateful my arm still constituted part of my body.

I started the engine and watched the amp meter. The charge indicator needle stayed motionless. What now! I scrabbled to lift the floorboard at the base of the companionway steps to expose the four house batteries and the melange of cables writhing over their tops. I found the problem. The positive lead had disconnected from the battery terminal. With the engine humming in neutral, I waited until the batteries had sucked up charge.

If we were going into the ice, close-quarter manoeuvring would have be under engine. Now was as good a time as any to check the drive. Up in the cockpit, I eased the throttle forward to engage. Horrendous clanking reverberated from the propeller shaft – metal on metal. I knew immediately that we had a very serious problem. I left the drive turning for 30 seconds, listening intently to make a diagnosis.

I slipped the engine back to neutral. What the hell had happened? How could it have happened?

I'd replaced the propeller shaft during the summer refit and paid particular attention to the engine and drive, anticipating the high mechanical demands of navigating in ice. The propeller shaft transmitted through the hull via a stern tube, part of the hull construction. Cutless bearings supported the shaft in the stern tube at the inboard and outboard ends, holding it firm. The cutless bearings prevented lateral movements and assisted the shaft to spin true. I got up from my seat in the cockpit and went below to examine the bit of mushed nylon Les had given me in Honolulu.

The curve of where it had fitted round the prop shaft was clear, the inside surface discernibly one piece and not a lot of fused strands as I'd originally thought after my cursory inspection in Honolulu, its grey colour the same as the cutless bearings. It wasn't fishing line but part of the cutless bearing that had worked its way out along the shaft and been mangled by the propeller.

This was a disaster! I had effectively lost use of the engine. How much of the bearing remained? Did it matter anyway? No, I decided, because the shaft was banging about clearly unsupported. The only way to replace the bearing was for *Barrabas* to come out of the water. The route to Provideniya was now blocked. I had to find a port where *Barrabas* could be hauled out.

But where?

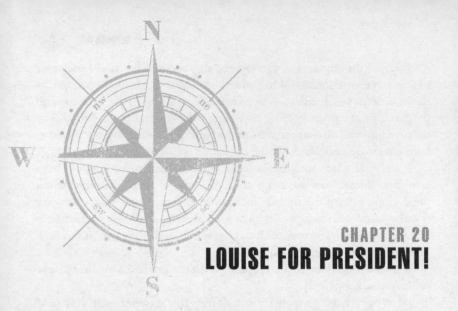

CHAPTER 20
LOUISE FOR PRESIDENT!

I PORED OVER THE CHARTS, calculator in hand. The conclusion was inescapable. The prospects of getting to the Bering Strait in time to have a sensible crack at the Northern Sea Route were receding fast.

I could not help but lower my head into my hands. With an effort, I overcame the rising mist of tears. I fought for control – this was no time for emotion. *Barrabas* was hurt. It was true that her hurt was my hurt, but I had to be pragmatic, assess the problem in the context of the rapidly shrinking time-window and find a solution.

Should I go into a Russian or an Alaskan port? After consulting my various pilotage books, I decided to put into Nome, self-styled 'metropolis' of northwestern Alaska. There would be no language barrier, parts were more likely to be available and customs procedures less involved.

The settlements dotting the western and northern Alaskan coasts are remote, but Nome is the largest of them with a population of 3,000. I reassessed my timings. If I could make it to Nome by 10th August, have the boat hauled out, repaired and back in the water by the 14th, make the short passage across the Bering Strait to be on station at the eastern entrance to the Northern Sea Route by August 15th, it might still be possible – just.

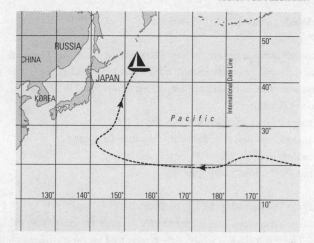

I fired off a series of emails to Louise. The Americans still used the imperial measuring system while *Barrabas*, being French, was metric. It would be easier to have replacement bearings sent out from the UK.

Louise contacted Vetus in Holland. Vetus led her to Denis Rawle at Exalto UK, their British distributor. Denis was happy to oblige.

In the dim light and windless conditions, the solar panels and wind generator were fighting a losing battle to keep the batteries charged. I turned the engine on again. Thirty minutes later when I shut it off and went to close the seawater intake, I found the service alternator lying in the engine well; its base plate had sheared, fatigued to destruction by the relentless vibration. Expletives coloured the air.

The second, engine-mounted alternator charged the engine-cranking battery. I could still use the engine to charge all the batteries by connecting the engine-cranking battery to the house bank using jumper cables. Another job for Nome – fabricate a new base plate. I could not go into the Arctic without a back-up alternator.

Despondency knocked at the door. I had to stay focused. The seriousness of the shaft problem lay in the solution rather than the problem itself. Would I find suitable facilities in Nome to lift *Barrabas* out and fabricate a new alternator base plate?

Louise wasted no time. She found out that the Nome harbourmaster was a woman called Joy Baker.

Louise: Wednesday 12ᵗʰ July 2006

Dear Joy

Adrian has some problems with his boat and we are trying to decide how best to proceed as it will definitely involve taking Barrabas out of the water. We were wondering what the feasibility of him getting things fixed in Nome was, so I pose the following questions:

1) Is there a lift-out facility in the port?

2) A marine stainless steel fabricator needs to be identified.

3) He needs to check the shaft for true alignment.

4) If the shaft is bent, straighten it.

Joy L Baker: Wednesday 12ᵗʰ July 2006

There are limited options in this community so it really depends on the weight of the vessel. There is a large 75-ton crane that is tied up on a construction project (more than likely not available since they'd have to set you down within reach of the crane). There are a few smaller lifts like a 40-ton rubber-tyred crane. Both are owned privately so you'd have to make arrangements personally. I am not aware of any local stainless steel fabricators. That would most likely have to be done out of Anchorage or even Seattle.

Barrabas nudged passed the northernmost North Pacific shipping lanes in poor visibility and deteriorating weather. Through this whirlwind of mishap and leaking time, a thought took root somewhere deep in my subconscious which, over the following few days, pushed itself to the surface like a deeply embedded thorn.

'I think it may be the only option,' I said to Louise. I'd outlined my thoughts in an email and she'd rung me back. She was crying.

'Are you absolutely certain?'

'There are too many unknowns and not enough time. Anyway, nothing is certain.'

'This is so difficult for you.'

'Difficult for you too,' I said. Louise had lived and breathed the expedition, picking me up when I was down, handling the press, maintaining the website, investing her energies in keeping the show on the road, finding sponsors, coaxing politicians, diplomats, billionaires and captains of industry. Had it all come to this?

'If you break the AGX in two, winter the boat in Alaska…'

'I know, I know. There are a lot of considerations – cost, not to mention having to psyche myself up again, leave the children…'

'I meant, you, what about you? How will you feel?'

The truth was that I felt okay about the decision. 'I'm okay. Sure, in fact. I can't control circumstances out here. There's no point in fighting what cannot be changed.' I resorted to my favourite expression. 'It is what it is.'

'Really?'

'What about you?' I knew she was exhausted.

'Whatever you decide.'

'We'll crack on, but we know what we do if time runs out.'

The decision to break the voyage and over-winter *Barrabas* in Nome, if that's what it came to, exhausted me. I went to my bunk, wrapped in the heavy-duty Arctic sleeping bag and slept solidly for eight hours.

Adrian: Saturday 15th July 2006

Message for John Mann…

'Hello John

I will put into Nome, Alaska, to make repairs. As for the escort vessel, my difficulty is this: without a good idea of the associated costs, I cannot determine feasibility and it is rapidly coming close to being impossibly late to raise the requisite funds.

I reckon that I have until August 20th to be on station at the eastern entrance to the NSR. If I can get to Nome by August 10th, repair the boat, then it is only a short passage across the Bering Strait to rendezvous with the escort.

Money and the extremely limited time in which to find it are likely to be the showstoppers unless we get some information very, very soon.'

John Mann: Monday 17th July 2006

Good news. I just talked to Zuev. He has received a list of available boats with NSR navigation certification from one of the ports he'd been talking to. He's going to go through it, pick one, and then determine the costs involved. He wants to meet with me tomorrow afternoon to present whatever it is he works up. So, some progress at last.

My schedule kept revising itself to accommodate the changing situation, deadlines shifting forwards, mission creep, like a gambler hoping the next spin of the wheel would go his way.

John Mann: Friday 21ˢᵗ July 2006 (14.21 Moscow time)

Zuev ducked out on me on Tuesday because he thought the trip was off. I can only assume Monko told him so.

Zuev was also apparently out of town again the past couple of days, which explains why he hasn't answered his mobile. Monko said that he had the same information that I did – that Zuev had found a boat and was coming up with the business plan side of things (i.e. pricing). He also said he'd go talk to Zuev to speed things along.

John Mann: Friday 21ˢᵗ July 2006 (15.41 Moscow time)

Talked to Zuev. Another reason he hadn't gotten in touch with me is that the people he'd been in touch with wanted $15K a day. He understood the insanity of that (and I'm not sure what kind of boat he was looking at). He said he'll be back in the office Monday and will make some more calls. I guess I'm going to need to call him every day to keep him on track!

$15,000 per day!

Well, whatever happened, we were heading for Nome. A friend in England dug up an excerpt from one of Michael Palin's television series when he had travelled through the town:

Nome is a very wacky town, taking pride in bizarre statistics such as the fact that it is 75 miles away from the nearest tree. It lies on the south-west coast of the 200-mile-long Seward Peninsula, named after George Seward, the American Secretary of State who bought Alaska from the Russians in 1867 for 7.2 million dollars. (Even though this worked out at roughly two cents an acre it was not a popular purchase and the territory was referred to at the time as 'Walrussia' and 'Seward's Ice Box'.) We are quartered at a seafront hotel called the Nugget Inn on Front Street next to the Lucky Swede Gift Shop.

There were in fact three Swedes who, in 1898, struck lucky in nearby Anvil Creek and started a classic gold rush, which in two years turned a stretch of Arctic desert into a city of 20,000. There are different versions of why it was called Nome, all of them suitably eccentric. One Harry de Windt who passed through in 1902 and described the gold-mad town as 'a kind of squalid Monte Carlo', claims that it derives from the Indian word 'No-me' meaning 'I don't know', which was the answer given to early white traders when they asked the natives where they were. The most popular explanation is that Nome came about as a misreading of a naval chart on which a surveyor had noted a nearby cape with the query 'Name?'

This piece of levity was welcome and a message from Henk put my troubles into context.

Henk de Velde: Saturday 22nd July 2006
A voyage including going over the top, like Adrian is doing now, is the most demanding. For example, look at the problems on my voyage in 2001–2004. First: expelled from Russia. Second: engine problems in Argentina – I lost six weeks. Third: struck by lightning north of Hawaii – I had to return to Honolulu and by the time it was repaired I was too late to go north so I lost six months. Fourth: wintering 10 months in Tiksi, Siberia because of too much ice. Fifth: rudders bent in very heavy ice and I had to get help from an icebreaker etc. All together it took me 3½ years. So you see, Adrian is not doing bad at all.

The Foreign Office had come up with a possible solution to the vexing question of a visa. The British Embassy would issue a letter of Consular Guarantee in lieu of a visa, effectively assuming responsibility for me. To lend weight to the idea, they first wanted Northern Sea Route Administration to issue an official permission. Chickens and eggs flitted though my mind. Would NSR Administration issue the official permission without my having a visa or something in its stead?

At the request of the Foreign Office in London, John Makin, the British Consul in Moscow, called on Nikolai Monko. The two men met to discuss the intricacies of my proposed transit. Monko had offered himself as a direct point of contact with the British authorities. Any concessions would, I guessed, be consequent to this meeting. It was a big step forward.

John Mann: Monday 24th July 2006
I spoke to Zuev today and he's got more people on board in the Far East identifying a suitable escort boat. He's thinking fishing boat now. We are scheduled to finally meet tomorrow afternoon.

The Aleutian Trench runs south of the Aleutian Island chain and plunges to depths of 9,000 metres, its north face rising to shoal depths around the islands themselves in the space of less than 60 miles. The waters driven by winds from the south-west towards the islands could, without too much provocation chuck up massive seas in the narrow gaps between the islands. I had to approach with caution. To give myself the best chance, I decided to pass the islands through the widest point available, between the westernmost of the Aleutians, Attu Island (US) and Ostrov Medynn (Russia). Stalemate Bank complicated the issue. Lying west of Attu Island, the water over Stalemate Bank shallowed to a mere 30 metres. To avoid the bank, I would have to stray into Russian territorial waters.

The great promontory of Poluostrov-Kamchatka dangles from the mass of the Russian mainland like an accusatory finger pointing at Japan (it was off this promontory that the Royal Navy team had rescued the trapped Russian submariners). Get caught in the lee of Poluostrov-Kamchatka and I could find myself with little or no wind.

Neither the charts nor pilotage gave the gap between these two islands a name, so I called it Stalemate Pass. Positioning was crucial – Stalemate Pass lay 100 miles distant. Winds were light. I set the mainsail at the second reef with barely any headsail flying to hold *Barrabas*'s bows high to the wind but with minimal boat speed. Like a leopard hunkered down in the long grass stealthily inching forwards, I had to keep *Barrabas* steady for 36 hours until the wind came round to the southwest to take us through the pass on a downwind run.

Before entering Russian territory, I advised the Maritime Rescue Coordination Centre (MRCC) at Vladivostok. Despite the fact that their phone wasn't working and the email address listed in the Admiralty list of signals kept bouncing back to me, the message got through. Equally bizarrely, MRCC Vladivostok couldn't contact me. Instead, they informed the United States Coastguard (USCG) at Juneau who then called *Barrabas*. I spoke with Lt Mara Miller who had 'googled' *Barrabas* and so knew all about us.

Together, Lt. Miller and I tried to decipher the email in broken English that Vladivostok had sent Juneau. The words 'shot', 'range' and the phrase '30-mile restricted limit' led me to suspect a firing range on Ostrov Medynn. Unfairly perhaps, the idea of some rookie Russian artilleryman eyeing *Barrabas* through binoculars and declaring enthusiastically while he loaded his shells that a yacht had been set up as target practice, sprang to mind. The ever-courteous Lt Miller agreed to converse with Vladivostok and find out more. A couple of hours later, she called back to tell me that no, it was not a firing range but a protected area reservation (presumably environmental) extending 30 miles offshore from Ostrov Medynn. With that bump ironed out, the winds swung round to the southwest as forecast and we began the run through the pass.

At close to midnight on Tuesday 25th July, a bout of food poisoning hit me. I now habitually checked the sell-by dates on all my food. My dinner of spaghetti with basil pesto, salmon and sardines was all in date. Everything had smelt okay before I cooked it. I eventually managed to get back to sleep at 6am, only to be woken again by the four-mile radar warning alarm with a contact dead on the bow. I managed to raise the ship on the radio and then proceeded to have a long chat with the radio officer who was interested to know all about the expedition. The ship was the *Long Beach*, registered in Panama with a Filipino crew.

At 1.30pm, we crossed northwards over latitude 54° north, marking a successful transit over the Aleutian Trench and through the Aleutian Islands/Komandorskiye Ostrova chain. I also breached the psychological barrier of less than 1,000 nautical miles to Nome and shortly afterwards crossed back west over the International Date Line, recovering the 24 hours I had lost earlier.

John Mann: Wednesday 26th July 2006

Here's a rundown of my first face-to-face meeting with Artur Mikhailovich Zuev.

I was expecting a frail, small elderly man given how he sounds on the phone. Instead, I was greeted outside his office by a large, jovial, potbellied gentleman of 78 years. His card says he works for a firm called Inter-regional Transportation Company or MTK for short. It appears to me that he does not work full time at this point, but is nevertheless a very respected man in the organisation and in shipping circles having spent 20 years on the Northern Sea Route. Also present at our meeting was Yevgeny Viktorvich Zvonov, his assistant and one-time seafaring engineer.

When we sat down, he informed me that he was in touch with yet another group of his contacts out in the Far East and that they were once again searching for a suitable escort boat after the last group came back with the exorbitant price I mentioned before. He explained that one problem was that the NSR is less used today than during the Soviet period and a lot of the ice-class boats that might have been able to make the trip are now in disrepair.

It was at this point that Zuev recommended sending Zvonov out to the Far East – either Petropavlosk-Kamchatsky in Kamchatka or Nakhodka in Primorsk. They believe that they could settle this whole problem in a matter of days if they had someone on the ground, given that the nine-hour time difference makes communication during work hours difficult. I calculated that with the airfare of $1,000, five days of hotel around $500, five days of per diem (their request) around $600, plus other expenses, we could be looking at $2,500 in costs.

After our meeting, I was treated to lunch with four shots of vodka (if you call that a treat… it basically killed my afternoon productivity), I explained that a) the expedition is working on a shoestring budget and b) I didn't have any authorisation from Governor Abramovich to get involved financially. As such, I explained that I could not promise that the option they presented would be accepted. I promised to pass along word to the expedition team, but nothing more.

Yesterday evening, I conferred with a colleague of mine who has spent a lot of time in Chukotka and who himself has carried out several land and sea expeditions of various types. My question to him was if, perhaps, he had any maritime contacts in Chukotka that might provide us with an alternative to Zuev. He informed me that most of the traffic on the NSR is west to east and that it will be very difficult to find someone going the other direction. Perhaps this is one of the challenges Zuev has faced, though he hasn't mentioned it specifically.

In short, I'm now not quite sure what the best course of action is. We're finally getting to that period where time is short and I don't feel much progress from Zuev's side. At the same time, he's the one Mr Monko has put on the case so I'm hesitant to circumvent him given that we need Monko to grant passage. I'm also worried how much Zuev would achieve if we don't take his solution. It's catch-22 in several dimensions.

So that's where things stand. I'll await word from you before I contact Zvonov (Zuev's put himself in the hospital for a few days) with our reaction.

Adrian (to John): Thursday 27th July 2006
Hi John,

Thanks for the summation. As for being on a shoestring budget, I have to tell you that I am now wearing flip-flops, shoestrings having long since disappeared.

I am 850 miles from Nome, Alaska, and should be able to be on station to RV with an escort by mid-August.

Every stage of the voyage presented a new set of challenges. The Pacific Ocean is very deep. The Bering Sea, north of the Aleutian Islands, is shallow.

Towards Nome, the seabed progressively shoals to less than 30 metres depth. A series of contour lines on the charts showed these progressions. My task now was to make sure we crossed these steps in light winds to avoid the vicious surface chop that even moderate winds could generate.

For the first time in a long while, blue sky showed through tears in the cloud. Barometric pressure started rising. I cooked and ate curry and stitched up the underarm seams on both sides of my mid-layer, which was beginning to fall to pieces.

The confused wave pattern rocked the boat from side to side. A 30-knot wind screeched in the rigging. The locker contents paraded around in their confined spaces, impatiently knocking as if clamouring to be free. Tension settled in my shoulders, roosting there. With every precipitous roll, muscles tightened and tension worked its way more deeply in, sapping and exhausting. I felt the weight of the strain beneath my eyes and in the heaviness in my limbs. I felt it in the hollow space excavated deep in the pit of my stomach. I set the boat to cope as best she could, then sat and waited for the weather to calm. When it did, the tension, with nothing left to feed on, crept silently out and away like an uninvited ghost and the exhaustion turned to sleep.

A red and white light hovered below the cloud base far behind the stern. Perhaps it was a plane or a helicopter too far away for me to detect movement. I switched on the VHF to Channel 16 and put on a masthead light. The red and white light remained for several hours, immobile in the sky, too low to be a satellite, too high to be the masthead lights of a ship. The light stayed stuck to the sky, immutable like an unblinking eye. Suddenly, it vanished. Gone, switched off. I have no explanation!

I spent the morning doing housework – disinfecting the heads and galley sinks, wiping the floors and generally tidying. Low grey clouds scudding to the east brought a chill wind. I didn't much like the look of them and shortened sail as a precaution.

The day had begun bright and blue but by mid-afternoon the light had dimmed to a steely grey. The low clouds moved over us. The seas became steeper. By 4pm, we were in 40-knot winds herding waves into a stampede. I sat in the cockpit and whilst my trusty Hydrovane steered *Barrabas*, wave action was slewing the boat so wildly that the headsail was backing. I kept the Hydrovane working while I faced backwards watching the seas, making steering corrections to take the more aggressive waves stern-on. The wind then shifted quite suddenly. It was not long before the seas crossed with breaking waves colliding almost at right angles to one another. After 25,000 miles, I had not experienced such confused water.

Three large waves rode up behind *Barrabas*, forming themselves into a crescent. I adjusted the steering to take the centre wave. My angle was just off. The foaming water got hold of the keel and slewed *Barrabas* viciously to port. At that moment, the left-hand wave broke and smashed into *Barrabas*'s port quarter. The water's grip was murderous. I braced myself in the cockpit and watched in fascinated horror as green water threw *Barrabas* over, rushing over the aft deck. The massive forces were too much for the rudder cables and the wheel spun freely as they parted. The water tore through the starboard dodger as if it was made of wet tissue. *Barrabas* spun through 180°, sails flogging as she turned head to wind.

I immediately fitted the emergency tiller, control lines already rigged and run through blocks to the cockpit so that I could control the rudder by pulling down on the starboard and port lines. There I stayed, beneath the protective cuddy, for the next two hours until the storm blew past.

I was grateful for the calm that followed. The Honolulu consignment contained 5mm gauge steering cables to replace the narrower 4mm cables fitted. I spent most of the day on Monday fitting these thicker cables, saving time on the ground in Nome. Four hundred and seventy-five miles now separated us from the settlement.

John Mann: Monday 31st July 2006

I spoke to Nikolai Monko today. He said the only remaining documentation he needs is:

A) Certification on the technical condition of the escort ship.

B) Your visa, if you've got it (I know you had something in the works on this) just in case you have to make landfall.

These are the only documents left to worry about for the NSR approval process.

Now for the unpleasant news. We've got a bit of a hold-up as Zuev went into the hospital for minor elective surgery last week and his assistant Zvonov took ill over the weekend. I've put Monko on the case in resolving the issue but it'll be tomorrow before I find out what comes next.

I was so grateful to John for his efforts but it seemed that this whole process was giving with one hand and taking with the other. At least I could deal with the visa issue.

'You're almost there!' Louise said. Excitement registered clearly in her voice.

'D'you mean almost there with the Russians or almost in Nome?'

'Both!'

'Well, we can't do anything about Zuev's medical condition, but can you ask Damian at the FCO to get onto Mr Monko and let him know that the British Embassy in Moscow will issue a Consular Guarantee in lieu of a visa?'

'I've already done that.'

I raised my eyes to the cabin headlining and thought to myself, 'This woman should be running the bloody country!'

* * *

Thunder filled the air around *Barrabas*. I rushed on deck just as a huge USCG C-130 Hercules screamed overhead at less than 500 feet. I ducked below decks flicking the VHF to Channel 16.

'US coastguard aircraft, this is sailing yacht *Barrabas*, do you copy?' I watched though the window as the great bird banked round to the north.

A low hiss of static, then, 'This is United States Coastguard aircraft, please identify yourself.'

'This is British sailing yacht *Barrabas*.' I spelled out B A R R A B A S phonetically.

The radioman repeated the spelling.

'How many crew on board? Please spell your name, sir. Callsign.'

'One crew.' I spelled out my name. 'Callsign Mike Hotel Delta Victor Three.'

'Your last port of call, Captain?'

'Honolulu.'

'And where're you headed?'

'Nome.' I figured they knew who I was from Lt Miller.

The aircraft hurtled passed once more, then climbed away to the south. The C-130 ranged in wide circles around us.

'Anything we can do for you, sir?'

'No, I'm fine, thanks.'

'Very well, sir. Have a good day,' the radioman said.

I watched the C-130 diminish to a speck then blink out in the low scudding cloud.

I found three more books, ones that Michael Roth had given me, hidden in the 'nuts and raisins' cupboard. I couldn't believe my luck. To celebrate, I gave myself a baby wipe bath in front of the heater outlet in the saloon. (I also wanted to test the heater. I had sat on the burner unit by accident whilst working on the steering cables.)

My mood remained buoyant all day because of the books and the flypast. USCG knew my position, knew my intentions. Lt Miller had agreed to call ahead to Nome and alert the customs and border control officer, Bob Gentz. As darkness fell, the distinctive sounds of whales' blowholes came from somewhere close by.

I spent most of the following day, Wednesday 2nd August, reading Tom Robbins's *Villa Incognito*. Part of my seeking solace in fiction was to quell the inevitable jitters about crossing the 200-metre contour line. We edged across at 10pm. From now until we reached Nome, the increasingly shallow water presented a constant threat.

Barrabas made steady progress towards Saint Lawrence Island. Mercifully, the forecast indicated fine weather. With winds blowing from the southwest, I decided to pass south of the island to avoid the wind shadow cast by its mountainous spine.

So taken was I with Tom Robbins, I immediately launched into the second of his books, *Fierce Invalids Home From Hot Climates*, silently thanking Michael for introducing me to this great writer.

Ricardo sent two satellite ice images lifted from the University of Bremen's Department of Environmental Physics website, in my opinion the best of the internet sites displaying this type of imagery (Eric Brossier also used this resource during his 2002 NSR transit in *Vagabond*). The pictures showed the ice receding to an almost unbelievable (and shocking) extent. It looked as though the ice might recede even further than it had the previous year when it had cleared completely from the Russian Arctic coast.

For an entire week, I had heard nothing further on the search for an appropriate escort vessel. The news from Ricardo plunged me into a monumental psychological battle between elation and despair. Could I get the repairs done in time? Would the repairs hold? Could the Russians find an escort vessel? Would the escort vessel be prohibitively expensive? Did we have enough time or not? Ice conditions looked like being the best (for my purposes) in recorded history. The tug-of-war between anxiety and hope was evenly poised. It could go either way. We were getting down to the wire.

The great, hummocked mass of Saint Lawrence Island slid by, invisible beneath my northern horizon. At 9.45am on Sunday 6th August we passed westwards over the 30-metre contour line. Taking advantage of the light southwesterlies, we ran dead downwind towards Nome, exactly 100 miles away.

By evening the following day, Alaska's mountainous coast loomed beneath blue streaked skies warmed by a soft sunset. I sat up on deck, the radiance of the sun gradually dimming from gold to orange to pink. Detail etched on the rugged rock faces faded with the light. Nome huddled beneath the mountains 20 miles away. I hove-to for the night, drifting gently eastwards. Despite my worries about how I was going to get *Barrabas* out of the water, excitement at making landfall flickered through me. This was frontier country. Nome would be a startling contrast to the glitz and wealth of Waikiki.

CHAPTER 21

NO PLACE LIKE NOME

I MADE IT TO WITHIN a couple of miles of Nome, but with no charts and no engine to manoeuvre into port, I put a call in to Joy Baker. A local fishing boat, *Juliana III*, came out and towed me into the sanctuary of the town's small, protected harbour. At 11am on Tuesday 8th August, I tied up alongside the harbour wall, throwing my lines to a baseball-capped, heavily bearded figure who spoke in a slow drawl. Like a number of people I was to meet over the following days, George Fullwood had sought the isolation and anonymity of the wild wastes of the Alaskan tundra two decades previously in the hunt for gold. Now he worked for Crowley Marine Services, whose 90-ton crane sat close by with its mighty boom reaching skywards above *Barrabas*'s mast. My heart sang. Could this be the answer to the question of how I was going to get *Barrabas* out of the water?

Bob Gentz arrived to check my papers. Joy Baker came down to say 'Hi' and introduced me to Tim Shields, Crowley Marine's terminal manager.

I clambered ashore after 83 days at sea, this time slightly less steady on my feet than I had been in Honolulu. Bob Gentz was a big man. He stood in front of me, feet apart, thumbs tucked in behind his belt buckle, navy blue uniform crisply ironed and adorned with a number of gold shields.

'We got ourselves a problem.'

I had made the mistake of calling him 'Bob'. 'What's the problem, sir?' I asked.

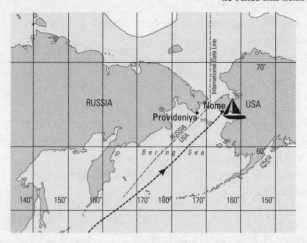

'Well,' he said, head crooked to one side, 'seems like you're an illegal alien.'

I couldn't help but think of the mysterious red and white light I'd seen hovering in the sky.

'How so?'

'You got no visa.'

I feigned ignorance. 'I'm British. Do I need a visa?'

'Yessiree.'

I was half expecting Bob to spit a dollop of chewing tobacco into the dirt.

'Well, there's a problem with the boat. I had to come in.' Quickly, I explained what I was doing, the Russians, where I was going.

'I checked you out,' Bob said proudly. Presumably, this followed the notification from Lt Miller that I was on my way in. He knew about Honolulu. 'You got emergency parole in Hawaii, right?'

'Right.'

'Parole for emergency visits is limited to one a year.'

I thought quickly. 'What period does a parole normally cover?'

'Thirty days.'

'I was in Hawaii for nine days, so might it be argued that I still have 21 days left?'

Bob thought about this for a while then said, 'Don't leave. I'll be back, probably tomorrow.'

'Do you mean I have to stay on the boat?' I needed to get to a supermarket. I was fantasising about fried egg sandwiches.

'Don't leave town.'

The roads from Nome led nowhere. Air and sea offered the only routes in or out. 'Don't worry, officer. I can't leave, not that I want to, of course. The boat's engine's out of action and I can't fly out because I've got no money.' Bob drove off, leaving a cloud of dust hanging in the air.

I strolled with Tim to his office, a 19th-century clapboard house up the road. He had heard most of what I'd said to Bob.

'Can we use the crane to hoist the boat?' I asked tentatively.

'What she weigh?'

'15 tonnes.'

'No problemo.'

Relief washed over me. I slumped back in my chair amidst piles of paper and files. 'That's great.' I smiled broadly.

''Cept one thing.'

'What?'

'Rick's away on a job. Rick operates the crane.'

'When's he coming back?'

'Dunno. Company business. Two days, a week.' Tim shrugged.

'I can't wait that long.'

'Dan could do it.'

'Who's Dan?'

'My brother. Works for Crowley up in Kotzebue.'

'Where's Kotzebue?'

Tim got up and stabbed at a map hanging on the wall. 'Half hour plane ride north.'

'Can he do it?'

'Sure, but you'll have to pay the fare, here and back.'

How much could it be? 'Okay, let's do it,' I said.

Tim reached for the phone while I wandered around the rest of the house looking at pictures of Crowley Marine tugs hanging in frames and some softball trophies won by the local boy's team, which Crowley sponsored.

'Yo! Adrian,' Tim called. I went back to his office. 'Thursday afternoon.'

* * *

Dale Whitney was more difficult to find. I trudged along the airport road out of town to a small settlement of dilapidated huts on the opposite bank of the river. Everyone knew everyone in this town. George had given me directions. The rusting domes of two Nissen huts concealed the front door of Dale Whitney's house. I knocked. The door opened. A small octogenarian (83 as it turned out) dressed in the thickest and oldest pair of woollen long johns I had ever seen stood framed in his doorway. A welder and steelworker, Dale Whitney had lived in Nome for 30 years. His hair was white, sticking up in places. Gold-rimmed glasses sat lopsided on the end of his nose. He looked like Father Christmas on his day off. Halfway through my explanation of who I was and what I needed, Dale ushered me inside. He lived with an army of cats. I finished my explanation.

'So,' I said. 'Would you be able to have a look at the prop shaft, see if it's bent and if it is, straighten it?'

'How long you here for?' Dale asked

'A few days.'

'Get George to bring the shaft round.'

I thanked Dale and left, stepping around trays of cat litter and discarded boxes of Corn Dogs.

I slept until midday. Bob Gentz collected me at the boat and we went over to his office to do the 'paperwork'.

'Okay,' Bob sighed, heaving himself into his swivel chair. 'We'll give you parole, extend your waiver for a visa over from Honolulu.'

'That's great,' I said.

'Normally there's a charge, but we're gonna waive that too.'

It seemed like I had a new friend. 'Well, thank you, sir,' I said, just to be sure it stayed that way.

On Thursday evening, Dan fired up the crane's massive diesel engine. The hoist was slow and even and as *Barrabas* cleared the dockside we turned her through 90 degrees using guy lines tied to the deck cleats. With the gentlest of motions, Dan lowered *Barrabas* onto wooden blocks just enough to 'ground' her without placing excessive load on the keel. Dan then locked the boom so that *Barrabas* was held firmly, securely suspended.

Another yacht entered the small harbour, tying up in the spot *Barrabas* had just vacated. Her owner and sole crewmember came ashore to spectate proceedings. With *Barrabas* settled, I then met Jerry, a retired ex-NASA scientist from San Francisco. Later he showed me round his boat, *Arctic Wolf*.

During the tour, I noticed quite a number of heating outlets. Jerry expanded on his various warmth-generating systems. The one part (or two, depending on how you look at it) of my anatomy that stubbornly refused to get warm when the temperature dropped much below 5°C were my feet. After Cape Horn, I was lying in my bunk (with cold feet) fantasising about electrically heated socks…

With barely controlled hand and arm gesticulations and rapid-fire speech, Jerry rummaged in an eye-level locker. He ripped out items of clothing, tossing them over his shoulder. They floated down and settled like giant, multi-coloured snowflakes. With an exclamation of delight, he turned, holding what looked like a regular fleece-lined jacket. What set it apart from the rest of the blizzard was the electric cable issuing thin and snake-like from its lining.

'This is what I do,' Jerry said, his excitement hampering his efforts to don the jacket. Then, finding the end of the cable, he shoved it into a nearby 12-volt socket. 'In 20 minutes, I'm toast!'

I was delighted at the display, but didn't mention that in England being toast was not a desirable state.

With tongue part way into cheek, I asked, 'You don't happen to have heated socks?'

'Oh, sure!' Jerry cried, arms spreading wide. 'And pants and gloves too!'

I was speechless. Here was my fantasy come true, the end of cold feet. 'I could really use a pair of these,' I said holding up the socks.

Jerry fired up his laptop, hooked into the local WiFi network and found the website for the magical manufacturer of heated clothing – www. gerbing.com.

With a possible solution to the problem of cold feet, I now had to sort out the problem of the cutless bearing. Inside *Barrabas*, I disengaged the steering quadrant from the rudderpost and loosened the prop shaft coupling. Clambering back to the ground, George helped me lower the heavy steel rudder so I could slide the prop shaft out. It was immediately obvious what had happened. The outboard nylon cutless bearing had melted with the friction of the spinning shaft. The bearings were seawater cooled and lubricated. Had I, at some time before arrival in Honolulu, run the engine in gear without opening the cooling valve? It was academic now.

George drove me to Dale Whitney's place with the shaft blocked and tied down in the back of his flatbed truck. We left the shaft with Dale then drove to the airport to take delivery of the new cutless bearings that Louise had sent to Nome via DHL. Back in Dale's huge workshop beneath the domed roof of one of the Nissen huts, we put the shaft in a lathe. The shaft was out of alignment by 30 thousandths of an inch. Dale (who held a Masters degree in engineering) reckoned it was as good as new.

I celebrated this piece of good news (not to mention saving the cost of replacing the shaft) with an enormous T-bone steak cooked in pepper and honey.

I called Louise the next day. 'The cutless bearings are slightly too large in diameter.'

'I've found someone in Anchorage who can make the alternator thingy, maybe he can help you. His name's Gary Feaster and his company's called Greatland Welding and Machine.'

'Fantastic – have you got an email address?' I scribbled it down on a cigarette packet.

I had already told Louise about Jerry and the heated suit.

'And I've been onto Jeff Gerbing…' Louise said.

'And?

'He's going to give you the full monty – jacket, salopettes, socks, gloves, the works.'

I was elated. I then called Gary Feaster. Could he fabricate a new base plate? 'No problem,' he said, 'just send me the bits to copy.' And the cutless bearings? Shave off $1/16^{th}$ of an inch? 'Send them too.'

I hitched a ride out to the airport and express-couriered the broken base plate and cutless bearings to Greatland Welding and Machine in Anchorage.

Rick Kostiew arrived back in Nome on Monday 14th August. Originally from Boston, Massachusetts, Rick was another stowaway, running from the urban sprawl and a broken marriage. In his fifties, his shock of white hair and distinctive Bostonian brogue made him instantly recognisable by day or night. At first shy, adopting a serious expression as he looked over *Barrabas* suspended in the straps slung from his beloved crane, Rick and I soon developed a strong rapport. It was not long before a smile split his lean face and the wisecracks started flowing.

'You wanna clean out the stern toob,' Rick said.

'You got a tool for that?'

Rick nodded towards the warehouse just across the street from *Barrabas*, Crowley's workshop. 'I got every type of tool you could imagine and then some. I got a tool for pokin', pushin', widenin', narrowin', cuttin', smoothin', you name it, I got it.'

'I've got a tool for poking too, but that's about it.'

Rick chuckled, shuffling his feet. 'I bet you don't done too much o' that out there,' and still chuckling to himself he went off to the 'shop' to fetch the reaming tool and flex extension to bring power out to *Barrabas*.

My mobile phone rang. Louise's number flashed on the small screen. I pressed the phone to my ear.

'I'm really sorry to tell you this…'

'What?'

'Someone in the Russian government has decided that a letter of Consular Guarantee from the British Embassy in Moscow isn't enough. They're insisting you have a valid visa.'

'Is this Monko?'

'No, I don't think so. Anyway, I've been onto Marie Forsyth…'

'Who's Marie?'

'She's the consul at the British embassy in Washington DC. This is the plan: she'll wait for the official permissions from Moscow to arrive at the Russian embassy in Washington. Once done, a British embassy car will drive your passport to their Russian counterparts. The Russians will then issue the visa and send the passport back to you in Nome via DHL.'

'So I need to send her my passport?'

'Yes and the completed visa application which I'll email. Can you print it out somewhere?'

'Shouldn't be a problem.'

I put the package together, including a US postal order for the precise amount of the visa and went to the airport to courier the package to DHL in Anchorage for onward carriage to Marie in Washington.

I had already been in Nome for longer than I planned, but then I had not expected the Russians to refuse the Consular Guarantee. My timings were slipping again. I was hoping for a three-day turnaround on the visa, but with no news of any progress on the escort vessel, that might prove to be unimportant. I could not leave Nome until the escort and its costs had been finalised.

While I was busy filling forms at the airport courier desk, the attendant said, 'Oh! Got a package for you right here,' and she hefted up a box. The new alternator base plate and milled down cutless bearings from Gary.

On the morning of Thursday 17th August, everything changed. The visa issue suddenly thrust itself forward as the crucial factor. The Iridium rang.

'You're not going to believe this!' Louise was breathless.

'What's happened?'

'They're letting you go! It's amazing. No escort, no ice pilot, no nothing.'

'What?' Had my ears deceived me? 'What d'you mean?'

'John sent me an email. I've forwarded it on to you. Mr Monko received instructions, orders to *make it happen*, get you through the NSR, solo!'

'I don't bloody believe this. Really?'

'Really!'

I fired up the laptop, waiting impatiently while the hard drive whirred and clicked.

John Mann: Thursday 17th August 2006

Well, it looks like your persistence has paid off, as well as the strategy of attacking on all fronts. Basically, as I understand it from conversations with Zuev yesterday and Monko today, the situation is as follows:

Monko received orders from the Ministry of Foreign Affairs to 'make this happen'.

Adrian will need to receive permission from the Federal Security Service (FSB to be present in high-security border areas). This is a regular process. I am to contact a Mr Igor Vasilievich Chomai tomorrow to find out what he needs to grant this permission, but according to Monko, he is predisposed to granting it (apparently, he also has orders to do so).

Monko wants all the contact information for Adrian to pass on to the people out in Chukotka and everyone else involved. Due to the good ice conditions, Alpha Global will be allowed to continue without the previously discussed escort boat.

He did add a caveat that, if by the time Adrian gets to Pevek (on Chukotka's northern coast) the situation has deteriorated at all, then the escort option might have to be revisited. If that is the case, then Monko's people would provide some sort of escort. No details on what that might be, but hopefully we won't have to cross that bridge.

Wow! How had this come about? Who had said what to whom? Ian's view was unequivocal. No one *ordered* the FSB to do anything. The Directorate of Internal Security was a law unto itself, even in so-called 'modern' Russia. Only the President's office could issue such a directive and President Vladimir Putin, being a former chief of the KGB, well…

I reeled at the likelihood that the Alpha Global Expedition, the boyhood dream of an anonymous Englishman managed by his equally anonymous

ex-wife from a village in rural Buckinghamshire, had percolated up to one of the most powerful political offices in the world.

The Russian Embassy in Washington DC would surely receive the necessary paperwork imminently. Maybe all the paperwork was already there. Louise alerted Marie Forsyth in Washington of this latest development.

Time began slipping by more quickly. Each time I looked at the clock, two hours had mysteriously disappeared. The new cutless bearings fitted snugly into the stern tube housings, the prop shaft was back in place and coupled to the gearbox. The heavy rudder was back on.

While I waited for my passport and visa, I scraped the last of the barnacles off the boat then washed the hull down with thinner. I had noticed tins of antifoul in the shop. Crowley no longer maintained their boats in Nome so the antifoul was surplus. Rick let me have as much as I needed and he laid on rollers, paint trays and masking tape.

John Mann: Friday 18th August 2006

I found out today that Adrian needs to stop in Provideniya (and maybe Murmansk) to say hello (and goodbye) to the Russian border guards.

When I spoke to the FSB border service today, they informed me that the only document they need to grant permission for Adrian's transit is a letter from the regulatory agency involved, which in this case is the good Mr Monko! I've already dropped a note to Monko asking him to write that letter. Below is the instruction from Monko:

> *Ministry of Transport, Russian Federation*
> *Federal Agency for Sea and River Transport*
> *17.08.2006*

> *To: O.N. Yanenko, Captain of the Sea Trade Port of Provideniya*
> *I.A. Boreev, Captain-Inspector of State Port Control of the Port of Provideniya*

> *I entrust you to conduct an inspection of the yacht* Barrabas *at the port of Provideniya in accordance with the shipowner's schedule.*

> *The yacht should travel in clear water along a coastal route through the Northern Sea Route under the instructions of the Sea Operations Staff, and in case of ice, with an accompanying boat with ice pilot on board.*

Upon receipt of permission from the RO UFSB RF for DVO (Regional Office of the Federal Security Service Directorate for the Far East Region) and the existence of an insurance policy, issue Permit No. 37/06.

Respectfully,
Head of the Department for Icebreaker Facilitation and Hydrography
Northern Sea Route Administration

N. A. Monko.

As the days ticked themselves off the calendar, my frustration returned. What was happening now? I was back on that familiar seesaw, bouncing up and down between euphoria and despair. My expectation of fast action from the Russian authorities following the stunning news from John had fizzled whilst people tried to figure out who should write which letter to whom.

'Be patient,' Louise cautioned. 'We've come this far. It won't be long.'

I busied myself with the logistics of the NSR transit. So late in the season, I might not have the luxury of sailing the entire route along Russia's Arctic coast. In light winds or headwinds, *Barrabas* had to keep moving forward. The consequences of becoming iced-in during the re-freeze did not bear thinking about. *Barrabas* had to be carrying enough fuel to motor the entire length of the NSR if necessary. I assessed my fuel stocks: 1,000 litres. With fuel for heating and fuel consumption at three litres per hour (running the engine at higher revs) factored in, I needed 2,500 litres. As a contingency, Louise had already sourced and ordered a further 50 x 5-gallon fuel cans. George drove me to Icy View north of town to pick them up in his flatbed.

Back at the 'shop', I lined up all 100 fuel cans in regimental array on the floor.

'What kind of fuel you got in there?' Rick asked.

'Regular stuff from the UK. Some from Honolulu.'

'You need winter grade. That stuff'll turn to wax at 0°.'

'Would this work – I decant 50 per cent of the fuel from 50 of the full cans to the 50 new ones so they're all half full..?'

'Yeah, yeah, yeah. We fill with winter grade, waxing point –60° and the mix should give you a waxing point somewhere around –20°.'

Rick started fiddling about with test tubes and pipettes, adding various chemicals and measuring colour changes against a chart to ensure this would work.

I decanted the fuel, then George filled the tank on the back of the flatbed with winter grade diesel and drove up and down the lines of fuel cans, topping them off.

On Wednesday August 23rd, Rick hoisted *Barrabas* back into the water. Getting the fuel on board occupied me for most of the next day. The combined weight, two tonnes, could raise the boat's centre of gravity, destabilising her. To keep the boat stable, I distributed the fuel as low down as possible, securing the cans with ratcheted webbing straps. With the operation complete, red fuel cans carpeted practically every inch of floor space on board.

John Mann: Thursday 24th August 2006

Got up early today to see what I could get done on this visa issue. I talked to my contact in the FSB and he's not yet received the letter from Monko's people. So I contacted Monko's assistant and he said he is unfamiliar with this specific issue. Furthermore, he's unable to issue such a letter himself until Monko returns next week. All together, I appear to be caught in a roundabout without an exit.

Nikolai Monko had gone on holiday!

I was tantalisingly close – one letter from the FSB. I could sense John's bewilderment and frustration mounting in parallel with my own.

'Look, what's the worst that could happen?' I said to Louise. 'I'm a lone yachtsman on a sailing boat moving at walking pace – hardly a threat to Russian national security.'

'You mean just go?'

'Yes. Mr Monko's issued the order, he's under orders, so if I just go now without this FSB letter…'

'You'll end up in some Siberian gulag.'

'Can you put it to the Foreign Office?'

Shane Jones: Russia Desk, Foreign & Commonwealth Office, Friday 25th August 2006

I would draw your attention to an incident last week in which, according to the Russian authorities, a Japanese fisherman strayed unauthorised into Russian territorial waters and was shot dead.

You will appreciate the FCO's concern to ensure that the arrangements required by the Russian authorities are in place before Adrian sets off to transit the NSR.

Maybe it would be better to wait! John rang round furiously, pulling in every contact he could think of and talking to every department in the Ministry of Transport's Sea Division, eventually ending up at the Security Department of the River and Sea Agency. They made enquiries and reported to John that the request for FSB clearance should come from the Russian Foreign Ministry and not Nikolai Monko!

Louise copied all the correspondence from the Foreign Office, John, British Embassy staff in Moscow and Washington DC, Sovcomflot and Ian's ongoing efforts with the Royal Navy to Sam Laidlaw. Perhaps one directed thrust might create a domino effect through the diplomatic inertia.

The Russian ambassador to the United States occupied the most sensitive and powerful office among the overseas diplomatic corps of the Russian government. Sam knew the ambassador personally. On 31st August, he wrote directly to His Excellency, Yuri V. Yushakov.

* * *

My days in Nome soon fell into a familiar routine. In the mornings, I downloaded the latest batch of emails and fired off replies. Then I walked to the supermarket to provision for the day, mainly because I enjoyed the exercise. After an article appeared in the local newspaper, *The Nome Nugget*, people regularly stopped me in the street asking about the latest developments with the 'Ruskies'. En route to or from the supermarket I detoured to the library, logging on to www.seaice.de to check the ice. Back on board *Barrabas*, I continually tinkered with the engine and the rigging, sometimes wandering up to the hardware store for bits and pieces to keep the boat in a constant state of readiness.

John Mann: Monday 4th September 2006
There is apparently some ice forming in Vil'kitskiy Strait so there could be problems passing through...

I spoke to Neil Abbott at the embassy. There's all kinds of activity on both the FSB letter and visa fronts but no results at present.

On Wednesday 6th September, a storm blew in from the west bringing 50 mile-an-hour winds. Whatever happened, the storm would keep me pinned down in Nome for 48 hours.

I found Rick in the shop.

'If I have to leave *Barrabas* here for the winter, what d'you think would be the best way?' I had mentioned the possibility to Rick already, so he'd had time to think about options.

'Come have a look out back.'

Rick led the way to a storage area behind the warehouse. A row of cradles the size of sea containers lined the back wall of a larger warehouse across the street. Each one held a massive gas cylinder. 'Lift out the cylinder and lower the boat down.'

I studied a cradle. 'Not enough height for the keel and I don't think it's wide enough.'

'You got the measurements?'

'No.'

'So get the measurements.'

'I can tell by eye.'

'Or,' Rick said, 'get two containers and put the boat between them.'

'Too much weight on the keel.'

'Or, dig a hole and lower the boat down so she's sitting on the ground…'

'Deep enough so there's no weight on the keel!'

I went to talk to Tim about the possibility of wintering the boat in Nome. I wanted to put the idea in play as a contingency. The ice edge appeared stationary. The window for 2006 looked as if it might be closing. By late evening, I fell into another exhausted sleep.

The mobile phone's chirruping woke me. I scrabbled for my watch – 6.30am.

'They're letting you through!' Louise exclaimed. 'The Russians are letting you go!'

I bolted upright. 'What?'

'John can't understand it and neither can I. But who cares?'

'That's great,' I said but my voice lacked enthusiasm. 'Big problem, though. The ice has stopped receding and new ice is growing at Vil'kitskiy Strait. You saw John's email. The western side is blocked.'

Two emails from John later in the day confirmed Louise's news.

John Mann: Thursday 7th September 2006 (15.08 Moscow time)
Update: Just spoke to Monko. He says go to Provideniya. I wish I knew for the love of all that's holy why they couldn't have decided this earlier...

John Mann: Thursday 7th September 2006 (17.54 Moscow time)
Dear god, could this get any more confusing?

OK, I spoke to Andrey Kechashin at Sovcomflot. He said he spoke to the border guard service and that everything can be done at Provideniya. His understanding is that the FSB's border guard service can grant the permit there on the spot. Apparently, it's a normal procedure when you've got boats transiting. Well, this flies in the face of everything we've been told.

So much for the letter of authority from the FSB, but did I need a visa or not? I called John.

Apparently not, according to Monko.

I called John in Moscow. Something did not stack up.

'I don't know...' Instinct was telling me that without a visa, the Russian authorities would either turn me away from Provideniya or worse, arrest me and impound the boat.

'I gotta tell you that I've had it from three sources now that new ice is forming,' John said.

'I know, John. I think it's too late...'

Damian Thwaites: Russia Desk, Foreign & Commonwealth Office, Friday 8th September 2006
Our Consul-General at the British Embassy in Moscow, Jessica Hand, called on Vyecheslav Pavlovskiy, Director, Consular Division of the Russian Ministry of Foreign Affairs (MFA), on 7 September to discuss the consular requirements relating to the expedition.

She informed him that Nikolai Monko, Director, Federal Agency for Maritime and River Transport, has advised Adrian that he does not require a visa and that he should proceed to Provideniya... Pavlovskiy made it abundantly clear to our Consul-General that Adrian would require a visa.

I should also add that Simon Smith, Director, Russia, South Caucasus and Central Asia Directorate in the Foreign & Commonwealth Office, has raised the issue of both visa and permission to transit directly with Andrey Chupin, Deputy Head of Mission at the Russian Embassy in London, requesting him to make representations to his colleagues in Moscow, on both counts.

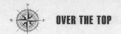

More confusion. I walked to the library on Front Street to check the ice. A massive floe of ice blocked the western side of the Vil'kitskiy Strait. It had grown, and north winds had brought down even more ice. I leaned back in my chair and stared at the library's Artex ceiling. Nome to Provideniya, three days, allow two days for the inspection, then 18 days to Vil'kitskiy. I didn't bother finishing my thought.

It was too late.

Barrabas would have to over-winter in Nome.

I trudged back to the harbour. The storm had passed but left a residue of low, grey cloud. I wandered about below decks, talking aloud to *Barrabas*, explaining the situation. I had to leave her. She would be safe. Rick was here.

The phone trilled. I smiled at Louise's rapid-fire enthusiasm. 'How are you?'

'Well…'

'I've got something to tell you…'

'The ice…'

'Me first,' she insisted. 'Sam just called. He's just spoken to a guy called Gulshko at the Russian Embassy in Washington. All the papers are at the embassy, MFA permission, the authorisation letter from the FSB. Gulshko can issue the visa now. You'll be out of there tomorrow.'

'Louise, I need to tell you about the ice.'

* * *

I was devastated. All that effort by so many people in various countries to send me on my way and now it was too late.

I distracted myself by keeping busy preparing *Barrabas* for her long winter hibernation, taking the sails off the rig and bagging them for storage in the warehouse, clearing the deck lines, oiling and stowing the blocks and then the back-breaking task of getting the 100 fuel cans off the boat and into the warehouse. I worked on silently, until darkness and exhaustion defeated me.

Eric Brossier: Sunday 17th September 2006
Hard to stop, but congratulations for having permission to sail single-handed! Good luck for the next part of the trip.

Rick used the crane to lift the mast from *Barrabas*. In pouring rain, I tidied the lines and shrouds and then wrapped the mast with industrial shrink-wrap and covered it with tarpaulin. With the mast suspended from the crane, we 'walked' it to the Crowley oil storage depot and laid it on palettes, distributing its weight as evenly as possible.

Rick then spent several hours digging out *Barrabas*'s 'pit' in an area of ground to the side of the Crowley warehouse, excavating a trench, 25 feet in length, 3 feet wide and 7 feet deep.

With tyres positioned around the lip of the trench, Rick carefully and expertly hoisted *Barrabas* from the water and lowered her gently into her winter home. The underside of her hull sat snugly on the tyres, her keel, skeg and rudder six inches clear of the bottom of the trench.

I packed the delicate electronic equipment and charts into boxes and stowed them in the attic of the Crowley office.

Cam Kristensen, one of Rick's team, carved traditional Inuit snow goggles as gifts for the boys. I bought Rick 200 cigarettes as a gesture. George drove me to the airport.

As I stared down through the small oval of Perspex locked in my own world of colliding emotions on the flight to Anchorage, I realised I had come know a certain truth. John Ruskin captured its essence when he wrote, *'There is no wealth but life – life, including all its powers of love, of joy and of admiration.'*

Barrabas and I had come far together, we had shared pivotal moments, weathered danger, rejoiced in the elemental beauty of the sea, taken care of one another and journeyed the hard road. I was anxious at leaving her but I knew that the remarkable people of Nome would care for her until I returned.

PART II
OVER THE TOP

CHAPTER 22
HOME AND AWAY

'EXCUSE ME, SIR. We have chicken or lamb today.' The flight attendant smiled at me offering the lunch menu.

The first-class section was half-full, the seat next to mine empty. At Dulles airport in Washington, a United Airlines representative had met me off the Chicago flight and whisked me to the executive lounge. 'Your wife called us, sir. My, what a voyage you've been on... we are happy to upgrade you for the transatlantic flight.'

The Atlantic Ocean spread endlessly beneath the aircraft's wings. The idea that I had traversed those spaces in a 40-foot boat was almost incomprehensible. Yet at sea, nothing had seemed more normal than sailing along day after day. Then, thoughts of driving to the supermarket, attending school plays, watching the evening news or flying on a plane had seemed bizarre. In the days of the Cold War, a lone Western yachtsman venturing into Russian Arctic territory would have been unthinkable. Today, it remained politically and militarily sensitive. Permission to attempt the passage single-handed was a huge break-through, a first, and I had to hold onto that to keep my motivation alive.

* * *

I glimpsed my sons' faces through the half-glazed doors of the arrivals hall – eager, expectant faces etched with excitement. I remembered all those years

before, the arrivals hall at Kai Tak, when the expectant faces had been those of my parents. Time had flipped the roles. I stood for a moment behind the doors, watching them and seeing the fathomless beauty that is only visible to a parent. Other passengers trundled past. All those miles, all that distance, all my thoughts. Now here they were, made flesh, like a miracle, two miracles. They were sitting on the floor at the end of a human corridor in front of Louise. Would time and distance have created space between us? Might some deep strand connecting me to my children have been severed? I pushed the door. Gabriel saw me first and was up and running. I genuflected to receive his little, airborne body. I squeezed my eyes tightly shut, but tears seeped out anyway. Benjamin, older, more self-conscious, walked towards us. When he got to me, he opened his arms and wrapped them around my shoulders, his face to one side against mine and in some minute but tangible way seemed to melt into me.

Louise and I hugged and almost together we said it seemed only a day or two since I had left. She persuaded a taxi driver meeting somebody off the flight to take some pictures and then we were out into the cold night and driving towards Buckinghamshire along familiar, unchanged roads. I sat in the back of the car with the children, no distance between us, no severed connections.

I turned 46 on 1st October. Louise threw a party in a marquee set up on the driveway. It was a Sunday. The party was as much for her as for me, a kind of release valve for all the tension of the last few weeks, a healing of sorts for the disappointment of having to break the Alpha Global Expedition. Sam arrived. I was glad of the chance to thank him. Ironically, he couldn't stay for long. He had a meeting in London with a group of Russians selling gas to Britain.

* * *

On 7th October 2006, one week after the party, a drive-by shooting in Moscow left a Russian journalist, Anna Politkovskaya, dead outside her apartment building. She had been an outspoken critic of the Russian government and in particular, the war in Chechnya. In London, Alexander Litvinenko claimed Politkovskaya's killing to be the work of the FSB. He had long been a thorn in the side of the Russian government. A former lieutenant-colonel in the FSB, Litvinenko fled Russia to Britain in 2001. The following year, he published a book, *Blowing up Russia: Terror from Within*. In his book, Litvinenko claimed that the FSB was behind the September 1999 bombings of apartment buildings in Moscow, Volgodonsk and the southern city of Buinaksk. The government blamed the atrocities on Chechen rebels, an allegation denied by separatist leader, Shamil Basayev. In the wake of the bombings, Russian forces launched a second offensive on Chechnya.

I called Andrey Chupin at the Russian embassy in London on Wednesday 1st November to arrange a meeting.

On the same day at 4pm, Litvinenko met Russian businessman Andrei Lugovoy at the Mayfair Millennium Hotel near Grosvenor Square. Later, he met Italian academic Mario Scaramella at the Itsu sushi restaurant in Piccadilly. Scaramella had been investigating FSB-related espionage. After returning home that evening, Litvinenko became ill and was admitted to Barnet General Hospital.

On Wednesday 8th November, Louise and I drove to London. 'Embassy Row' is a grand avenue of grand houses, gated and secured at both ends. I parked up across the street from the Russian Embassy twenty minutes ahead of our allotted appointment. A junior staffer showed us to the Orangery overlooking the formal gardens of the residence, complete with tennis court. I was expecting a youngish, Armani-suited diplomat of the new order. Instead, Andrey Chupin was in his late fifties, reed-thin, wearing a tweed jacket, bespectacled and slightly stooping – more professorial than new-generation egalitarian. The table was set with a bone-china service, pastries, hand-made Russian chocolates, silver cutlery and linen napkins. Andrey Chupin listened intently while I précised events that had led to my decision to delay the Alpha Global Expedition in Alaska. Despite everything that had gone before, I needed to reapply for permissions to transit the NSR. Would he, I asked, act as our liaison to ensure the application followed a smoother path this time round?

'Well, you see, it's not possible for me to become directly involved.'

'Of course. I understand that various government departments in Moscow act with a degree of autonomy.'

Andrey Chupin cracked a small smile at this reference to the FSB.

'But, I believe that were we to gain the support of the ambassador, then the Foreign Office and your Ministry of Foreign Affairs [MFA] might be able to have a more productive dialogue.'

The First Minister ruminated. 'Perhaps.'

'Rather than direct involvement, I am thinking more in terms of a recommendation.'

We admired the room, spoke about the ambassador's prowess on the tennis court and returned to the matter at hand.

'I will consider putting this to the ambassador,' Andre Chupin said. 'I see him daily.'

'Does His Excellency know of the Alpha Global Expedition?'

'Of course.'

We parted with the knowledge that Andrey Chupin had a fondness for English pubs and warm English beer and the promise that he would table my request for some kind of intervention with His Excellency, Yury Viktorovich Fedotov. I was to call the following Tuesday to find out what, if any, result had materialised.

On 11th November, Litvinenko spoke on the BBC Russian Service. He claimed to have been the target of a 'serious poisoning'.

Three days later, on Tuesday 14th November, I waited anxiously while somebody summoned Andrey Chupin to the telephone.

'I have spoken to the ambassador and I have to tell you, Mr Flanagan, that His Excellency is fully in support of your expedition.'

'That's very good news, sir.' A cool wave of relief washed through me.

The Litvinenko affair was now commanding headline space on front pages and news bulletins across the country.

'Can I ask you, Mr Chupin, what's the next step?'

'I myself will prepare a document and this will be signed by the ambassador and sent to the appropriate officials within the relevant departments of the MFA. It is a matter for them to decide whether to distribute the document to other relevant government departments and agencies.'

'I am very grateful.' Pressing my luck, I said, 'May I ask, sir, what the document suggests?'

'The ambassador will be recommending that the relevant departments support the Alpha Global Expedition in granting clearances for a transit of the Northern Sea Route in 2007. Once we have heard back, I shall let you know the outcome.'

I followed the Litvinenko story closely. His dissident status was well known. So far, doctors had not been able to identify the cause of his illness. On 17th November, Litvinenko was transferred to University College Hospital. Suspicions mounted. Scotland Yard placed an armed guard outside his door. Any implication of subterfuge by the Russian government would strain diplomatic relations with Britain to breaking point.

On 19th November, doctors concluded that thallium poisoning (a highly toxic chemical once used to poison rats) was to blame. Litvinenko suffered a heart attack on the night of Wednesday November 22nd and died the following day. Doctors revised their diagnosis, discounting thallium poisoning. Scotland Yard's counter-terrorism unit began pursuing a rigorous investigation into Litvinenko's 'unexplained' death. Eventually scientists identified a radioisotope, polonium-210, as the poison that had killed Litvinenko. The police found traces of polonium-210 at the Mayfair Millennium Hotel, in cars and in a British Airways jet on which Lugovoy had flown to London. The trail led directly back to Moscow.

* * *

I heard back from Andrey Chupin in early February. The Ministry of Foreign Affairs had been in touch with him to say they would agree to distribute the ambassador's report to the appropriate departments within the Russian government: Interior, FSB, Defence, Transport and Northern Sea Route Administration.

'I am very grateful to you, Mr Chupin. I hope that the ice lets me through, but if it doesn't, the fact that I would be the first to enter the Northern Sea Route alone will make a small piece of history.'

'Yes, yes. I should say to you, Mr Flanagan, His Excellency believes that your voyage could make a positive contribution towards Anglo–Russian relations.'

I almost fell off my chair.

* * *

John Mann was still co-ordinating activity for the new permission in Moscow, liaising regularly with Nikolai Monko. He emailed us to say he would be in London in March. We arranged to meet at one of the hotels in Chelsea Village.

When John walked into the hotel foyer, I was surprised at his youth. More importantly, the rapport both Louise and I had developed with John through innumerable emails and telephone conversations, catalysed no doubt by the intensity and urgency of the situation that had thrown us all together, continued on without missing a beat. We went to a bistro across the road for lunch.

'This is just so weird,' I said to John. For a moment, his expression seemed uncertain. 'Sitting here in a restaurant in London with you.'

Of course, to John perhaps the encounter was not so surreal. He travelled extensively on business as head of Roman's public relations and media management. To me, Russia was another country, unseen and ill understood. Not to John. He was fluent in Russian, married to a Ukrainian and had made his home in Moscow. Meeting all types of people, from adventurers to politicians to corporate executives, was all part of his daily agenda.

'So,' I said, 'I guess you must have studied Political Science and Russian at Harvard.'

John looked startled. 'How did you…'

'Just a wild guess,' I said. It was an educated guess. I figured Roman Abramovich would only employ the best and in the States, that usually meant a degree from Harvard. John came from Washington DC, with a background as a former vice-president of US PR giant Burson-Marsteller, the company that represented Ford and Coca-Cola in the United States. Whatever his education, John was well schooled in circumspection. Dealing with Russia's labyrinthine bureaucracy required a practised hand and John agreed to continue liaising on behalf of the Alpha Global Expedition. Winning the requisite permissions for a transit of the NSR that summer would, we agreed, likely be a formality. How things might turn out in the hostile and unpredictable Arctic environment was less certain.

In the frantic race to get to and through the NSR the previous summer, I had not followed up on MDA's promise of providing satellite imagery to assist with navigation of the passage. I reprised that promise in an email to Simon Chesworth, MDA's sales director for Europe, the Middle East and Africa.

On 4th May 2007, John sent me a copy of the instruction from Nikolai Monko to the port authorities in Provideniya requesting that on completion of a satisfactory inspection of *Barrabas* they issue me with permit number 18/07 to transit the NSR. On the same day, I received the draft acquisition plan for satellite imagery from MDA.

To slot the final piece of the jigsaw, the visa, into place, I needed an 'invitation' from an appropriate organisation in Russia. John arranged for the invitation to come from the Administration of Chukotka province of which Roman Abramovich was still governor. After registering the invitation with the Ministry of Foreign Affairs in Moscow, John sent me a copy which I in turn sent on to Andrey Chupin.

Nikolai Monko had also copied his instruction to Nikolay Babych at Western Marine Operations Headquarters, the traffic co-ordination centre controlling shipping through the western part of the NSR, including the Vil'kitskiy Strait.

John said, 'The Murmansk Shipping Company operate the icebreakers under government contract. Western Marine Operations Headquarters controls their activities, guidance, navigation, that sort of thing.'

'And Babych?'

'He heads up WMOHQ.'

'So he works for MSCO?'

'I guess.'

'Do I need some kind of contract with MSCO, then, in case I get into trouble?'

'I spoke with Babych. He says an exchange of contact details is all you need. If you get in trouble then they'll come help, presumably with some cost.'

Adrian (to: Simon Chesworth, MDA Geospatial Services): Thursday 14th June 2007
Tim and I have discussed the best way to proceed with the ice routing. The plan is that Tim will use the www.seaice.de website to get an overview, check on what the ice is doing on a daily basis. He will cut the relevant section relative to my current position and email the image (reducing file size as much as possible) so that I have

a general idea of what's happening with the ice edge. As I approach more ice-congested waters – likely to be near Vil'kitskiy Strait – Tim will contact you (with as much notice as possible) with requests for the satellite image needed (long/lat/ resolution etc). If you can then take the shot and pass it to Tim, he will contact me for my current position and then plot the route and advise me accordingly by either email or voice. I have asked Tim to call you to discuss image formats etc and other technical details to max the accuracy of his interpretation.

Meanwhile, John had finally received the vital authorisation from the FSB. On Friday 22nd June, my last full working day in England, I drove to the Russian Embassy in London to meet with the head of the Consular Section. I left an hour later with a three-month visa. On Monday 25th June, I flew from Heathrow to Chicago on United Airlines flight 931, the first leg of the long haul back to Alaska and *Barrabas.*

CHAPTER 23

STAMP OF APPROVAL

I STEPPED OUT OF THE SMALL terminal building at Nome Airport. The muddied pick-ups in the car park, the distant buzz of quad bikes zipping along on the airport road and the treeless tundra surrounding the airfield were immediately familiar. Low grey cloud dropped sheets of drizzle. I lit a cigarette and waited for Tim to collect me.

As we turned onto the dirt road leading to the Crowley shop, I glimpsed *Barrabas* behind some earth-moving trucks that Rick had parked around her as protection. My heart leapt at the reassuring familiarity of my beautiful boat like spotting a cherished face in an anonymous crowd. On board in the dim light, I made a quick inspection. No damp, just the musty smell of disuse. The heater's fuel tank was full. The batteries had held their charge through the polar night. I fired up the heater and soon a wave of warm air began dispelling the scent of neglect.

I found Rick in the shop. 'So, Rick, what's that bloody huge dent doing in the side of the boat?'

He was wise to me now. 'Drove a truck into her, sorry 'bout that, you know how it goes, dark and that.'

We shook hands. 'How've you been?'

'Good, you know, not bad.'

Later, I learned from Cam that Rick's wife was in hospital in Anchorage, desperately ill, fighting cancer. She was due for major surgery to rebuild her spine. How typical of Rick to bear it all with a grin.

I set straight to work, unwrapping the mast where it lay in the oil storage facility, overhauling the engine and installing the new Furuno Radar that DHL had air-freighted to Nome ahead of me. The radar was fitted with an integral GPS unit. I ran the cable below decks from the chart table to the aft frame. But how to mount it? Rick had a look.

'What's'd'matter widge you? You got a problem with this?'

'Yes, Rick. You got a solution?'

'Sure.'

Off he went back to the shop. He reappeared fifteen minutes later. Using plastic plumbing pipe, Rick had constructed an angled support mount for the GPS receiver with a curved base plate that sat perfectly on the tubular structure of the aft frame. He tapped it in with two screws and for good measure bound it with Jubilee clips. I tested it for strength. Rock-solid. I reckon I could have hung off it with my full bodyweight.

Over the following days, while *Barrabas* sat squat in her trench, I organised the deck gear, set up the two laptops and rimmed out the mast radar cable outlet.

Adrian: Sunday 1st July 2007

Glad the boys have settled back quickly after I left. I have to confess to a mighty bout of depression when I left you at Heathrow. Once I'm on the water I'll be fine…

On Wednesday 4th July, Rick came into work to help me. We lifted the mast horizontally with the crane, up and over the fence of the oil storage facility and 'walked it' towards the shop. Still suspended four feet off the ground, Rick welded reinforcing seams around the upper spreaders. As an Independence Day parade rolled by on the dirt road, I stood on *Barrabas*'s deck guiding Rick in the crane's cab with hand signals. We stepped the mast in a perfect operation. With the new radar scanner mounted on the mast, the mast electrics hooked up and the forestay and furling gear back on, we could now lift *Barrabas*.

With *Barrabas* held in slings, Rick locked the crane while I applied a fresh coat of antifoul. Cam, working as a mechanic with Crowley but an artist by training, temperament and inclination, 'tattooed' *Barrabas* on her starboard and port quarters with an image of a păl-ai-ŷuk, a mythical serpent-like creature from Inuit tradition, usually painted on hunting kayaks. Being fierce, the păl-ai-ŷuk would frighten other sea creatures away and protect *Barrabas*.

Later that afternoon, with *Barrabas* in the water and moored alongside the harbour wall, Rick left for Anchorage. It was a difficult farewell – Rick had been unstinting in his support for the expedition and me. Without him, this Alaskan hiatus would have been much more difficult.

On Sunday, someone tapping at the bow interrupted my routine of work and worry. Two young guys stood on the harbour wall. I recognised something distinctly non-American about them. It turned out they were French – Sebastien Roubinet and Eric Andre, who had just sailed in on a small Kevlar catamaran, *Babouche*, so called because its shape was reminiscent of a Moroccan slipper. The boat's odd appearance was by design, the idea being to meet low pack ice at speed, climb up onto the ice and continue sailing on top of the pack. They were going to try the Northwest Passage. Sebastien and Eric, all lantern-jawed, tousled-haired, broken-nosed Gallic confidence, had no engine, no radar and only two hand-held GPS units for navigation.

While Sebastien and Eric made final preparations, tied up to the fishing boats' pontoon across the harbour, I bent on the mainsail, laid out the running rigging and filled the fuel cans, lined up on the floor of the shop.

I learned from some of the crew on the local gold dredgers about 'Splash Zone', a two-part underwater cement that set like rock to repair small holes in the hull. The risk of a hull rupture sat ever-present like an unwelcome guest long after the party is over. I ordered some Splash Zone from Katchemak Gear Shed in Homer.

Cam and his wife, Malinda, appreciating that I would not be sitting down to home-cooked food for a while, invited me to dinner several times – steak, pasta, salads, puddings, beer.

On Saturday 14th July, Malinda drove me to the A&C store out of town. I bought basic provisions: 60 litres of long-life milk, tins of fruit, chilli beef, creamed corn, cheese, salami, butter, jams, biscuits, tinned milk, energy bars, sweetener, fruit juices, assorted nuts, confectionery and paper towels (for mopping up oil and fuel spillage when I made filter changes on the engine) plus the essential coffee, tea and drinking chocolate.

The next day, I started loading the fuel and completing my list of final jobs. At dinner that evening, Malinda and Cam presented me with a box of food: Malinda's 'historic' fried bread, jams and wild Alaskan blueberries. Cam had made me a fishing line with a lure carved from bone and an amulet carved from moose antler.

'See, here's how it goes.' Cam leaned forward. The lid of the box was carved with a face. He pulled it away. 'This here's grizzly fur.'

'You shoot the bear?'

'Yep. See, when a grizzly meets a polar bear, the polar bear backs off.' He pushed the lock of fur back into the box and closed the carved lid. 'The idea's you hang it in the boat someplace. It'll ward off any polar bear attack.'

'Thanks. Really appreciate this, and everything else you two have done for me.'

Cam waved these sentiments away. 'How you feeling 'bout things?'

'Nervous. Colliding emotions, I guess. There's the desire to be under way and I'm eager for what lies ahead, but then there's the fear of the unknown, the consequences of a misjudgement or of pure bad luck.'

'You can bet your ass the Ruskies'll be watching you.'

'Good!'

I hung the amulet from the cabin headlining alongside the tea leaf lei from Hawaii.

I finally got away from Nome at 2.30pm on Tuesday 17th July, three weeks to the day and almost to the hour since I'd arrived back in Alaska. Winds were light and out of the west. Provideniya lay 200 miles across the Bering Strait so I expected to make port sometime on Friday, but crossing the International Date Line westwards would warp me forward 24 hours.

The Crowley team and Joy Baker saw me off. I discovered the boat's main GPS unit was not working. The instruments relied on signals from the GPS. With no signals, the displays were blank. I switched to a hand-held GPS back up and then traced the problem to a section of cabling in the dark recesses of the lazarette. A sharp edge had abraded an area of the cable sheath and corrosion had broken the core connection. I cut, cleaned, spliced and soldered, tried the unit and bingo, we picked up six satellites and *Barrabas* and I were back in business. I followed this with a meal of fried eggs, Malinda's fried bread (which was indeed truly historic), salami and fresh wild Alaskan blueberries.

Barrabas settled comfortably on the open water. I kept the engine running but not engaged for 24 hours; after nine months of standing I wanted to make sure she worked well and that the fix to the cutless bearings had held true. I was close enough to Nome to return, if ignominiously, to sort out any problem. As it was, the engine ran sweetly.

Adrian (to Cam & Malinda): Wednesday 18th July 2007
I wrote a letter to Rick in Anchorage and I will repeat some of the things I said to him. The hallmarks of greatness lie within the simple courtesies of everyday life – generosity of time and spirit, concern and thoughtfulness, the expenditure of effort on behalf of others in return for no reward. All these things you have shown to me and I am deeply grateful to you both.

Louise had learnt from her previous experience of managing the expedition. This time round she had hired an au pair to help with the boys.

Louise: Wednesday 18th July 2007
All is well here – Rosanne took the boys out all day to give me time with my beloved computer. Rosanne is really working out way better than I expected. She has a lovely calm manner about her – she is absolutely on the boys' level which they love. Never tires of running around with them and playing tennis and football in the garden.

At 1.05pm on Friday 20th July, we passed into Russian territorial waters, crossing the International Date Line at the same time. I raised the Russian courtesy flag on the starboard shroud.

Three large whales, brownish in colour, surfaced off the starboard beam. I heard their blowholes. When I came on deck, the mountains of the Russian coast loomed ahead, shrouded beneath eiderdowns of fluffy mist.

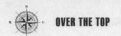

Louise: Saturday 21st July 2007

*Off to see Harry Potter this morning then I have to go and buy some new jeans…
seem to have crept from a size 10 to a size 12 – only temporary though! I must be
feeling very relaxed… the Rosanne effect. Last time with no help I was in such a
high state of anxiety all the time. I worried constantly how I was going to juggle
the AGX and kids and took virtually no time for myself. It was all wrong and I see
it very clearly now. Can't wait to hear what awaits you in Provideniya.*

I motored the last 10 miles to reach Provideniya's natural harbour carved
from the mountains at the head of a deep-water fjord. Wreathed in layers
of mist, precipitous scree slopes showed through like a massive granite and
cotton millefeuille. I made it to the town at 6am. Great rusted dockside
cranes reached towards the sky like the curved talons of some long-dead
prehistoric bird. Someone instructed me by radio to berth at number two –
it turned out to be crane two. Three federal internal security guards ordered
me to stay on the boat.

A posse of uniformed officials from various state departments
instructed me to take *Barrabas* to another quay. It had been a jetty at one
time, the concrete long since crumbled away, leaving the twisted, rusty
steel frame poking dangerously towards the hull. The guards produced
a bevy of forms to fill, all in triplicate, then flanked by guards, we made
our way across the dock to a neighbouring tug. In the relative comfort of
the wardroom, I produced my wad of Russian permission letters. A brief
discussion followed about the need for an ice pilot. I ruffled through more
papers, incomprehensible documents in Russian. The answer seemed to be
contained among them, rapid-fire Russian was followed by a consensus of
nodding heads and any thoughts of an ice pilot quickly dismissed.

At noon, one of the uniforms gave me my permit to transit the NSR,
numbered 18/07, stamped and approved. I was free to go!

I decided to stay the night alongside. Internal security allocated a
two-man detail rotating in six-hour shifts to stay with the boat. We tried
to communicate in the universal language of broken English, mime and
gesticulation punctuated with groans of frustration as meanings were lost.

I needed to top up on fuel. The master of the tug called the oil terminal –
no one answered so he gave me some of his at no charge. I gave him a bottle
of rum and a bottle of sloe gin from *Barrabas*.

Uran, the tug's mate, spoke some English. He led me into town to buy
onions. There was no shopfront as such, just a wooden door, bent by years

of freezing winds. Inside, the place reeked of ancient wax and cabbage. A single, naked bulb cast a dull yellow light. The shelves were almost bare: a few tins here and there, some dusty bars of chocolate, candles, cooking oil. I imagined post-war rationing in a deprived area.

Back on the tug, Uran offered the use of their shower, which I readily accepted. The tug's master knew Henk de Velde from his attempt at the NSR in 2003. So even in this strange forbidding land that time seemed to have forgotten, it was still a small world.

On Monday morning, 23rd July, I was ready to leave. The FSB commissioner came to the dock at 10.45am, handed my papers over, indicated for me to sign more documents in Russian and then I was free to go. I started the engine and slipped my lines at 11am.

Under full sail during the night, *Barrabas* touched 6.5 knots despite her 6,000lbs of fuel and water. If ever a boat had real guts, it was this one. While she battled on, I slept for a few hours. Our great adventure together into the unknown had begun.

Barrabas passed Cape Dezhnava and crossed the 66° north parallel, the eastern entrance to the Northern Sea Route at 12.50am on Wednesday 25th July, the first yacht ever to do so single-handed. I murmured silent but heartfelt thanks to the very many people in London, Moscow, Washington and elsewhere that had made this possible.

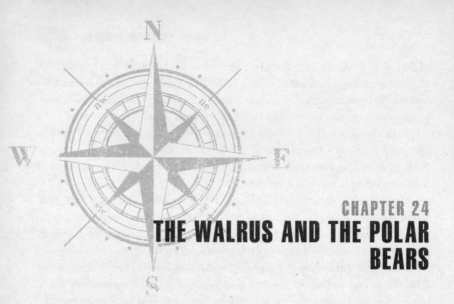

CHAPTER 24

THE WALRUS AND THE POLAR BEARS

Louise: Thursday 26th July 2007

I almost killed your sons tonight. They were playing with the hand shower in their bathroom and managed to flood my office, wiping out my external drive, my mobile phone, my cordless mouse and key pad. Thank god the computer is OK otherwise… As it is they are in their rooms for the rest of the evening (since 5.15). I have never been so angry in my entire life.

By Saturday 28th July, we had covered 500 miles from Provideniya. Wrangel Island lay due north as we passed from the Chukchi Sea westwards into the East Siberian Sea. On deck, the weather was fine, a beautiful 'blue' day, the coast discernible eight miles off the port beam wreathed in mist but the air warm despite our latitude at almost 70° north.

Malinda: Monday 30th July 2007 (sent via Louise)

I hope that things are going well. We are checking Adrian's page daily. I just needed to relay a message to him. They are doing a huge recall on some canned chilli from Alaska and I think that he bought some when I took him shopping. Please let him know not to open the cans or eat anything inside. The cans could contain bacteria that cause botulism.

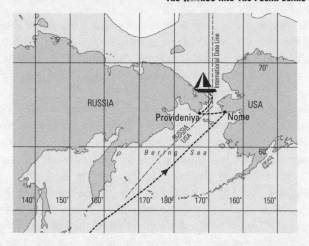

I had bought eight cans and already eaten one! I punctured the remaining seven and chucked them over the side: the idea of botulin toxin on board outweighed my environmentally friendly instincts.

On the last day in July, the easternmost of the four islands of the Ostrova Medvezh'i slid into view. I altered course to pass north of Chetyrokhstolbovoy Island (what kind of name is that!). Its neighbour, Puskaryova Island, sat dough-like on a flat, shimmering sea. Sea mist rolled in ahead of a depression. It had an icy look to it. I knew the land would be gone within minutes. The depression laid a mantle of thick cloud over this small part of the earth's apex, reducing visibility to half a mile. The light dimmed to grey. The sea became slate. Winds shifted to the northwest and built. We pushed into this wind for the next 24 hours, striking two precious miles off our track each hour.

Nikolay Babych at West Marine Operations Headquarters finally responded to my requests for weather information. The Maxsea GRIBs data did not extend much above 70° north. Tim provided forecasts by email, but I figured that WMOHQ would have access to more detailed reports specific to Russia's Arctic coast. He also sent through email contacts for two icebreakers operating on the eastern side of the Vil'kitskiy Strait with the instruction that I should copy the icebreakers on all communication to WMOHQ.

Barrabas bashed on through the night. I marked up the chart. In spite of the headwinds, we had reached the halfway point to Vil'kitskiy Strait.

Like a phantom echo, my appetite hovered somewhere distant. My body had shut down into some deep, primeval survival mode able to sustain itself with no obvious source of energy. The muscles of my belly became defined, my cheeks hollowed. I started heaping sugar into tea and coffee, the only sustenance I wanted or, it seemed, needed.

The land of northern Russia's remote wilderness scrolled slowly by, soft hills sliding gently to the sea treeless and brown, mottled in places with snow, white flags testifying surrender to the previous winter's bitter cold.

Whenever *Barrabas* was happy sailing without me goading her on, I read, as much to hide from my anxiety as for the enjoyment on the page. I had already digested Paul Torday's *Salmon Fishing in the Yemen*. The thought of the dry heat of the Arabian desert seemed like Nirvana. By now, I was well into *The Road*, Cormac McCarthy's novel on the hell of surviving a post-nuclear world. I'm not sure reading of a holocaust was the most apposite choice – descriptions of a grey cold wasteland did nothing to lift my spirits.

At 2.30pm, Friday 3rd August, the radar registered a contact at two miles, 20° off the port bow. A patrolling icebreaker, perhaps? Tim had warned me to expect ice at 153° east. I glanced at the GPS. We were close. I grabbed the binoculars and went on deck. I couldn't see anything. I ducked my head below the companionway to watch the radar sweep. There it was again. I glassed to the fore. A massive chunk of sea-ice floated like a carcass abandoned by the herd. I played the binoculars along the line of the sea. More lumps of ice dotted the horizon carved by wind and water into strange, alien shapes. I passed another one, a tiny island, streaked with blue and green. It looked like a swan the size of a family car, its head bent low on its icy neck as though being drawn inexorably into the melt. The ice edge stretched away to the north, intra-lit by the Arctic sun.

These were orphans, cut adrift from the southern bulge of the ice edge by the west wind, outriggers to the main pack. I approached the edge of the pack southeast of Proliv Dimitriya Lapteva, looking for a way round. Hummocks of ice stretched away in all directions, projecting cold like a solid wall. I estimated the ice at 30 per cent cover, the safe maximum in which *Barrabas* could manoeuvre. I was dressed warmly, helped by my heated mid-layer. A ski mask protected my eyes, preventing the frigid air from drawing tears and obscuring my vision. I edged forward along a narrow channel. The entire ice mass was moving and shifting on the currents, openings slowly closing, new channels widening, contracting and expanding as though the ice itself was drawing breath. Seals rested on level shards, curious at the low growl of the engine. Whiskery faces bobbed up around me at this unexpected interruption to their day. As I drew nearer, the seals' curiosity gave way to anxiety and they slid quickly to the sanctuary of the water. I stayed in the ice for six hours, steering cautiously. The ice was soft but submarine edges could still be razor sharp. *Barrabas* nudged and bumped. My heart fluttered at each grinding contact. In that small footprint of the earth's surface, in that tiny fragment of time, I felt truly humbled.

Barrabas came through the ice field. Were there others close by? I managed a few hours' sleep. Like a siren, this icescape was as deadly as it was beautiful. The possibility of ice collision now became my central concern.

At some point while I was below, I heard the sound of something metallic falling on deck. Rousing myself from the warm innards of the sleeping bag, I clambered on deck and found a nut on the starboard side, nestled against the toe-rail, level with the mast. A jolt of panic zinged through me. I looked up. The split pin at the end of the through-mast bolt securing the lower shroud tangs had failed. The nut had worked its way off the bolt and dropped to the deck. The bolt was eking its way out too, the starboard shroud tang literally hanging on its very last thread. Had that gone with full sail set, the mast could have buckled in the middle! Part of the thread was damaged, so I drilled out the inside of the old nut (thanking my lucky stars I'd kept it from Honolulu) to use as a washer. Loosening the shrouds, I hefted the tang firmly up the bolt, slid the 'washer' home, tightened the nut and put in a new split pin. Freeclimbing the mast, I inspected the intermediate tangs and the cap shrouds at the mast top. They, thankfully, were fine.

Cam: Monday 6th August 2007

Rick update. Hannah is doing better. She is up walking around (with some trouble), so that is a good sign. Rick is doing good, well as good as any guy that can't sit still more than two minutes can do sitting around.

Ever since reaching the halfway mark to Vil'kitskiy Strait, the wind had stayed stubbornly in the west at 25 knots, forcing us to bash into uncomfortable seas. Sleep was difficult. Instinct, sharpened by time and experience, tugged at me. I could not afford to relax the ceaseless rounds of inspections and maintenance checks. I spotted a problem. The starboard forward lower shroud was unravelling. I gybed *Barrabas* onto port tack to take the pressure off the starboard rig and then went aloft to have a look.

The damage was not so bad. One strand had broken. Still, a break was a break, and more worryingly, if one strand could break, others might follow.

I called Louise and asked her to find out from Tim when this depression would blow over. She called back to say, 'The worst is over.'

The engine demanded regular attention to ensure it kept running sweetly. In close ice conditions, loss of the engine would be catastrophic. I ran the engine routinely, to keep it warm and prevent any type of seizing. On 8th August, the engine suddenly cut out. My heart skipped a beat. I knew immediately it was a fuel problem – no coughing and spluttering before dying, no blue, black or white smoke. I checked the fuel system. Everything appeared normal, no leaks or disconnected piping. The filters were clean. I called Louise. She called the engineers at Golden Arrow. Together we isolated the problem to a failed fuel solenoid, a type of electronic fuel flow controller. I switched the engine to a mechanical override and off she went. Nevertheless, the combination of events and conditions were enough. Seeds of doubt sprang from their pods and quickly took root. I found my thoughts turning as bleak as the sea around me. I had to snap out of this, give myself a talking to, which I did, aloud. I talked to *Barrabas*. Because of the impenetrable ice ahead, I put the idea to Nikolay Babych of finding an anchorage to wait for the ice to clear from the Vil'kitskiy Strait.

Nikolay Babych: Wednesday 8th August 2007
The passage through Vil'kitskiy Bay from the east at the present is not available. Awaiting ice conditions improvement in the west part of the Laptev Sea can be of long-term period – about 20–30 days. In the area of Begichev and Peschanyy islands drift ice is observed. The place of stoppage for waiting of best weather conditions is recommended to be area of Stolbovoy Island or to make the call to port Tiksi.

Stolbovoy Island lay 30 miles north. Tiksi, the main port along the NSR, was deep into the south of the Lena Delta. *Barrabas* answered. The water rushed rhythmically against her hull like the passing of rail track beneath a speeding carriage. Press on... press on... press on, she seemed to be saying.

Sea and sky were a monochromatic continuum of grey. The wind carried a bite. The sea clutched at *Barrabas*, pinching, shoving, prodding. It was difficult to rest. With the horizon veiled by curtains of mist and sea fog, the radar swept a constant vigil. Fatigue began corroding my resolve, abetted by the cold.

Just as my endurance seemed to have given out, the next morning broke clear and blue. The wind backed south, carrying with it the warmth of the land close by. *Barrabas* barrelled along under full sail at over 6 knots, nose to target, eager to make up lost ground. I fell into an exhausted sleep for six hours. Two hundred and twenty miles remained to sail westwards and then we could turn north for the ice.

Louise: Saturday 11th August 2007

Benji starts his cricket course on Monday – and they both have their swimming course next week as well. They have had a very active summer. Has been wonderfully hot and sunny this week but forecast is for change... more rain starting tomorrow. Ian says land temperatures in Russia are unseasonably high right now. This is such good news for you...

I consulted my charts and found a promising looking anchorage 75 miles west on the eastern side of the Taymyr Peninsular. The northern end of the peninsula formed the southern side of the Vil'kitskiy Strait. From the chart, the anchorage appeared well protected and out of the tidal stream. I could hole up there for as long as necessary, then as the ice allowed, inch northwards towards the Vil'kitskiy Strait, seeking out anchorages as required.

By the evening of 12th August, I saw drift ice ahead, vanguards of the main pack. This was a bad sign. We were still miles from the peninsular. By 10pm and still 50 miles offshore we hit the edge of the pack ice. My heart sank. The ice edge was much further south than I had expected. With the engine on low revs and all sail down, I steered *Barrabas* through these outliers. Ahead, a white line looked like the leading edge of the solid ice sheet, but I knew that as I drew closer, this line would break up, revealing channels though the pack.

I found a gateway in. Large pieces of ice formed an intricate mosaic. Something moved in the water. At first I thought it was a bobbing ice chip, but it was moving too fast. I looked again. Two black eyes stared back at me. Now 20 metres in front of my bow, the polar bear lifted his snout to sniff at this strange thing in its midst. He swam off to one side, checking repeatedly over his shoulder. I circled round. The bear reached ice and lumbered up out of the water, a young male with an immaculate coat. He shook himself and studied *Barrabas* from a better vantage point. He sniffed vigorously, confused. As I came closer, he loped off and slid back into the water, swimming away though the ice maze.

I carried on, passing through two more lines of denser drift before getting to the edge of the main pack that curved away in a great arc to the northeast. I manoeuvred *Barrabas* deeper into the ice for a couple of miles. An unbroken carpet of white covered the ocean for as far as I could see.

The sun dipped to kiss the horizon. Then, like a huge orange ball, it bounced back into the sky, climbing ever higher as *Barrabas* nosed her way gently between the massive floes, 24-hour daylight making this foray possible.

The ice became too dense for me to go any further. I worked *Barrabas* back to clear water and headed south. Anchorages along the north Russian coast were impossible to reach in a vessel drawing much more than three feet. In most places, mud banks extended up to 15 miles offshore covered only with waist-deep water. Where did I go now?

Clear of the ice pack with open water to the south, I set the boat and went below. I had not slept for almost 30 hours. The prospect of a hot, strong cup of sweet tea was more appealing to me than anything else (with the exception of being teleported to a tropical island paradise). I never had the tea. I sat on the saloon banquette and immediately fell asleep.

A terrible screeching from the bow jerked me awake three hours later. *Barrabas* had collided with a chunk of drift ice. Dread surged through me like a cold rain. I grabbed a torch and scrambled to the forecabin to inspect the forward part of the hull. Stripped of insulation and fittings, I could see the inside of the hull plates: no gaping holes or splits, no frigid water rushing in. We pressed on. After a further 12 hours, I could evade sleep no longer. I laid out my sleeping bag on the floor of the galley because my starboard berth was on the high side of the heel and the port berth unserviceable, covered with fuel cans.

Sometimes, the most logically founded decisions are wrong. I believed I was clear of the drift. There hadn't been any ice at this latitude on the way up. I should have stopped the boat to sleep. Three hours later, I woke to the same screeching sound, a shudder and then stillness, not even the gentle side-to-side motion of a boat floating. I tore topside. We had collided again, only this time *Barrabas*'s bow had ridden up on to the ice. The wind had died. As the ice spun beneath us, pressed down by *Barrabas*'s weight, she slid off, leaving behind gashes of red anti-foul paint like smears of blood.

Louise: Monday 13th August 2007
How thrilling to see a polar bear. What a bummer about the ice. On the sea-ice maps there has been a marked melting on the other side of Vil'kitskiy Strait. Hope the rest follows suit and soon! We picked blackberries yesterday and I made a huge crumble today. Thought how much you would have enjoyed it. Hope you find good spot to stop soon.

The many ice scientists and organisations I had consulted, among them America's National Ice Centre, Russia's Arctic and Antarctic Research Institute and the Scott Polar Research Institute in Cambridge, agreed that the North Polar ice cap achieved its minimum extent by 15th September. I still had one month.

The next day, I received an encouraging update from Tim.

Tim Thornton: Wednesday 15th August 2007
Good news, the Uni Bremen ice image shows that the ice has thinned significantly. There appear to be two passages opening up: a narrow one right along the coast, and a much larger one further north.

Three days later, *Barrabas* nosed through scattered drift ice towards the low-lying Ostrov Peschanyy, not so much an island as an ovoid sand bar rising no more than two metres above sea level, enclosing a lagoon. The island measured four miles across at its widest and was home to a defunct light and walrus rookeries. I tried manoeuvring into the lagoon but *Barrabas* bottomed. I backed out and finally anchored off the northwestern side.

Tim Thornton: Sunday 19th August 2007
Definitely thinning out now and more so along the coastal passage than the one further to the north.

According to an environmental congress in Norway, the North Polar ice cap was melting faster and earlier than at any other time previously. Polar bears and walruses were suffering. Permanent ice had disappeared, revealing new islands.

My experience was different. Despite that, the ice at Vil'kitskiy Strait stubbornly refused to yield and Peschanyy Island looked like market day in Hong Kong with the huge number of walruses snorting and hooting.

Nikolay Babych: Thursday 23rd August 2007

There is much drift ice in Vil'kitskiy Strait. Powerful and strong vessels having special ice class only under nuclear icebreaking assistance are able to sail through Vil'kitskiy Strait. As to your vessel, such sailing is not admissible even with nuclear icebreaker assistance. We have received more or less favourable forecast of improving ice condition in Mope Laptevych (Laptev Sea) in September.

I began to have serious doubts about the feasibility of getting through the Vil'kitskiy Strait. In 2002, Eric Brossier was through by 29th July.

In the respites between storms, I slept, attended to various ongoing jobs, read or watched the wildlife. The walruses, by now used to *Barrabas,* became more inquisitive, approaching the boat in pairs or trios. Their long tusks gave them lugubrious expressions and their eyes, situated shark-like at the sides of their heads, were small, mean and bloodshot, swivelling as if controlled by wire in need of fine-tuning.

A permanent ring of ice surrounded the island. Depending on wind direction, the ice either closed with the slender spit of sand or moved off like the bellows of some meteorological accordion. As the end of August approached, I needed a breakthrough.

Tim had ordered up a Radarsat image. I emailed John Mann asking him to contact Nikolay Babych to get a more detailed prognosis of the ice and conditions at Vil'kitskiy Strait. While I waited for information, the island gained three new inhabitants: polar bears, a mother and two cubs.

John Mann: Tuesday 28th August 2007 (sent via Louise)

OK, I had a long chat with Babych.

Right now, as Adrian noted, the temperature has dropped and winds turned to the north. That means ice is coming down from the north and nothing is opening up.

There is a 60 per cent chance that the winds will change to southerly. This would mean ice pushing north and a chance for Adrian to make a run through the Vil'kitskiy Strait.

BUT, the current view is this won't happen now until around 3 September. Then it would take a few days for the change to have its corridor-opening effect. The problem is that new ice will start to form around 20 September. In other words, the window is going to be very, very short.

There are three small ships in Tiksi waiting to travel. A Dutch yacht crew is waiting in Dikson wanting to go east. Right now, Babych isn't giving any of them clearance to make a run for it.

Further to the west, drift ice had cleared. Nikolay Babych recommended that I move to Preobrazheniya Island 50 miles away to await further developments. Meanwhile the American National Centre for Snow and Ice published a comparison of the current melt with the previous minimum recorded in 2005. In October of that year, the North Polar ice cap shrank to 5.32 million km². On 22nd August, just a week before, the ice cap occupied an area of only 4.92 million km².

It was getting late in the season. The opportunity to get through the ice might remain for only a few short weeks.

CHAPTER 25

A SLICE OF CHOCOLATE CAKE

PREOBRAZHENIYA ISLAND SAT like a giant wedge of chocolate cake laid on its side in the grey syrup of the ocean, sheer cliffs rising from the water on the north side with a slope covered in cocoa-coloured tundra running down to a gravel beach.

A disused polar research station was marked on the chart, but as I came into the bay, a small supply vessel rested at anchor and men moved about on shore. I coasted towards the other vessel and dropped anchor in the lee of a spit, flat and straight like a man-made breakwater. A skiff broke away from the beach.

Through a combination of sign language, broken English and my Russian paperwork, I managed to establish my credentials and explain that I planned to stay for a few days while awaiting clearance to sail north towards Cape Cheluskina, the eastern gateway to Vil'kitskiy Strait. I had no idea who these people were – maybe researchers, itinerant hunters, government employees. The two men in the boat, Valerie and Vladim, told me they were heading out the following day, Friday. They duly did, leaving me alone once more with my boat, the walruses, and my hopes that a sustained southerly wind would clear the ice and give me passage west to the Kara Sea.

Sitting at anchor off Preobrazheniya Island, I was isolated literally and figuratively. The Iridium could not support detailed satellite ice

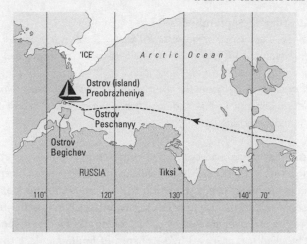

images and with no pictures to look at, I was relying completely on Tim's interpretations. The time delay between Radarsat taking shots and my receiving Tim's interpretations on board was too long. By the time it reached me the information was out of date.

'I've been in touch with AARI,' Louise said. Outside, strong winds were blasting the northern cliffs of the island and screaming down the southern slope into the bay.

'Who's Harry?'

'Not Harry, AARI – Arctic and Antarctic Research Institute.'

'How did you manage that?' It was a stupid question in light of everything Louise had achieved.

'It was Ian's idea. I called them up.'

'Just like that?'

'Yes. Anyway, I spoke to someone called Vasily Smolyanitsky. He's head of the climate laboratory. He's going to help. I've sent you some information.'

I couldn't believe this development. The elapsed time between a satellite snapping an image from space and the interpretation reaching me would be much closer to real-time.

'I need sustained southerly winds, three days minimum, five days would be better to blow the ice off the coast.'

'You're going to get them in a couple of days according to Vasily.'

AARI: Saturday 1st September 2007

The area of the Laptev Sea adjacent to Vil'kitskiy Strait is blocked by Taymyr ice massif, though the Vil'kitskiy Strait itself has only ice stripes and patches. According to the forecast for the next days (1st–3rd September) northeastern winds will preserve the ice near the coast of the Taymyr Peninsula. Not having high-resolution imagery, I cannot advise either going close to the coast or trying to use the stated weakenings.

The North Polar icecap had continued contracting and now covered only 4.42 million km², a 10 per cent decline within the last fortnight. Despite this, a 200-mile-wide finger projected south from the main ice pack and clung to the eastern side of the Taymyr Peninsula, blocking my path. I favoured the inshore channel over any openings appearing among the offshore floes. If the ice blocked me, at least I had a chance of finding a place to anchor. Offshore, with nowhere to go, the ice would embrace *Barrabas* and then crush her to death.

The temperature plummeted. Freezing north winds dusted the rugged mound of the island with frost. Hail and snow fell steadily. Between me and the open water of the Kara Sea on the west side of the Vil'kitskiy Strait, 100 per cent ice cover in places presented an impenetrable barrier and yet the North Polar icecap had reduced to a staggering historic minimum. The only way through would come with sustained southerly winds.

AARI: Monday 3rd September 2007

Our expert strongly advises Adrian to wait where he is for changes in ice situation due to favourable winds. Pending stable south and southwesterly winds for a couple of days, the Taymyr ice massif will swiftly move in NE direction so that a good opening near the shore will form. Adrian still has three weeks before new ice formation and may wait for up to 10 days for changes in wind situations. Also, it is much more reasonable for the yacht to use near shore opening than try to use very risky seaward weakenings as due to winds and currents, the ice situation in the NW Laptev Sea may change too swiftly for the yacht.

At least the confirmation of using the inshore channel was heartening. Now I could eliminate any thoughts about an offshore passage. Vasily compressed the Envisat images he was receiving and sent them to Tim who forwarded them to me. I now had pictures. But until Nikolay Babych agreed the viability of the inshore passage, with the implication for icebreaker support, that route remained closed to me as well. I had to get agreement from West Marine Operations Headquarters.

Adrian (to: Nikolay Babych, WMOHQ): Monday 3rd September
The latest satellite ice image from AARI shows an open water channel inshore along the coast of the Taymyr Peninsular. Is this the best route? Please advise soonest.

The tension nestled in my shoulders. The route was fraught with danger. South winds had to open the channel and keep it open for long enough for me to make the 100 miles to open water in the Vil'kitskiy Strait. If Babych gave me a 'Go', I would need 48 hours. If the winds reversed before I was through, the ice could pin me to the coast. The Taymyr Peninsula was crawling with polar bears. If the boat foundered in the ice, I would be in real danger. I had the shotgun, but only 50 rounds of ammunition, and the very idea of shooting a polar bear was so appalling that I would not risk being caught in the ice. Only an open channel sustained by southerly winds would do.

AARI: Tuesday 4th September 2007
The ice situation remains completely unfavourable for the yacht going westward as Taymyr ice massif blocks the way to Vil'kitskiy Strait due to the prevailing winds of NW-N sector. The same unfavourable perspective is for the next 1–5 days. However, long-term synoptic forecast for the period 9th–15th September points out for a high probability of the SW/S/SE winds. If there will be such S-sector winds blowing for a couple of days the Taymyr ice massif would move swiftly NE, thus opening a free water channel near the coast. Based on the above we recommend you to wait till the stated period 9th–15th September.

'This is really desperate,' I said to Louise. 'I was supposed to get south winds today. Things ain't looking good.'

'Vasily says wait.'

I waited at anchor, anxiety and tedium vying for supremacy. I read, slept, tried to eat, paced the deck and occasionally listened to music. Time was fast running out.

Vasily came through with confirmation that winds would veer south the next day and hold for at least two days. I bent over the charts. Eighty miles to the entrance to the inshore channel, one day's worth of sailing leaving me only a day to navigate 100 miles along the channel. Too tight. Or was it? How much drift would there be in the channel? I had no way of knowing. I had not heard from Nikolay Babych about the feasibility of the inshore channel, but on Friday 7th September, I got my answer.

Nikolay Babych: Friday 7th September 2007
AARI's information about the existence of a coastal route without ice along the Taymyr Peninsula coast is inaccurate. In reality, that area to the north from 75N, due to the long-term action of north/northwest and northeast winds, is blocked with very serious ice.

Inaccurate? How could AARI's information be wrong? Tim had looked at the US GFS weather model, which confirmed Vasily's opinion that south winds would blow from 9th September. Babych was telling me that forecasts predicted south winds on the 15th September. Who was I to believe? Both AARI and WMOHQ were experienced interpreters of ice-imaging, but AARI had no vested interest in me. Was Babych playing it safe?

I wanted to go for the inshore channel. I could leave the following morning at dawn. The south winds would drive me to the channel's southern entrance. I could cover the 100 miles inside the channel in 24 hours and even if the wind changed, I would still have several hours before the ice started closing with the shore. It would be damn tight, but could I escape the channel into open water and get west fast and out of danger? The critical piece of information was Babych's view that floes of impenetrable ice were blocking the northern exit of the channel. He was offering an alternative.

Nikolay Babych: Friday 7th September 2007
I want to inform you that a caravan of not large boats called Osipenko, Orekhovo-Zuevo *and* Novoulyanovsk, *led by Captain Valery Petrov, departed from Tiksi on September 6. These boats have been told to wait for an icebreaker at 7530/11700. We plan that the icebreaker* Taymyr *could go to these boats on the morning of September 10.*

The southern winds that we expect after September 8 could change the situation favourably, as long as it lasts for 3–5 days or more.

I can't give any guarantee that the three-boat caravan's attempt will be successful. In any case, I suggest you join up with this caravan.

Could I keep up with a convoy? The route would be offshore, in deeper water, a total distance of 250 miles from the rendezvous to open water. At a constant 5 knots, travel time would be a minimum of 50 hours, probably longer. At no point during the passage would I be able to sleep. This would be tough. Even getting below to make a brew would be a challenge.

Things were now down to the wire. The winter re-freeze was imminent, ambient air temperature was falling and, another factor I had to consider, in sub-zero temperatures ice could accumulate on *Barrabas*'s deck and rigging, raising the boat's centre of gravity to a dangerously destabilising extent.

If the icebreaker decided to give it a go, I would emerge into ice-clear waters at the western end of Vil'kitskiy Strait with perhaps only hours to spare.

Louise: Saturday 8th September 2007
Good luck for tomorrow – at least you will be moving again. Start eating, otherwise you have no chance of having the strength to stay awake whilst in convoy.

I weighed anchor at 10am the following morning. A dense line of sea-ice showed the southerly extent of the massive ice bridge reaching down from the polar cap. Beyond the ice, the snow-dappled mountains of the Taymyr Peninsula floated on a bed of ground mist. The inshore channel meandered somewhere between the ice and the coast, open or closed, navigable or not, I didn't know. The rendezvous lay 80 miles north-northeast. I made good progress, averaging 6 knots, but recent satellite pictures had clearly shown large tracts of drift ice south of the RV position.

At 6pm, I went on deck to check my horizon as I had done regularly throughout the afternoon. A piece of ice was bobbing in *Barrabas*'s wake 50 yards astern! We had narrowly missed another collision. More alarming was the sight to the front. A small ship was passing right across my bow. Two similar vessels followed astern of her. These had to be the three boats that together with *Barrabas* and the icebreaker would make up the convoy! Four miles north, the horizon was phosphorescent with ice, extending as far as I could see along the horizon. This was ominous. We were all still 40 miles south of the rendezvous. I hove-to. The three-ship convoy passed without altering course. Were the ships heading west to find a way around the drift? Maybe operations HQ was routing them through to the RV. I judged their speed at 6 knots and thought about tagging along behind but worried that I might not be able to keep up and, if I had to come back east again, I would be head to wind.

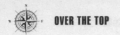

While *Barrabas* held station, I went below and called on the radio.

'No English, no English,' came the reply.

'Tiksi, Tiksi, Taymyr, Taymyr,' I said, hoping that someone among their combined three crews would assimilate the information and draw the conclusion that I was talking about the icebreaker. Surely Nikolay Babych had told Captain Petrov that a yacht might be joining the convoy. Static crackled from the radio and nothing else. I tried calling again several times but no one answered.

Daylight faded fast, the drift too thick to penetrate alone. The latest forecast from Babych indicated north sector winds from 11th to 16th September. I computed the options. The best alternative was to wait here south of the ice until daylight and get an update from Nikolay Babych in the morning.

Just before midnight, I went on deck. Three miles astern, I saw the lights of the three ships blazing brightly, but the small convoy was now sailing due east. They had failed to find a way through the drift ice to the rendezvous.

I called Louise and explained the situation. 'It can only mean that the three ships are not being routed by Babych.'

'What do you want me to do?'

'Can you email Babych? We're all here in the same place, so ask him to get the icebreaker to come to us. That way, we'll have a path cut through the drift.'

'I'll do it now.'

'Babych won't be in his office, but he'll get it first thing. The problem is I can't communicate with the ships. No one speaks English. If I could get them to agree to wait here with me…'

I slept for eight hours. The wind died to a zephyr. Drift ice framed the eastern horizon. By morning, the ships had gone. The radio had been on at full volume while I slept. If anyone had tried the VHF, I would have heard it. I checked my email for any response to my suggestion of re-designating the RV. Nothing. Had the ships met up with the icebreaker or turned back for Tiksi? By 2pm on Monday 10th September, I still hadn't received any communication from Operations HQ. According to forecasts from WMOHQ and AARI, southerly winds would continue through the day. I had missed the RV and it was too late to try the inshore channel. Setting course for Tiksi meant battling head to wind. The only option for the moment was to wait.

Louise called me at 7.30pm. John had spoken to Nikolay Babych. The other three ships had not made the rendezvous and were 'circling'. The icebreaker *Taymyr* was still escorting large ships through difficult ice up to three metres thick in places. New ice was forming between the floes. The cargo ship, *Kapitan Danilkin*, en route to Tiksi to pick up her load of timber, was stuck fast in the ice, awaiting the *Taymyr* to break her out. Nikolay Babych's recommendations mirrored my own bleak assessment: either winter *Barrabas* in Tiksi or get her transported on the *Kapitan Danilkin*. The convoy option was dead. The *Taymyr* had not even gone to the RV.

'Please wait where you are,' Louise said, her voice cracking with emotion. 'AARI are holding an emergency meeting to look at the inshore channel. It might still be on.'

'Don't cry,' I said. 'It is what it is.'

'Just wait there, promise.'

'Okay, I can't go anywhere until the wind swings round anyway.'

'I've also sent AARI's satellite pictures to Babych. We'll see what he says.'

Nikolay Babych: Tuesday 11th September 2007

We have received the picture that Louise sent to us. As a comment, I would note that it's necessary to know how to decode such pictures. A lip of solid ice that moves on to the south following the contours of the coast is very visible in this picture. There is clean water between the massif and the coast up to latitude 75.35N… to the north from 76.03N parallel the ice is from 6 up to 8 points. In the area of Ostrov Petra (Peter's Island), extended strips of ice of 9–10 points attached to islands are observed.

As we said before, there is no through passage along the coastal route through clear water. It's also necessary to keep in mind that the coastal area has a wide zone with the depths less than 10m. The icebreaker Taymyr has a 9m keel and it's forbidden for it to enter into depths less than 10m.

Finally it's necessary to know that when eastern and northern winds blow, such a pass could close in just six hours and it becomes a trap from which it is impossible to escape neither to the south, nor to the north, nor to the east.

The yacht Campina, which entered into this pass without our permission, crashed in a similar situation approximately at 75.45N latitude.

I sent to John our picture dated September 10 on which it's possible to see that a lip of solid ice pressed to the coast of Taymyr at the lat 7520–7530N. The trap has slammed. It's very good that there is nobody there at the moment.

CHAPTER 26

THE SHIPPING NEWS

I TURNED FOR TIKSI BENEATH GREY SKIES. Darkness reduced any prospect of spotting drift ice so, at 10pm, I gybed *Barrabas* and backed the sails to let her drift while I slept until daybreak at 3am.

The *Kapitan Danilkin* had broken free from the ice and was now steaming for Tiksi. She would load her cargo of timber over a ten-day period. I checked the chart – 250 miles to go.

Tim Thornton: Friday 14th September 2007
I just looked at the last two Radarsat images from today and yesterday. These confirmed what the Russians said – the broken ice isn't too dense, but there is a lot of new ice forming in between and Adrian probably wouldn't have been able to get through. At least that confirms we made the right call.

I guided *Barrabas* into the lee of the Olenek and Reka deltas. The wind calmed. Dense veils of cloud that had persisted for weeks finally cleared and by nightfall stars glimmered and moonlight struck a reluctant flame in the ocean. The cabin was snug and warm, lit by the dull glow of a single reading light. With no evidence of drift ice, *Barrabas* sailed on through the night under reduced canvas. I burrowed into my sleeping bag, too exhausted to concern myself further and slid blissfully beneath the blanket of sleep.

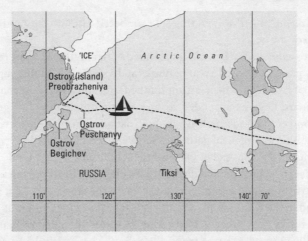

My bodyweight had fallen substantially. I felt drained. That evening I forced myself to cook spaghetti with fish sauce (clams from Honolulu) and sardines. A wave strike sent everything loose in the cabin flying, including the pot on the stove. The concoction of hot, stinky fish went all over me. I wiped myself down and retreated to my bunk while *Barrabas* nudged southwards at 3 knots. Just as nature had thwarted me, the dawn cheered me with blue skies and sunshine at long, long last.

Studying my only chart of the area, I spotted a small cove 15 miles from the port of Tiksi. I could anchor in the bay and rest up before facing the inevitable avalanche of bureaucracy in port.

The smooth-sided hills sloped cautiously towards the sea, suggesting that the bottom would be sand and mud shoaling gently. I dropped anchor at 8pm in the still waters of the bay. In the lee of the hills, *Barrabas* sat quietly at her chain, sheltered from the west wind. Two small huts stood at the southern end of the beach. I sat up on deck appreciating the tranquillity of the scene until the last light crept silently away.

I woke to the noise of an outboard engine buzzing around *Barrabas* like an angry hornet. On deck, I watched a skiff came alongside, its floor tiled with freshly caught Arctic cod and its driver grinning widely and jabbering in Yaktucsh. He introduced himself as Slava. He rummaged among the fish, selected the two biggest ones and offered them up. I took the gift and laid them out on the aft deck. Keen to show me his world, Slava suggested coffee by pointing to the huts on the beach then making a drinking gesture whilst uttering, 'Koff' several times. I clambered into his skiff and we sped off towards the beach.

Slava's cabin, hewn from logs and lined with cured seal skins, measured 12 foot square, contained a pair of bunks and a single cot, a table supporting a variety of radio equipment, an unplumbed sink and a wood-burning stove. An outboard engine suspended from a trestle outside the hut generated electric power to a single, naked light bulb dangling from the low ceiling. My efforts at internationalism gathered Slava's story. He owned seven knives, three guns, had a wife called Ola and two children – a boy, Ura, 12, and a girl, Viola, 10. A brother had died, shot through the heart during a hunting accident the previous season. Slava was 34. In the summer, he cut and sold wood and in the winter hunted reindeer. Of his two dogs, one was a sweet-natured husky, the other a Cujoesque monster of indeterminate breed (thankfully chained to a tree trunk). We drank coffee, smoked a couple of cigarettes together and inspected the new hut Slava was constructing. Back on board *Barrabas*, I gave Slava a litre of long-life milk, two tins of fruit, a jar of jam and two bottles of olive oil. Our comradeship forged, we bade one another farewell and I was alone again with my ship.

I weighed anchor early the next morning and as I rounded the headland, a cargo ship operating three deck cranes came into view. I asked for identification on the radio. In fluent English, the chief mate responded that the ship was the *Kapitan Danilkin* of the Murmansk Shipping Line.

Through various dialogues between myself, Louise, John and Nikolay Babych, we had agreed a plan B – to transport Barrabas to Murmansk on the *Kapitan Danilkin*. The ship's company had been expecting *Barrabas* and arrangements were in progress to transport the yacht through the ice. As I passed close to their bow, the chief mate, Dimitri, came back on the radio. The immigration authorities were on board and insisting that I was forbidden from entering port, that I did not have clearance, the border was closed and that I should instead sail out to 'international waters'.

'Dimitri, please tell the immigration authorities that I cannot do that. It is unsafe. I am not going to place myself or my yacht in danger.'

A pause as Dimitri conferred. 'They are insisting.'

'They can insist all they want, Dimitri, I'm not going out there. I'm going into port.'

'Okay, I will talk to the Captain.'

The captain, Alfred Zagorsky, was MSCO's experienced skipper and he spoke good English.

'Adrian, hello.' Captain Zagorsky's voice was a growl, his words heavily accented. 'I speak with immigration people. They say is impossible for you go in Tiksi, but I have idea.'

I was intrigued. 'Do the immigration people speak English, Captain?'

'No, no. So listen.' I heard a quick burst of Russian and then Captain Zagorsky was back on the radio. 'If you have damage to you then you go to port.'

'You mean an injury?'

'Yes, yes. You have one, no?'

'Yes, yes I do. My wrist is dislocated, broken.'

Another burst of Russian. Captain Zagorsky sounded irritated with whoever he was speaking to, presumably an immigration officer. 'Okay, I tell them you break hand. They say you can get x-ray.'

They wanted to check? Fine. Any film of my right wrist would show the unstable scaphoid.

'They can check if they want to, Captain.'

'Okay, good. You go to port. They say is okay now. I call you on radio later.'

I grabbed a bandage from the first-aid box and quickly strapped my right wrist.

* * *

Piers radiated seawards from the town like splayed fingers. I slowed *Barrabas*, looking for a mooring place. Car headlights pierced the driving sleet. A figure emerged, then limped to the edge of a pier, leaning heavily on a cane. He stared at me without expression then gave orders to another man, a stevedore, who directed me to the western pier. Someone was screaming over the VHF on Channel 16 in Russian. It sounded to me like invective. I discovered later that I had sailed ominously close to an unmarked wreck lying submerged between two piers. The western pier was dilapidated, bristling with iron spikes that at one time had secured timber joists, long since decayed and broken off. I moored in a 'clean' spot. The man with the cane, who clearly viewed my arrival as a nuisance, turned out to be the harbourmaster. As politely as I could, I protested about the dangerous, protruding spikes and the boat's exposure to west winds, but he brusquely dismissed these concerns.

The expected phalanx of uniforms quickly descended. A research vessel, *Petrov*, had followed me into port, berthing at the eastern side of the dock.

Its compliment of German geologists came to say hello. In unequivocal language, the authorities told them to get lost.

I was processed, then handed over to some branch of the military – expressionless faces, khaki camouflage, high-laced boots. They passed my papers around amid much discussion until eventually a slightly built local man of Yakut descent was brought to the boat to act as a translator. His name was Vissarion and he'd learnt his English on a language exchange course in Oxford. I was delighted. Through Vissarion, I explained the nature of my situation, my need to come into port because of my 'injury', the plans to transport the yacht and my desire to leave just as quickly as possible.

The following days brought repeated visits and more questions. Each time, Vissarion was present to translate. These Q&As took place either in a military vehicle parked dockside or on *Barrabas*. One of the officers, the designated photographer, began snapping the Russian chart open on the navigation table. Where did I get it? England, I explained. I opened the chart table and showed them the 30 or so others detailing the north Russian coast. He gave up taking pictures of the charts after that.

During the Soviet period, Tiksi's population had swelled to 30,000. Now, many of the buildings were derelict, windows broken, roofing tin torn off by the winds. Concrete tenement blocks housed the 2,000 diehards clinging to a meagre living. Military uniforms and vehicles predominated. There were no visible shops, only peeling signs of 'bread' or 'tomatoes' hung askew on doors that slatted on loose hinges in the constant wind.

I went to the bank to exchange some US currency. The bank teller handed most of my 20-dollar bills back with the exclamation, 'Niet!' Eventually, a hundred bucks was accepted and exchanged after careful scrutiny. I discovered some shops on the ground floors of the tenements – no windows, just doors off long, straight corridors. I wanted eggs. In one shop, I flapped my arms and made clucking noises. The babushka behind the counter gave me a blank stare and an apathetic shrug. I drew a picture of an egg. No recognition. Then an arrow pointing to a fried egg. Still nothing. On the other side of the egg picture, I drew a chicken to illustrate the entire sequence: a chicken produces an egg, which is then fried. The rouble dropped. The babushka's face creased. She called other shopkeepers. They locked their doors and hurried to the impromptu summit. The babushka handed round my drawing and explained. It seemed that I had provided the amusement of the week. I left the 'arcade' some time later with eggs, bread, tomatoes, onions and bacon (I had to draw a picture of a pig). On the walk back to the docks, I bumped into the German geologists. Who are you? Where are you from? How far have you travelled? They invited me on board the *Petrov* to take a shower any time I wanted. The *Petrov* was in port for three days.

At Captain Zagorsky's instruction, I made drawings of *Barrabas* detailing approximate measurements to help him assess the logistics of getting *Barrabas* onto his deck and shoring her up for the passage through the ice. At 7am next morning, a tug nosed into the pier and I handed the drawings over. The tug's skipper made little effort to guide his vessel gently towards the quay. He simply crashed his huge boat into the pilings. Later, on board *Barrabas*, I heard a thudding against the hull. When I went topside to check, I saw a great raft of timber floating past that the tug had dislodged from the pier.

At 10am, I went to the *Petrov*. The ship ran to Moscow time. Everyone was asleep. The first officer, a Russian, was on duty. I drew a picture of a stick man taking a shower and he led me below. The shower was fantastic – powerful and hot. The last decent shower I'd had was in Nome, in Rick's 'shop'.

Louise had been liaising constantly with the Murmansk Shipping Company. They in turn had agreed in principle to transport *Barrabas*, but the final decision would be down to Captain Zagorsky. On Thursday 20th September, Dimitri called me from the ship.

'We will take you, but we are waiting for authorisation from Murmansk.'

'I was under the impression they had left the decision to you.'

'Yes, it's true,' Dimitri said, 'but you must have a contract first. This you must agree with them.'

I called Louise. She had discussed the contract with a man called Antonov. Murmansk would email the contract to Louise. She could sign it on my behalf.

The weather deteriorated. The wind kicked in from the west, gusting to 40 knots. By some fortuitous foresight, I had scavenged among the piles of debris on the dock and found some old car tyres which I'd hung from the quayside to cushion *Barrabas*'s hull. By Saturday lunchtime, the seas were hurling *Barrabas* against the dock. The tyres undoubtedly saved the boat from serious damage. I called Dimitri and asked him to contact the harbourmaster. I needed a tug to pull me off and get me to a more protected berth.

Eventually an ancient tug puttered around the corner, approached *Barrabas* far too closely, lost control in the high winds and collided. The tug got away from *Barrabas*'s side, spewing oil all over her deck from the exhausts. I threw the towing line. The tug then dragged *Barrabas* along the quayside. Metal spikes dug into her hull. The spikes would have ripped a fibreglass boat to pieces. I ditched the tow line as soon as *Barrabas* was clear and motored to the other side of the quay, completely protected from the strong winds forecast to continue from the west over the next 48 hours. I tethered *Barrabas* to a rusted crane platform moored deep in the recess between two piers so she would rise and fall with the tides without me having to adjust her lines.

Louise: Saturday 22nd September 2007
I am so sorry – it sounds like hell but the best news is that next week you will be out of there!

Early on Sunday morning at 1am, I was woken by someone on board *Barrabas* shouting 'Sorry gentleman, sorry gentleman!' Who the hell was this? Drunkenness and vagrancy were rife in Tiksi. My hunting knife hung in its scabbard near the chart table. I kept the blade honed to razor-sharpness. With the knife in my hand, I opened the companionway hatch. The reek of stale alcohol made me retch. I recognised the man as one of the crew on the tug. He wanted to sleep on the boat! I got rid of him as diplomatically as I could with constant shrugs as though I did not understand what he wanted.

After 10 days in port, I had still not received permission from the military authorities to leave. Captain Zagorsky was concerned. The ship had to sail on the 26th September. She was to be the last vessel through the Vil'kitskiy Strait before Nikolay Babych closed the route for the winter. The gaps between the ice floes had now frozen.

Lack of money to winter the boat for another season, the slim chance of getting another Russian visa, the difficulties of regaining permissions from NSRA and my refusal to be away from the children for another extended period meant either *Barrabas* sailed with the *Kapitan Danilkin* or I faced the hideous prospect of abandoning her in this Arctic hellhole.

A light tapping came from somewhere on deck. It was lunchtime. Vissarion was throwing small pebbles to attract my attention. I motioned for him to come on board.

The head of the border guards in Petropavlovsk had sent the order to give me clearance to leave.

'But,' Vissarion said, 'you have to go into Murmansk to check out of customs.'

'Okay.' I expected this.

'The border guards told me that information about you is being sent to Murmansk. If you do not go into port, then they will intercept you at sea.'

This whole experience was rapidly deteriorating into an Orwellian drama. I immediately called Captain Zagorsky.

'You must to wait in port on standby for loading.' Sweet words. I was getting out of here!

'What time do you anticipate calling me, Captain?'

'I think 5pm. The weather today is good, but not so good for tomorrow.'

'I'm ready when you are.'

I stayed on board, tidying the cabin and preparing *Barrabas*. At 5pm, the radio crackled. The ship was standing me down!

'What's the problem, Captain?'

'There is no contract.' I heard Captain Zagorsky speaking Russian. Dimitri came onto the radio. 'The captain says that you must have a contract with the Murmansk Shipping Company.'

'I do.' Louise was dealing with this.

'Murmansk say they sent the contract but they have not yet received it back.'

'Bloody hell. Okay, Dimitri, I'll sort it out. I'll call Louise now.'

'Okay. There is something else. We need two sea containers to place either side of the yacht on the deck. The port is refusing to send them to the ship. They must have authorisation from Murmansk, but with no contract, Murmansk cannot do this.'

'Leave it to me, Dimitri. I'll get on it now.'

I called Louise. 'What's happening with this contract? I can't…'

'There's a problem. I wasn't going to tell you. John and I are trying to sort it out…'

'What problem? The ship's leaving.'

I had to sit down as Louise gave me the bad news. The cost of the transport quoted in the agreement recently sent to her by MSCO was $52,000!

'But Babych quoted $10,000 and that was three weeks ago. The ship's leaving in 24 hours and they come up with this?'

It was impossible to raise $52,000. Because of the time differences between Tiksi, London and Moscow, we only had a few short hours to try to resolve the situation.

I radioed the ship and explained the situation. Captain Zagorsky agreed to stand by until 11pm, six hours, otherwise preparations would be made

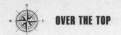

for sea and *Barrabas* would be left behind and me with no option but to fly out of Tiksi and abandon *Barrabas* to her fate.

John Mann: Tuesday 25th September 2007

Not good news. Antonov (MSCO) said that Babych was very wrong to have given us that $10K figure at the beginning. He insists that this was done without consultation with the commercial freight division (not what Babych told me before).

The $52K price includes taxes, fees, etc… in conclusion, Antonov said he couldn't do this operation for any less than the price listed in the contract. He insisted they are a commercial organisation, blah, blah.

Louise and John set to work making calls, exchanging opinions, revisiting history, recalling decisions, negotiating and finally reaching agreement with contracts written, exchanged, signed and returned. I interjected the to-ings and fro-ings with numerous calls on the satellite phone and settled to wait as the clock ticked through half past ten. At five minutes to eleven, Louise called with the outcome.

'They've cut the price of the transport!'

We were back to Babych's original quote.

At two minutes to eleven, the deadline only 120 seconds away, I radioed the ship to tell Dimitri, standing by on the bridge for my call, that we had an agreement.

Adrian: Tuesday 25th September 2007

Hi there… you must be mentally on the rack. Well done! I am still pretty sick at the amount but still, it's 'doable'. I always believed you would be able to negotiate an acceptable solution and so you have… if the AGX has delivered anything it should be in you believing in yourself in a way that perhaps you have never done before.

Please pass this msg on to JM

Hi John

Once again, I am deeply indebted to you. I am beginning to understand how difficult it can be dealing with the Russians. I realised that the only solution was going to have to be a face-saving compromise on both sides. Whilst the amount is (in my opinion) steep, it was clearly the result of skilful negotiation on your part and Louise providing succinct appraisals of the situation on the ground here. What started out as a 'single-handed' expedition has become anything but that.

* * *

On arrival alongside, I met Dimitri, the chief mate, who was very amiable and younger than I'd expected, and then Captain Zagorsky. At 72, small but toughly built like a jockey, he scrambled down the rope ladder onto *Barrabas*'s deck. Despite the diminutive stature, his greeting was akin to having my hand slammed in a closing elevator door. He then immediately yelled for light in the gathering dusk and almost instantly, *Barrabas* was ablaze beneath the port side floodlights. I watched him carefully. Hooded eyes flicked across the yacht's deck, up the mast then down again, shrouds and stays tested for tension. Rapid-fire Russian peppered the chief mate, who fed the questions back to me in English. How strong was the mast? Could I disconnect the backstays? How? Was it possible to rig a jury stay leading aft from the mast? How quickly could I get it done?

I accompanied the captain onto the deck of his ship, watched by the assembled crew. He wanted to show me the arrangements he had planned for taking *Barrabas* on board. In a quick aside, the chief mate told me that the captain had not slept well for three weeks over the problem of how to stow *Barrabas* and get her through the ice. He had conducted brainstorming meetings with the ship's company, made scale drawings and tested different options. Two sea containers barged out to the ship by the port authorities and fixed on the port and starboard hatches of the central cargo wells provided lateral support. The yacht's keel would sit on wooden blocking laid in the central gallery running between the hatches.

By midday on Friday, with the hoisting straps in place beneath *Barrabas*, the crane swung outboard and the great block lowered precisely between the yacht's twin backstays. Slowly, the crane lifted her from the sea to her new resting place. The crew then set to work, evidently rehearsed, shoring up the yacht's sides. We lashed two of the ship's fenders, each 12 feet high and 4 feet wide, vertically in the spaces between *Barrabas*'s bows and the sea containers. To prevent any side-to-side or forward and backward movement, the crew tethered *Barrabas* to the deck of the ship with strapping from her forward, midships and stern cleats attached to chains made off to secure lashing points and then tensioned almost bar tight.

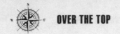

The *Kapitan Danilkin* weighed anchor in the late afternoon, turned hard to port and nosed eastwards out of the Tiksi harbour. I watched from the bridge. To the west, the pewter skies had burnished to silver. Feathery cloud moved listlessly aloft. From high on the bridge deck, I watched the cranes' derricks lowered to their sea-going positions, one of them crossing over *Barrabas*'s stern deck like a protective arm.

CHAPTER 27

FROM RUSSIA WITH LOVE

MY CABIN COMPRISED TWO adjoining rooms on the fifth level, part of the officers' quarters just below the bridge. One contained a drawing room with sofa, armchair, coffee table and large desk and the other, a bedroom with an en-suite shower room. After supper in the mess, Captain Zagorsky knocked on my door and came in carrying two glasses and two tins of Tuborg. He moved with repressed energy. The dome of his head was bare. Under different circumstances, the pale blue of his eyes might be cold and intimidating, but some inner zest set them alight.

'You know, the carriage of the yacht is illegal.' The captain poured beer carefully, gave a small shrug. 'No insurance, no papers.' He sipped. I sipped. 'Babych is my friend. He say to me you must to take the yacht to Murmansk, so I help you.'

'Thank you, Captain. I am very grateful.'

'But, why you do this thing?'

'Sailing around the world?'

'Yes. It's crazy. And in the ice, bah!'

'Well, lots of reasons but mainly because I wanted to.'

Captain Zagorsky looked baffled. He was a contradiction, a company man raised in the strictures of the Soviet regime yet a maverick who made his own laws and bent or simply ignored the dictates of others if that suited his purpose.

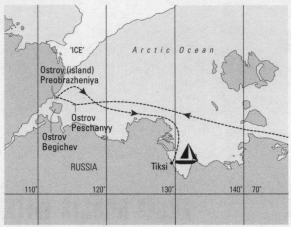

After a while he said, 'Okay. You know, I see this.' He nodded, not approval but certainly understanding. 'But I am seaman for fifty years. Is dangerous for small boat to sail with big ships, no?'

'Yes.'

'If you are only one on board, how can you see ships coming?' He told the story of a Danish fishing boat run over by a Russian ship with the loss of all hands.

'There is a risk which any single-handed sailor must accept, a responsibility.'

'And you children?'

'Two boys.'

'What they think of you do this?'

'What can I teach them? To work hard, to play hard, to be good, respectful, polite. But also to show them to be true to themselves, to do what they believe. Like you, Captain. To make their own rules.'

I learned later that the captain's nonagenarian mother had recently died. Normally, he would have flown to his home town of St Petersburg on compassionate leave. Instead, he had chosen to stay with the ship to get *Barrabas* safely out of Tiksi.

'I have two daughter. One is married. He is painter.' The captain made brush strokes in the air. 'I not like him.'

'Why?'

'No job…'

'Like me.'

'You write book, no, this is your work, this why you make voyage.'

He was twisting the order of things to accept me more comfortably, bending his own rules this time to suit his purpose.

I began quite quickly to form a deep affection for Captain Alfred Zagorsky.

On 30th September just before midnight, the ship made its rendezvous with the icebreaker, *Russiya*. I walked from the bridge in a snowstorm as we headed through early bands of progressively thicker drift ice. I wanted to see the ice. A question still hovered. Could I have made it through on my own? I stayed up into the early hours of Sunday morning observing the ice from the freezing prow. Ice was at 100 per cent cover, several metres thick. I spent some time on the aft deck with the captain. The reason for my vigil was to answer a second question. Could a ship, maybe one in the convoy, have towed *Barrabas*? The icebreaker ahead crunched through the frozen sea leaving a path strewn with ice boulders in her wake. The *Kapitan Danilkin*'s 38mm-thick steel bows pushed this debris aside and in turn left a trail of open water. Captain Zagorsky explained that pieces of ice pressed beneath the bows could ride along the ship's keel and emerge at the stern. Ice chunks breaking the surface from the depths of the ship's draught, 25 feet, each weighing up to one ton, would cause devastating damage to a yacht following behind. As the captain and I stood in the warm lee of the funnel stack looking sternwards, I saw boulders of ice breaking the surface. A single impact from one of those would have sent *Barrabas* to the bottom.

* * *

My few days on board the *Kapitan Danilkin* quickly fell into a routine governed by rigid mealtimes and the two periods I spent with the captain: morning coffee (which usually ran on until lunch) and tea or a drink in the evening in the conference room annexed to the captain's cabin. Dimitri always joined us for coffee. Occasionally, the chief engineer dropped in to share a drink after supper. Between times, I checked on *Barrabas*, showered, rested, read, talked to Louise and spent time on the bridge with the officer of the watch, marking up my charts. Sleeping in a heated cabin was blissful. The food was unimaginative, but I still did not have much of an appetite anyway. Meals tended to be quiet, even silent affairs, more a refuelling pit stop than a forum for social interaction. The officers ate separately from the rest of the crew. Often the captain and I were the only ones who spoke. I made a light-hearted comment to the captain about the paltry breakfasts, usually a bland pancake or cold sausage and coffee.

'What you like?'

'Well, you know, English breakfasts, eggs, bacon, sausage, bread, jam and best of all, a glass of ice-cold milk.'

'Bah!'

Captain Zagorsky was interested in many topics and our conversations ranged widely: oriental philosophies, religion, future population migration and national cultural influences. The captain's favourite subject revolved around the concept of freedom. He was keen to delve further into my rationale for making the voyage and the consequences of it. He was, I think, using me as a sounding board, perhaps to better understand the artistic temperament of his son-in-law or in some way to reconcile that difficult relationship. The conversation continually returned here, to this blight.

'You have another daughter?' I asked.

'Yes.'

Perhaps his second daughter had married a better proposition. I noticed that the Slavic lift of his eyes that usually lent his face a cunning expression had dropped, the mischievous blue light momentarily dulled. 'But she has died,' the captain said quietly.

'I'm sorry.' Hopeless words. 'What about grandchildren?'

The light returned. 'Twins. A boy and a girl. They are five. I walk them in St Petersburg and take them to the hut in the woods… a small place. My son-in-law, he is doing it up.'

We spoke about the hut in the woods. His wife was ill. His child had died and most recently, of course, he had lost his mother. Captain Zagorsky needed to make sense of what he had left. I felt drawn in. Like a son.

I mentioned I wanted to wash some clothes. One morning after breakfast, I found Captain Zagorsky in my cabin stringing up a clothesline. He then marched me along the corridor to the laundry room and showed me how to operate the washing machine.

I turned 47 at sea, with the ice safely astern and a 50-knot wind screeching across the deck. I got up late and went down to the mess hall on the first level. Everyone else had finished. The dining-room hostess came out of the kitchen, beaming. She set a tray down and placed a plate of fried eggs and sausage, bread, jam and a tall glass of very cold milk in front of me.

'Kapitan!' she said triumphantly.

I pointed to the plate. 'Kapitan Zagorsky?'

'Da!' she replied, nodding happily.

'Speciba!'

At morning coffee in the conference room with Dimitri and the chief engineer, the captain presented me with a bottle of 18-year-old Chivas whisky. That evening after supper, the cook brought up my 'birthday cake', an apple tart on a sweet bread base. After the anxiety and exhaustion of the NSR, it was a happy time. I had been holding onto another worry. I decided to speak to the captain.

'I'm getting a bit anxious about going round North Cape in October,' I said to the captain at morning coffee the next day.

Dimitri was there. He had spent two seasons in Cape Horn, as chief mate on a passenger ship plying between Ushuaia and Antarctica. 'We call North Cape the Cape Horn of the northern hemisphere. In October is very bad, very dangerous place.'

The captain was not quite as fluent in English as the chief mate. He spoke fast, often tripping over English words, checking his step and continuing in Russian. I heard the word 'fjord' several times.

Dimitri was nodding, then turned to me. 'The captain says you can go through the Norwegian fjord system. He has done it once in winter. You go below North Cape.'

'I don't have charts.'

The captain got up from the table, a stream of Russian spilling over his shoulder. He picked up the telephone.

'The captain will call one of the cadets to get charts from the chart room for you to see.'

Fifteen minutes later, Captain Zagorsky and I bent over the charts laid out by the cadet.

'You go here,' the captain said, his finger tracing the route through the fjords down as far as Vestfjorden.

The *Kapitan Danilkin* dropped anchor a mile offshore from the port of Murmansk late on Friday night, 5th October. Early on Saturday morning the wind stood still. It was time to put *Barrabas* back in the water. The hoist was smooth. Captain Zagorsky barked commands, radioed instructions to the crane operator and pulled on guy lines to orientate *Barrabas* for her descent to the water.

My pilot, a quiet man called Yevgeny, boarded the *Kapitan Danilkin* at 9am and he and I were soon underway. As my engine fired and the lines let go, a cheer erupted from the crew, led as always by Captain Zagorsky.

'I come to see you later,' Captain Zagorsky had told me. His rotation on the *Kapitan Danilkin* was over and he would be returning to St Petersburg in the next day or two, back to look after his sick wife during four months of shore leave.

During the unloading procedure, Dimitri had worked up quite a sweat. He was suddenly incredulous at the successful delivery of *Barrabas* to Murmansk. We stood together on the side deck shaking hands before I scuttled down the rope ladder to the deck of my own ship.

Barrabas eased away. I turned hard to port as instructed by the pilot and then gave the wheel over to Yevgeny to steer us the two miles to the customs quay. Within minutes of arrival, uniformed officialdom descended. After an hour of questions, form-filling and document stamping, we were done.

Yevgeny reappeared, directing me to a new mooring on Pier 16. A 300-metre quay jutted westwards and another protruded southwards, both occupied by 50,000-ton ships. A rag-tag assortment of floating pontoon barges, tugs and bunker vessels hovered in the crotch between these two limbs. I tied up to one of the floating barges. A doghouse enclosed a small office manned on a 12-hour rotation by 'watchmen'. Ura and Ghena were on duty. Ghena had one of those fascinating faces – the features unequal, lopsided, crunched, akimbo as though moulded from a softer, more pliant material. I showed him a long piece of flex with American plugs and asked (through various gesticulations and diagrams) if he had a Russian plug so I could get power to the boat. Ghena eventually got the picture (literally). He insisted on doing the splicing. To support the cable while he worked, he ran it through a small steel loop welded to the door (I did not see this at the time because I had retreated to the boat). He called for me when he'd finished. I made suitable expressions of pleasure, then saw the run of the flex and pointed out to him that the plug would not come back out through the steel loop. Ura thought this hilarious. Crimson patches bloomed on Ghena's ravaged face. We sorted it out second time round.

Captain Zagorsky arrived with Nikolay Babych at noon on Sunday, bringing with him a bottle of cognac, which we attacked with the eagerness of comrades who had shared a unique experience.

I pulled up satellite images on the laptop. Nikolay Babych interpreted them.

'Impossible for you to go ice,' he concluded, shaking his head solemnly from side to side. 'But you the first to be in North Sea Route alone. This is great honour for me to be on boat,' and with that he raised his glass and we all drank.

Captain Zagorsky said, 'I give you this.' He handed me a piece of paper, a number scribbled in pencil. 'This my telephone in St Petersburg. You to call when you in England. Then I sleep okay to know you are safe!'

After polishing off most of the cognac, it was time for them to leave. I embraced Nikolay Babych and then turned towards Captain Zagorsky. He wrapped me in a bear hug. I responded in kind.

'You promise to call me, yes?' he said releasing me.

'I promise.'

Later, nursing the kind of hangover that afflicts the unaccustomed, I took a stroll along the docks. When I got back to *Barrabas*, Ura pointed to a package in the cockpit.

'Mr Babych,' he said. Inside the bag, I discovered bread, cheese and various Russian salami and sausages.

On Monday 8th October, Port State Control visited the berth to check my safety equipment. Having passed muster, I ordered a weather file. A vicious depression north of Murmansk would keep me pinned down for the next four days.

Igor Melnikov appeared with a bright smile on his fresh 24-year-old face announcing himself as my 'new' agent from the MM agency, a necessary requirement for foreign vessels in Murmansk.

I explained to Igor – who spoke very decent English – that I needed an external heater to combat the plunging night-time temperatures. Igor disappeared, returning at 6pm with a heater. He refused to take any payment. When Igor arrived at the pontoon the next morning, *Barrabas* was as warm as toast and I was down to a T-shirt.

'I was talking to my family about you and your voyage last night.' Igor clambered down the companionway steps clutching packages. 'My mother made these for you.'

The packages, wrapped and tied with ribbons and bows, contained a freshly made mince pie and dried fish.

I was astonished. 'Please thank your mother.'

'I will, yes. This is no problem.'

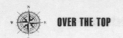

'What's her name, your mother?'

'Lubov.'

I nodded.

'It means love,' Igor said.

He disappeared with my driving licence to get a pass for me to leave the high-security dock area. With two of my empty gas bottles in the trunk of his car, we eventually found a filling station, left the bottles and drove to his home for lunch with his brother, Dimitri. The apartment building was a featureless concrete box in a rank of many identical structures that constituted an estate, dilapidated and careworn, its common areas pocked as if strafed by gunfire. Graffiti adorned the hall. This was 'middle-class' living by Russian standards. The flat was small: a hallway shared with another apartment, a sitting room, tiny kitchen, bathroom with a separate toilet and two bedrooms. The whole family lived here.

After lunch, Igor and I visited bookshops in search of something in English. I managed to find copies of *Lord of the Flies* and *Sons and Lovers*. At a supermarket, I stocked up on milk, biscuits, bacon, sugar and Nesquik, and after that, at his office I emailed 12 pictures to Louise on a high-speed internet connection.

A more recent weather file decided my departure date – Saturday October 13th. A 40-hour window of south winds would see me to Vardo in Norway.

Two nights of sub-zero temperatures had left Murmansk sheathed in white and *Barrabas* painted with a veneer of ice. Stepping carefully onto the treacherous deck, Alexandre Kondakov, a director of the Murmansk Shipping Company and Sergey Minchenko, head of the MM agency, visited me on *Barrabas* and presented me with a beautiful crystal polar bear on behalf of the company.

Igor drove me to a vantage point to the west of the city, the largest settlement north of the Arctic Circle. Descending to the urban sprawl, its centre ringed by sentinels of ugly, grey apartment blocks we came across a shopping complex, newly opened and inside, a revelation of European chic and modern design. The place was buzzing with young women. Their objective was clear – to see and be seen. Collectively, these girls were monumentally attractive with an apparent genetic predisposition towards an extra six inches of leg length above standard proportions and a startling array of eye colour (either that or some wily entrepreneur was making a killing in the coloured contact lens business). The fashion: jeans so tightly fitting as to suggest aspirations towards painting them on rather than pulling them on and boots, winkle-picked and stilettoed to the limit of walkability. After months on a visual diet of water, tundra and Tiksi, this parade of beautiful women was vastly more appealing.

By 3pm, I was back on board from my city sojourn (during which, ironically, given the city's predilection for fashion consciousness, I was unable to find a comb) to meet the press. Two television crews and a clutch of print journalists, attracting with them a small crowd of bemused dockworkers, arrived at my berth. I showed them *Barrabas*, answered questions, posed and said 'Hello' to Murmansk on cue through several takes because the interviewer could not quite wrap her tongue around 'Flanagan'.

Louise's diary: Wednesday 10th October 2007
Sunk to the very bottom. Spent most of the day in tears, a cumulative effect of everything. Tired from the stress of the expedition, worried about what dramas may unfold next, desperate for Adrian to get home but with no clear sign of timings in sight, lost all tolerance and patience with the boys and it is so unfair on them. Wondering what my life is going to be all about when this is finished and pissed off that I spend my whole time looking after everyone else with no one looking after me.

I was talking to a journalist friend in England on the sat phone.

'Do me a favour. Louise is pretty down right now. Can you organise a bunch of flowers for her.'

'Consider it done. Anything on the card?'

I thought for a moment. 'From Russia with Love.'

CHAPTER 28

MAYHEM IN MEHAMN

I SLIPPED MY LINES ON 13th October, a gusty, dismal Saturday morning. The pilot on board was called Andrey. He spoke no English and we soon lost any reason to communicate. He'd joined me on *Barrabas* shortly after a small army of officials arrived from the immigration authorities to give me permission to leave.

Seven miles out, Murmansk radio ordered us to stop. 'Why?' I said to the pilot, palms upturned, arms outstretched, shoulders shrugging to get my question across. A Russian naval vessel was coming in to Severomorsk. This restriction came with no warning. We moored up to a buoy and sat down to lunch. After getting underway at 3pm, we reached the pilot station two hours later. The pilot vessel, a powerful tug, drew close. I asked the helmsman to hold a steady course at 4 knots then brought *Barrabas* in on an elliptical sweep, coming alongside so that our decks were 12 inches apart and my pilot could step onto the tug.

Clear of the traffic separation scheme at the entrance to Kola Bay and the zones restricted for military use, I steered *Barrabas* around Rybachiy Peninsula beneath a wondrous display of the Northern Lights, green and blue illuminations seeping through the night sky like coloured inks on wet blotting paper.

Barrabas crossed the border into Norwegian territorial waters just after midday on Sunday 14th October. I stayed awake through the night.

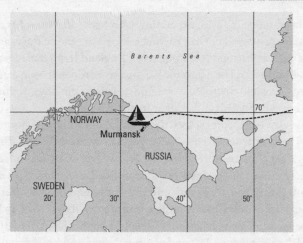

Situated on a small island connected to the mainland by an under-sea tunnel, Vardo is the oldest settlement in northern Norway, with a population of 2,000. I entered through the harbour wall into a merciful calm. Pretty, colourfully painted houses dotted the hillsides. Clean, modern cars zipped along unblemished strips of tarmac in contrast to the ancient jalopies coughing along the fractured roads of Murmansk. I moored *Barrabas* against a barge just inside the harbour wall. To get ashore, I had to step onto the barge and then, on the other side, onto a Norwegian search and rescue vessel, the *Oscar Tybring IV*, and up a gangway. I introduced myself to the captain of the rescue vessel, Roger Pettersen. He invited me on board. Could I have a shower? No problem, he said. Further, he was cooking dinner and I was welcome to join the rest of the three-man crew, which I did for a traditional Norwegian dish of soupy cabbage and lamb chops followed by nutty custard with a fruit jelly sauce. I ate three servings of each. After almost 40 hours awake, I collapsed into my sleeping bag.

Next morning Roger came to have a look at *Barrabas*. We went over my charts. Roger gave me some useful local knowledge for sailing in these waters. The coast became a treacherous place when the wind blew from the north. *Oscar Tybring IV* belonged to Redningsskoyta (The Rescue Company). A fleet of similar vessels, powerful twin diesel tugs, was located at strategic points along the Norwegian coast. The organisation was part-government funded and relied on public donations and membership fees to cover the rest of its operating budget. Unknown to me, Roger had been onto his head office in Oslo, explaining who I was and what I was doing. Redningsskoyta offered me free membership to the end of the year.

To be back in Europe felt wonderful. England had seemed so distant while I was in Russia. The 100-mile passage to Vardo had been a great leap homewards. I visited the town, wrote postcards to the boys, found a John Grisham novel in English and bought fresh provisions.

On Tuesday 16th October, with the promise of another 40-hour weather window, I set sail from Vardo. As Roger had warned, I soon discovered that navigating close inshore along the Norwegian coast was a hazardous business. The long, high-sided fjords amplified the wind. Crossing the mouths of the fjords took me into 50-knot maelstroms. During late afternoon, Vardo radio issued a gale warning of Force 8. I gybed and reefed the main. Through another sleepless night, I put into the small port of Berlevag at dawn. After a few hours' sleep and breakfast of coffee, eggs and bacon, I went in search of fishermen to tap them for some local knowledge. I told them I was heading for Gamvik before the weather closed in. Immediately and in unison they shook their heads.

'Gamvik's got a no good harbour,' one said.

'Ja,' the second agreed. 'Mehamn's better.'

So Mehamn it was. I had enough time. With the wind light but steady from the northwest, I made good time under full sail around Nordkynhalvoya, an island bounded on the east by Tanafjorden and on the west by Laksefjorden. As I turned the corner into Mehamnfjord and picked up the occulting white, red and green light providing guidance towards the harbour entrance, darkness had already descended. I dropped all sail. *Barrabas*, ever true and seeming to know my intentions, nosed gently round in tight circles as I tidied halyards and sheets and rigged mooring lines and fenders. Then, with the engine humming sweetly, we eased round the headland and picked up the fixed green light of the harbour entrance. Within the safety of the breakwater, I steered *Barrabas* around the harbour perimeter. An assortment of fishing boats occupied all the quays and sidings, but in the northwestern corner, I found a pontoon and tied up alongside in pouring rain just as the clock struck midnight.

By morning, the rain had stopped. I climbed a hill past neat houses and down the other side over tundra towards a small beach. Breakers goaded by the wind shattered onto rocks. A seagull watched silently from a narrow promontory. Together we surveyed the innocent violence of the sea.

I thought of my sons. Today was Gabriel's sixth birthday. I should have been home by now.

I stopped at a supermarket and the town's bakery. When I returned to *Barrabas*, the wind was screaming. I set a bowl of fresh fruit on the saloon table, a visual reminder of domestic normalcy. Next to the bowl of fruit, six candles cast a soft, sputtering light. I'd bought a small cake. While the wind shrieked and the rain clattered down, I toasted Gabriel with the last of Captain Zagorsky's French brandy, then called Louise and spoke to the boys.

Oddvar Jenssen owned Nordkyn Seafoods. The wood-clad office block and processing plant stood on the harbour's edge just up from the pontoon. Two fishing boats tugged angrily at their lines against a quay in front of the buildings. I climbed the stairs to the offices and introduced myself.

'My wife told me she met you,' he said.

'Your wife?'

'In the bakery, yesterday.'

'Otto Jenssen's bakery, is that you?'

'My father. Now my wife runs it.'

'So, Oddvar, you know the fjords?'

'Ja, I often go to Tromsó. That's my boat.' Oddvar pointed through the window. A cabin cruiser tied to a mooring buoy bobbed close to the pontoon. 'But now, this time of year…' He gave a few small shakes of his head.

'Can you show me anyway, on the charts?' I had brought them along. There was really only one way to go and Oddvar pointed out anchorages, chin tucked in, peering over the top of his reading glasses.

Outside, the weather was atrocious, constant gales howling in from the west. Oddvar logged onto a local weather site. Wind speeds just offshore were touching 50 knots. All the fishing boats had stayed in port. How far would I get bashing head to wind in open water against the prevailing south-westerlies?

Inshore, the step-sided fjords funnelled the wind so for the moment this route was not an option either. North Atlantic low-pressure systems travelled eastwards between Norway and Spitsbergen and as at Cape Horn, moved unopposed with no landmasses to break, slow or decay the depressions. Conditions would worsen going into November. England was so tantalisingly close, yet between northern Norway and the English south coast, I was facing the prospect of the worst sustained conditions of the

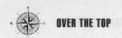

entire voyage. Charts in hand, I wandered back to *Barrabas*, brewed a fresh pot of coffee and sat there for a long time, thinking.

All circumnavigations conform to a guiding principle: you hit the hotspots at the best time of year. I made it round Cape Horn just in time, at the end of the southern hemisphere summer. The delay in Honolulu meant I was late getting to the antipodal point and the risk from typhoons became very real. I was lucky to get away without a serious encounter with big weather. Sea-ice presented a unique aspect to the 'vertical' route, a physical barrier rather than a weather danger and (in my case) west of there, the Norwegian Sea and the North Sea. Delay at any critical point and the ramifications transmitted down the track. My plan had me past the ice by the end of August with September to get round Norway and home before conditions turned perilous.

Force 7–12 conditions plague the Norwegian Sea 30 per cent of the time in November and through the winter months. Unmarked rocks litter the coast south of Vestfjorden. Savage seas build quickly over the shoals and in the prevailing winds the Norwegian coast is a lee shore. I watched the weather and waited. The conclusion was inescapable. I had missed my window.

I waited through the weekend, popping into Oddvar's office to check weather forecasts on the internet. Each day I downloaded fresh GRIB files and walked along the coast, staring seawards.

Oddvar came to the boat on Sunday.

'So, what have you decided?'

I blew out my cheeks. 'Leave *Barrabas* here. Come back in April or May.'

Oddvar nodded. 'Good. The right decision.'

'Will *Barrabas* be okay?' There were no facilities to lift her out anyway.

'My boats stay in the water all through winter. It's no problem.'

The water was cold enough to prevent barnacles encrusting the hull but the warm Gulf Stream prevented the sea from freezing over. My concern about leaving *Barrabas* in the water for six months must have been obvious.

'Don't worry,' Oddvar said. 'You will show me how everything works, the bilge pumps, battery isolation, the windmill (wind generator) and I will come to the boat each day to check.'

Louise: Sunday 21ˢᵗ October 2007

You are right – no one apart from you knows the real sea conditions where you are at this time of year and I do understand. If it really means putting yourself in grave peril and still not being home for two months then it is more sensible to come home.

If Oddvar Jenssen dominated on the west side of the harbour – he also owned the Arctic Hotel in town and had bought up a group of dockside buildings – then Kare Karlstad dominated on the east side. His company owned the main quay where the small cruise ships plying the fjords tied up, a trading company and a parade of shops. He came to have a look at *Barrabas*. A one-time naval officer, twice married (his second wife was a Russian model) Kare spent the winter months in Thailand. We talked boats for a while.

'I had for many years a Baltic 43. I sailed her up to Spitsbergen but mainly near Oslo.'

We were driving west in Kare's Mercedes. I wanted to see something of the countryside and he was happy to show me. Over lunch in a bistro in Kjollefjord, I asked Kare about the sense in trying to sail home at this time of year.

'I answer with a story,' he said. 'Some years ago, I sailed with a French couple to Spitsbergen, they in their 35-foot yacht and me and some crew in the Baltic. The French couple went down to Bergen. They wanted to go back to France. It was October, so I said to them it was crazy to try this now. Anyway, they went. In the North Sea, they were in many storms. Usually, they dropped the sails and drifted, lying ahull. Then, in big seas, their boat rolled over and they lost the mast. Scottish rescue services saved them, but they were lucky. For you, I think it is crazy to try this now.'

When I spoke with local fishermen, they all said pretty much the same thing. My main concern though was not the weather nor *Barrabas*'s ability to cope with extreme conditions. After all, we had both been round Cape Horn. I was physically and emotionally shattered. The sea would ruthlessly exploit any weakness. To put to sea in my state of deep fatigue would be a misjudgement and the consequences might easily be fatal.

I called Louise. My decision was final. I would fly home on 1st November. She was getting ready to go out to dinner.

Louise: Wednesday 24th October 2007

Benji was violently sick last night before I went to the Chapmans' for dinner. It happened in the downstairs loo and it took me two full rolls of kitchen paper and 25 minutes to clean up – no area of the room was left unsplattered! He apologised

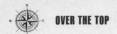

profusely to me and I said, 'Don't be silly, this is what being a parent is all about, Benji,' to which he replied, 'Thank God I've got about 30 years to wait, then!'

Kare's house stood alone on its own small island, which enclosed the northern part of Mehamn's harbour, connected to the mainland by a man-made isthmus. I walked to the house. Across the dark waters of the harbour, Mehamn's twinkling lights banked up the shallow hills. Inside, the house was warm, floored and walled in polished pine. Another friend was there, Gunmarie, a town councillor.

'We have something special for dinner,' Kare announced. 'Whale meat.'

The cooking smell was meaty, but not quite beef. I bit into a texture somewhere between liver and lamb with a flavour of fishy beef. It was a great evening of jokes and laughter which I needed after the hard decision to over-winter *Barrabas* for a second time.

The following morning, the sails came off and went into the attic of Oddvar's warehouse. I rinsed the watermaker with a biocide solution, flushed antifreeze through the engine cooling chamber, shut off the fuel, electrics and sea cocks, checked the stern gland, cleared the deck lines and finally laced tarpaulin over the cockpit area. While *Barrabas* was alongside Nordkyn's quay (his boats were out fishing), I showed Oddvar how to operate the bilge pumps.

With the help of two local men, Roy and Marinius, who, under Oddvar's direction connected a new chain to the harbour bed, we set *Barrabas* to her mooring buoy. Below decks, I kissed my faithful yacht. As in Nome, I knew the people of Mehamn would keep her safe. Then they rowed me ashore.

PART III
HOMEWARD BOUND

MY TIME IN ENGLAND PASSED QUICKLY. The last phase of the Alpha Global Expedition would be short. I wanted to enjoy it and to do that, I had to go back to *Barrabas* feeling rejuvenated.

During the school holiday in April, Louise took the children to Mauritius, to the same resort they had visited during my first Christmas at sea in 2005. I drove them to the airport. Four days later and four weeks before flying back to Norway it dawned on me that I'd never enjoyed a proper holiday with the children. Despite my creaking finances, I called Louise and we agreed I would fly out to join them.

After a blissful two weeks of tropical sunshine, I felt recharged and eager to get back to *Barrabas*.

* * *

I arrived in Mehamn late on Sunday evening, 27th April 2008. A mantle of thick snow draped the hills around the town. The temperature was close to freezing. I'd spotted *Barrabas* from the air and my heart lifted at the sight of her. I spent the first night in the Nordic Safari Lodge then went aboard the following morning. *Barrabas* was as familiar as a well-loved armchair or a favourite coat. The first order of business was getting the engine started after her winter hibernation. I replaced all the fluids – oil, coolant, transmission oil – and the oil filter.

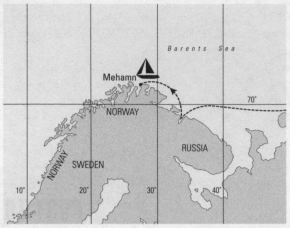

I brought her alongside and rigged the sails. Preparing to depart is always a tense time for me so I was glad of Kare's invitation to dinner at the Nordic Safari Lodge. He had just returned from a business trip to Moscow. We ate two local delicacies, cod tongues (sounded revolting – I was seriously dubious but it was delicious) and air-dried cod boiled and served up with potatoes and mashed carrot.

'So, how long to get to England?' Kare asked.

'With a following wind all the way I could do it in two and a half weeks.'

Kare nodded sagely. We were chasing our courses with shots of aquavit and my head was beginning to spin. 'It's possible. Now we have north winds.'

'It's not going to happen, not all the way to England. I'm figuring four to six weeks. I've set a target of 31st May.'

Kare refilled my shot glass. 'We drink to this.'

I tipped another dose of fire liquid down my throat.

The town's council members were dining at the neighbouring table. Kare knew them all. He introduced me and I suddenly found myself standing up in the middle of the restaurant delivering a mini-talk on who I was and what I was doing. They all knew *Barrabas*.

By mid-afternoon the next day I'd checked all the onboard systems: engine, rigging, electronics, heating, electrics, navigation, computers, Iridium. All that remained was to ship extra provisions to bolster the stock already on board. In the Co-op supermarket, I asked the checkout lady whether she could call a taxi. Instead, she offered to deliver my groceries to the boat herself after work.

Thursday 1st May was Louise's birthday and a national holiday in Norway. It seemed an auspicious date to leave. I filled the water tanks. Roy, who had helped put *Barrabas* to her winter mooring, came by with a gift of seagull eggs, warning that I had to boil them for 15 minutes. A friend of his disappeared and came back some time later with beer from Tromsø – apparently I had to have the beer and seagull eggs together, a Norwegian tradition. It was a beautiful day – blue sky, warm in the sunshine with light southerly winds to get me north out of Mehamnfjorden and into the Barents Sea. I said my goodbyes to Oddvar and Kare feeling peculiarly emotional and deeply indebted to them both, set the ship's clocks to UTC and slipped my lines at 12.30pm. The log showed 28,961 nautical miles.

Despite over-wintering the boat, time compresses. Back at sea, it seemed I had hardly been away at all. The following day at 8.38am, *Barrabas* passed westwards across the longitude of Nordkapp (North Cape), the northernmost point of the European mainland. As soon as we were safely past, I dropped the mainsail and let out full headsail so *Barrabas* could bear away and introduce some south into our course. It was cold and grey.

By the early morning of Saturday 3rd May, the wind had settled in the east at 30 knots, more or less dead astern. A combination of getting back into my shipboard routine and wary of the jagged coast close by, I had managed only one hour of sleep since leaving Mehamn. I nestled down into the thick warmth of my sleeping bag, but sleep would not come. It had turned bitterly cold with a blanket of grey cloud pasted over the ocean. But at least we were sailing downwind and pulling further from the Norwegian coast.

I'd been expecting a hard beat into prevailing westerlies to get around northern Norway, but here I was already sliding down the west coast towards Vestfjorden with following winds 48 hours after leaving Mehamn. Just after 8.00pm that evening, we passed south of the latitude of Mehamn. We were now making south *proper* and truly homeward bound.

Louise: Sunday 4th May 2008
All well here. Lovely day with the boys yesterday – football in the sun, movie (Nim's Island, the one about the little girl whose father gets lost on his yacht!).

*Went shopping for new summer jammies for the boys then lunch at the Chinese –
had the most amazing dish of chicken in satay, coconut and lemon grass sauce –
then I gave Benji a REAL treat… I bought him a pair of running spikes. He is
completely ecstatic. He wrapped them up with a ribbon for bed. We vaselined the
spikes before we put them in as the lady had told us to do so in the shop. I have
never seen him so excited by anything before. He can't wait to get back to school
on Tuesday. Also don't forget safety harness!!!!!!!!!!*

Dear Daddy
Hope you are having a grait time. Please come home soon. Love Gabriel.

Dear Daddy
*I am really missing you and I hope you will be back soon. I can't wait for us
to play cricket and sport again. Mummy bought me 3 tennis balls and a pair of
spikes. I'm really missing you. Love Benji.*

The bone-marinating cold of the last few days and the pitiless grey of the
seascape put me in mind of the Russian Arctic. Not only were thoughts of
home fuelling my quest to make south but my feet felt like blocks of ice,
just as they did going around Cape Horn. This time round, I had the heated
socks although I couldn't move far from the 12 volt socket! With the short
distance to the English south coast, I was less frugal with onboard power. I
didn't ration the heater to the same extent as before. I sat on the floor with
my feet against the hot-air outlet and luxuriated in the simple sensation of
comfort. A school of large black porpoises swam around *Barrabas* at mid-
morning and a little way off, plumes of spray betrayed a solitary whale. I
was back in the groove of sailing *Barrabas* with all my onboard routines re-
established.

I slept. When I woke, the skies had cleared. For the first time since
leaving Mehamn, I didn't feel cold. The 24-hour light of the polar day in the
far north was rapidly changing even though we were only 120 miles south
of Mehamn's latitude. It was still light at night but increasingly dimmer.

Adrian: Thursday 8th May 2008
*Still a nip in the air here. Made 100 miles nose to target over the last 24 hours.
Just about 1,000 to go! Today is slow, maybe 60 miles south and west then should
pull in another 100–120 tomorrow. The wind will be on the side so* Barrabas *will
be sailing fast. Your banana cake is still alive and well. The first one is gone. Half*

the choc biscuit cake left. My diet is great. Coffee, tea, cigarettes, chocolate. Had a shave today but can you believe it, I haven't got a razor handle on board! Must have taken it home by mistake. Anyway, did an OK job just holding the blade between my fingers... kisses for u 3... Ax

I expected heavy weather on Saturday evening. The winds were not overly strong, touching 40 knots at times, but somehow the collusion of wind and water conjured a monstrous demonstration of raw, unbridled power. I shortened sail to second reef – most boats would be down to storm sails, but I wanted to generate good boat speed as a defence. The light dimmed to a grey so resonant that it appeared blue. A bizarre band of pink striped the gunmetal sky. *Barrabas* ripped into the feast, insatiable it seemed. I was over-canvassed but *Barrabas* was talking to me. 'Let me fly, let me fly.' Green water spumed over her decks as waves, bayoneted by her prow, collapsed. She took some truly jaw-shuddering impacts. *Barrabas* performed magnificently. I could not sleep simply from the noise and pounding of the boat. I did try to get my head down, arranging cushions on the galley floor and snuggling down into the sleeping bag with my head by the companionway steps so I could see the instruments over the chart table. After 10 minutes, a massive wave strike sent water streaming through the gaps in the closed companionway hatch, soaking my head and the top half of the sleeping bag. I gave up on sleep after that.

By midday on Sunday 11th May, the winds had calmed to 12 knots from the north. I downloaded a four-day weather file. My next obstacle was crossing the 200-metre depth contour 120 miles to my south from the deep water of the Norwegian Sea onto the shallow plain of the North Sea. I needed light, downwind conditions and the forecast promised exactly that: north sector winds at 12 knots. Perfect! I did a little gig around the deck, feeling the first real twinges of gut-tingling excitement. The battle into headwinds that had been a distinct possibility in the North Sea had given way to a perfect scenario. It felt like a reward after the storm. We were entering another high-pressure system, this one centred over northern France. I was passing from one high-pressure system to another like a relay baton and this new system was providing the gentle following winds, blue skies and warmth.

With the boat stable, I slept on the starboard bunk, crashing out for nine hours. It was luxury being able to stretch out fully and not be cramped on the floor with my knees bent.

I set the sails in a goosewing, an arrangement which had served me so well before, the headsail poled out on the port side adding 1 knot of boat speed. At 2pm on Monday 12th May, we passed over the 200-metre contour and shortly after that, the log clicked onto 30,000. In the pink-tinged dusk, I saw Unst, northernmost of the Shetland Islands, some 20 miles west – my first sighting of UK territory from the deck since the Cornish coast faded behind me in the mist on a drizzly November morning in 2005. Entering UK territorial waters brought a blessed comfort; even the place names on the Shetland Islands conjured a soothing familiarity – Sullom Voe, Muckle Flugga, Lerwick. Since departing UK shores, I heard my first British weather broadcast courtesy of Shetland Island Coastguard at 6pm. I had been fabulously fortunate with the weather so far. I held the rising tide of excitement in check and concentrated on my plan to make for Kinnaird Head across the open space of the Moray Firth. Beyond there, I would hug the east coast of England and when I'd hugged it all I could I'd get off my boat and kiss the ground – that was the plan.

I'd spotted three trawlers and two ships during the day. Not every vessel showed up on radar, so I stayed awake through the night. It was a good time to think. My thoughts and feelings were changing, morphing, as the end neared. I sailed the boat, attended to routine maintenance, but I was preoccupied with the sensation of change. A hugely important chapter in my life was drawing towards a close and with it came a peculiar juxtaposition, a rising euphoria set against the ebb of impending loss. The euphoria was easy to understand, the loss less so. Perhaps it was the ending of this profound experience I had shared with *Barrabas* as she carved her own unique track around the world or the ending of that special relationship between a sailor and his craft that manifests on the open sea. Or, I thought, it could be the fading out of that peculiar limbo of the lone sailor, the absence of the usual markers of passing time and the vaulting sense of freedom.

Past the Shetlands and Fair Isle with the Orkneys below the horizon on my right, I thought, 'I'm closer to London now than some people in northern Scotland!' That raised morale, not that my morale needed too much feeding. The following winds were set to continue driving us south at a good lick.

I'd left the dense clusters of oil platforms of the Brent, Viking Bank, Bergen Bank and the Fladen Ground far to my left, but there were others closer inshore. I passed by the Buzzard platform at the southeastern end of the Moray Firth as I angled my course due south towards Bridlington on the Yorkshire coast.

Adrian: Thursday 15th May 2008
Hi… sleeping as much as poss. Weather kicks off tomorrow around 2pm and goes on for 36 hours, otherwise all OK – I would say arrival on Wednesday 21st is now 'probable'…

Poking around the boat looking for food I may have forgotten about, I found a stash in the forward storage bin below the starboard bunk – stuff I'd bought in Alaska, mainly tinned fruit (always good) and wonder of wonders, a tin of 'American' baked beans with bacon and cane sugar. I couldn't resist. I had one egg left so I quaffed the lot.

Louise: Friday 16th May 2008
Boys and I will come out to meet you with Tim on a Beneteau (44ft). Wow… almost there… I'm so excited for you. Lx

If this wind pattern held, it would be the perfect window to see me home – 375 miles was all that remained. So far, magical winds had touched this final leg from Mehamn. I cleaned the galley and the heads and rigged up a deck shower. I'd been running the engine to charge the batteries and generate hot water. With the pressurized water switched on at the galley pump, I had a glorious hot shower in the cockpit, the shower hose led up from below. Why hadn't I done this before? I must have been daft, although there was always the concern about conserving power. Without the need to keep an eagle eye on fuel reserves any longer and with plenty left over from the Arctic phase, I was being much more liberal. I used cabin lights at night instead of candles and oil lamps. The radar was on 24/7 – necessary now that I was in relatively congested waters, and the VHF was permanently tuned to Channel 16. Even though there was only a short distance to go, I had to stay focused and concentrate on the job in hand. One octogenarian lady in Holland who had been following my journey warned me to stay vigilant. A lapse would be all too easy while, as Bé Vonk put it, my mind was '…milling around the end of the affair'.

It was a good thing I had a shower earlier. That evening I had some unexpected visitors. With the sea calm and only a zephyr to nudge *Barrabas* along at a couple of knots, I was lying on my bunk reading while waiting for the forecast northeast winds. At 7.30pm, the radar alarm squawked. A contact had entered the guard perimeter I'd set at six miles. I watched the blip on the radar screen from my bunk. Whatever it was, this vessel was moving fast and seemed to be heading directly towards *Barrabas*. I got up and set an electronic bearing line (EBL) onto the contact. If a contact stays on an EBL, then the collision risk escalates. I rushed up to the cockpit, grabbing the binoculars on the way. Magnified, the ship was grey, moustached by a great white bow wave. Just then, the radio crackled to life. 'Sailing yacht *Barrabas*, *Barrabas*, this is Warship *Mersey*, Warship *Mersey*.'

I spoke to Lieutenant Commander Alan Wilson. 'How did you know I was here?'

'We have our spies,' he joked. They had checked out the Alpha Global Expedition website. Lieutenant Commander Wilson and the ship's company wanted to stop by and wish me well for the rest of the voyage home. 'We have a small gift and a donation from the ship's company for your expedition's charities,' he said.

I hove-to while HMS *Mersey* nosed to a stop 200 yards off. What a welcome back into British territorial waters! A RIB was lowered into the water and buzzed alongside *Barrabas*. Her crew passed on the good wishes of the ship's company amid much smiling and hand-shaking. I joked and chatted with the RIB's crew. They then handed across a cheque for the charities and a bottle of Special Reserve port.

I really appreciated the gesture by the Royal Navy and said so to Lt Commander Wilson over the radio.

CHAPTER 30

PROMISES

AT 7.50AM ON SATURDAY MORNING, I went on deck and for the first time since my departure, I saw the UK mainland – green hills somewhere between Hartlepool and Middlesbrough. I looked at *Barrabas* as she creamed the sea at fabulous speeds touching 9 knots, at her tired decks, her paintwork broken and peeling from excesses of sun and ice. Now she was back, almost, to where she started.

Louise: Saturday 17ᵗʰ May 2008

Hello speedy! Boys and I will be setting off around lunchtime on Tuesday. We said tonight whilst watching Britain's Got Talent *that this time next week you will be watching it with us! I also said to Benji that if Chelsea wins the Champion's League on Wednesday, it could turn out to be the happiest day of his life! Maybe we can watch it in the bar of the Royal Southern YC!*

Far to the south at his home in Lisbon, Ricardo was tracking my progress home. He sent an email to Louise that she forwarded onto me.

Ricardo: Saturday 17ᵗʰ May 2008

For years I have looked at that stretch of ocean between Norway and Iceland and Scotland and wondered what it would be like to be up there so far away and so far north. It is so inhospitable and rough. The lowest of lows go through there and yet

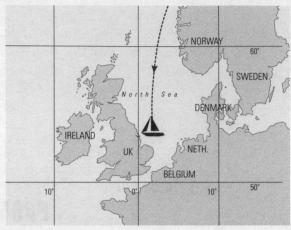

there Adrian is blessed by unbelievable weather, a perfect direct course. He will be only too aware how dangerous the last dash is. Dover sucks. It is a major shipping and navigation nightmare. I really hope he has the wind to get through there fast.

I looked at a fresh weather forecast. It showed north sector winds with moderated wind speeds to a maximum 16 knots. Ricardo was right. I was blessed. If the previous forecast was near ideal, it was perfect now. I recalled my dinner conversation with Kare in Mehamn: *'a following wind… it's not going to happen, not all the way to England…'*

The wind either on or behind the beam would put *Barrabas* on her fastest point of sail.

Adrian: Saturday 17th May 2008

Going really well – in amongst the oil and gas platforms – Barrabas humming along at 7–8 knots and been at it since 5am – would you believe the fastest sustained sailing of the entire voyage!

I called Humber Coastguard to request information about active exclusion zones around the platforms. They put me in contact with one of the standby vessels that protect the rigs. The instruction was not to venture within one mile of any installation. As I passed the Minerva oil platform two miles off my port side, I could see five other rigs at various points around the horizon, colossal alien-looking structures. I figured I'd be through the bulk of the rigs by 8am Sunday morning – it was going to be a sleepless night.

Coming through the gas fields at night was a fascinating experience. Lit up, I could see them dotted all about the horizon. It's like Piccadilly Circus in there; not just the rigs – each platform has a standby vessel holding station close by to warn off possible interlopers. Busy ferry lanes criss-cross with commercial shipping routes. Just after 2am, I counted 13 platforms and seven ships, four of which were within a mile of me.

Adrian: Sunday 18ᵗʰ May 2008

Posn at 0800 UTC 52.49 north 01.41 east (basically east of Great Yarmouth on the Norfolk coast). There must be a massive current here (in my favour) or a bunch of dolphins has fed Barrabas steroids – she was cruising at 10 knots for a couple of hours just now – and that was with shortened sail! Tell Benji I want to watch the Champions League final with him – that's why I'm breaking my neck trying to get back in time. Ahead of schedule so far – I set my markers at midnight – at midnight yesterday I was right on the money to make the Isle of Wight by midnight Tuesday!

Louise called on the Iridium.

'Are you sure you gave me the right position?'

'Yes. Well, I mean, I think so. I always check positions before I send them. Why?'

'Well, I think you're wrong. I plotted it and according to my workings you're in a field somewhere in Norfolk.'

'Pretty waterlogged field.'

'Ha, ha! So what is your position?'

'What I sent you.' I thought for a moment. 'I think I know what you've done…'

'What?'

'You've plotted my longitude as west instead of east.'

'Oh.'

'I'm about three miles off the Norfolk coast. I can see a beautiful stretch of beach with trees. It's a fabulous day here – blue sky, warm, 14-knot breeze – glorious sailing.'

'Okay. Well, you're right. Anyway, so you're not in Norfolk. Can you do something for me?'

'Yep.'

'I need you to write something for the Press Association. Keep it short and sweet.'

'You'll have it on your desk in the morning, by the time you wake up.'

I was in for a second consecutive night without sleep. That's the problem with single-handed sailing in congested inshore waters. Hazards pepper the East Anglia coastline (as testified by the amount of wrecks dotting my charts).

I made my turn south of Great Yarmouth putting the wind directly astern. Without a spinnaker, I resorted to my favoured goosewing sail plan, the headsail poled out on the port side. We were going along nicely at 5½ knots.

As I approached the start line on that blustery October morning in 2005, someone on a press boat asked me for a comment. I had yelled back, 'Two miles down, 30,000 to go!' Less than 200 miles now stood between the finish and me. After all *Barrabas* and I had been through together, it seemed implausible that the end was almost literally in sight. I glanced at the log – 30,608 nautical miles.

With darkness falling, I called Thames Coastguard to obtain clearances to enter the shipping traffic scheme offshore from Harwich and Felixstowe. The tide had turned in our favour and *Barrabas* was now surging ahead at 7 knots. I sat for a while on deck as we passed through deep-water anchorages and the turning areas where several traffic lanes converged. I was thinking about the Press Association bulletin. I did not like the idea of writing about the completion of the voyage before I had actually finished, but I understood Louise's shore-based world. She had steadily involved the media in my imminent arrival home and forward planning was all part of the package. I went below, sat at the chart table and fired up the laptop.

Adrian: Monday 19th May 2008
Release for Press Association

Barrabas has carried me almost 31,000 miles around the world. I feel immense relief that I have fulfilled a boyhood dream and huge pride in my yacht Barrabas. *She has seen me through fair weather and foul. The voyage has been long and hard at times, filled with moments of joy and terror. Facing down the challenge of Cape Horn against wind and currents presented the greatest physical peril. To have become the first solo yachtsman to enter the Russian Arctic is a huge privilege and my heartfelt thanks go to everyone involved. I owe much to Louise, my ex-wife, who has managed the Alpha Global Expedition. Without her, I would not have succeeded. To live and not to dream is pointless, but to dream and not to live it is worse. I hope the legacy of the Alpha Global Expedition will be as inspiration to my sons, Benjamin and Gabriel, and to anyone else to chase their own dreams.*

Monday broke clear and blue. Unbelievably, the winds veered from northeast to east, following me round as I progressively pulled my course up from southwest to due west past Dover, Dungeness and Beachy Head. Finally, at 2pm and well clear of the shipping lanes and traffic schemes, I crashed onto my bunk and slept for four and a half hours. By 9pm on the evening of Monday 19th May we were south of Selsey Bill and entering the eastern approaches to the Solent, that stretch of water which separates the Isle of Wight from the mainland south coast. *Barrabas* had covered almost 300 miles in 48 hours, her fastest run of the voyage. We had arrived in the Solent 27 hours ahead of my most optimistic prediction.

Louise had been gunning for an arrival date of Wednesday 21st May. I had two choices: either I sailed around in circles, hove-to for the next 36 hours or I found somewhere to anchor. I decided the most sensible option was to anchor, get some sleep. Some part of me wanted to sail up the Hamble River, moor *Barrabas* and steal home on a train or in a taxi without fanfare. Instead, I navigated into the narrow confines of Chichester Harbour. It was past 2am on Tuesday morning when I finally dropped anchor in the Chichester Channel. The air was still and cool. I stayed on deck for a while contemplating the pre-dawn peacefulness.

Below decks, I switched on the heating, cooked spaghetti and sardines then turned in, cocooned within *Barrabas,* who sat rock steady on the still waters of the channel. When I woke at 7am, a bright sun warmed my face.

The Iridium trilled.

'You're not going to believe this!' Louise exclaimed. 'The Royal Navy are going to lay on an escort for you!'

'You're kidding.'

'Nope. HMS *Trumpeter* – good name, don't you think? It's a fast patrol boat. They'll escort you up the Solent.'

I was amazed. It was an honour.

'We'll see you at the waypoint.'

I'd emailed coordinates of the rendezvous where Tim should bring the yacht that would be carrying Louise and the children. It was the east cardinal mark at the eastern end of the Solent's north channel, two and a half miles from the finish line between the Calshot Spit and Hillhead.

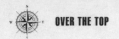

'Where are you?'

'In the car coming into Southampton. I'm going to the BBC Radio Solent studio for an interview, then onto the Royal Southern Yacht Club.'

I spent the rest of that day preparing *Barrabas* for her final steps home and enjoying the tranquillity of the Chichester Channel. Shallow water inside the harbour and *Barrabas*'s 1.9-metre draught together with conflicting tides prevented me staying a second night. Before weighing anchor at 11.50pm, I sent Louise a last email that she would pick up the following morning.

Adrian: Tuesday 20th May 2008

Good morning! So, if we'd known on 28th October 2005 that a) I'd finish and b) the time and date would be 10am, Wednesday 21st May 2008, I wonder what we'd have thought. This has been a long, hard road for both of us… know that without your involvement it would never have happened. So, thank you. I'll see you at 10am. Ax

I sailed to Gilkicker Point, anchoring on the west side in Stokes Bay for the night. HMS *Trumpeter* under the command of Lt Will King found me at 9am the following morning. I'd been up since dawn doing nothing much but savouring the moment, waiting. The sun had pulled back the curtain of night on this final day. Snapshots of the voyage flickered through my mind: hugging the boys as I prepared to depart, being swept from the deck, the tropical cyclone off the Canary Islands, beautiful blue sailing in the Atlantic trades, arming myself as suspected pirates tracked me off the Brazilian coast, the capsize at Cape Horn and reaching in the southeast trades towards Hawaii. Honolulu, an ice-cold Guinness, Michael Roth, Ivan Chan Wa, Ernie Woodruff and Bobby Jennings. Astro-navigation, making the antipodal point and turning for the ice; Nome, Rick, Cam, Malinda, the Russians and frustration at having to break the voyage. The ice, the danger, the cold, Tiksi. I smiled as the rugged face of Captain Alfred Zagorsky flashed and faded, Murmansk, Igor, Vardo, Kare and Oddvar in Mehamn. Then this final leg and the best sailing of the voyage. I saw myself on my ship, reading, writing, eating, shaving, sleeping, studying, laughing, crying, joyous, terrified, bored, euphoric. I stood and looked along *Barrabas*'s deck then up to her mast, squinting in the sunlight.

She knew. I knew. Only the two of us. Our secret. When I had been swept over the side, this boat had stopped. As sure as I had been of the certainty of death, I knew she had stopped and let me clamber back on board. My partner, my friend, my teammate, my protector, I owed *Barrabas* more than gratitude, more than love. I owed her my life. I walked to the foredeck, knelt, rested my forehead on her firm, steel skin and pressed my lips to her.

'Thank you,' I whispered in the gentle breeze.

I weighed anchor at 9.30am. HMS *Trumpeter* took up station at my stern. With the wind behind, I goose-winged the sails for our run home. At exactly 10am, we made the east cardinal mark. Press boats and an eclectic mix of launches and yachts had swelled our small convoy. I could see Tim's yacht heeled over coming towards us. She went wide, tacked round and came up on our starboard side. I waved to my children and blew a kiss to Louise.

HMS *Trumpeter* pulled alongside and one of her crew handed me a cup of tea. *Barrabas* sailed on sedately at 5 knots. I didn't record exactly when we crossed the line between Calshot Spit and Hillhead. It was sometime around 10.30am. Whenever it was, we'd 'tied the knot', completing the loop of our track around the surface of the planet. I dropped the sails then motored up the Hamble River with HMS *Trumpeter* leading the way. Two of the harbourmaster's launches flanked me, sirens blaring while a busy swarm of dinghies and inflatables buzzed all around.

30,825 miles. That's what the log read when I tied up at the Royal Southern Yacht Club just after 11am on Wednesday 21st May. Tim had brought his boat in ahead of me. Louise and the boys emerged from among the throng of journalists and camera crews. They clambered aboard. I ushered them below into the cabin.

'We did it,' I said to Louise as we hugged.

'You did it.'

'We did it.'

I kissed Benji. He looked up at me. 'Will you watch the football with me tonight?'

'Of course,' I said. 'Why d'you think I arrived back today!'

Gabriel clung to me. I kissed his soft cheek. His blue eyes flicked uncomprehendingly over the 37 fuel cans lashed in the cabin. 'It's smelly in here,' he said.

* * *

Much later that evening, the boys tucked up in bed in the clubhouse and Louise asleep, I stepped back aboard *Barrabas* in the quiet of a still summer's night. Below decks, I sat in the buttery glow of a single candle.

I had made three promises. I'd promised the child I had once been that I would sail alone around the world and I'd promised my sons that I would return to them safely. Then I reached for the Iridium phone and dialled Captain Zagorsky's number in St Petersburg.

EPILOGUE

After the Alpha Global Expedition, Louise, me and the boys moved to France; Louise to a converted barn on a wine estate near Bordeaux, me to our friend Karen's house twenty minutes up the road while she worked in Dubai. The main purpose was to give the children an opportunity to learn a second language.

Louise, a fluent French speaker, felt immediately at home. My limited language skills, on the other hand, made life a bit more tricky although thankfully, I didn't have to draw any pictures to make myself understood.

We returned to the UK four years later.

Benji is studying Fashion and Design at university. Gabriel is working towards his goal of becoming a music producer, composer and DJ.

Barrabas lives in Germany now and has spent recent summers travelling around the waters of Scandinavia.

Louise and I both live in Hampshire. We see each other often. She is evolving her passion for photography. I work as a sculptor.

www.adrianflanagansculpture.com

SINGLE-HANDED, WESTABOUT ROUNDINGS OF CAPE HORN

Name	Nationality	Boat	Date
Al Hansen	Norwegian	*Mary-Jane*	1934
Marcel Bardiaux	French	*Les Quatre Vents*	1952
Chay Blyth	British	*British Steel*	1970
Edward Allcard	British	*Sea Wanderer*	1973
Kenichi Horie	Japanese	*Mermaid III*	1974
Eilco Kasemier	Dutch	*Bylgia*	1977
David Scott Cowper	British	*Ocean Bound*	1982
Jonathan Sanders	Australian	*Parry Endeavour*	1986
Mike Golding	British	*Group 4*	1994
Samantha Brewster	British	*Heath Assured II*	1996
Philippe Monnet	French	*Uunet*	2000
Wilfried Erdmann	German	*Kathena Nui*	2000
Jean-Luc van den Heede	French	*Adrien*	2004
Dee Caffari	British	*Aviva*	2006
Adrian Flanagan	British	*Barrabas*	2006
Minoru Sait	Japanese	*Shuten-dohji III*	2009

YACHTS THAT HAVE SAILED RUSSIA'S NORTHERN SEA ROUTE

Date	Master	Country	Vessel	Crew	Ice Pilot
1991–1993	-	Russia	*Yakutia*	Full	Yes
1991: Tiksi–Chukotka, 1992: cargoed back to Tiksi, 1993: Tiksi–Murmansk					
1998–1999	Nicolau Litau	Russia	*Apostle Andrew*	Full	Yes
East to west, wintering in Tiksi					
2000–2002	Sergei Cherbakov	Russia	*Sibir*	Full	Yes
West to east, including two winterings					
2002	Eric Brossier	France	*Vagabond*	Full	Yes
West to east, first passage without wintering					
2002	Arved Fuchs	Germany	*Dagmar Aaen*	Full	Yes
West to east					
2003–2004	Henk de Velde	Netherlands	*Campina*	2	Yes
East to west, wintered in Tiksi, 2004: ice damage, cargoed to Murmansk					
2004–2005	Jarlath Cunnane	Ireland	*Northabout*	Full	Yes
East to west, wintered in Khatanga					
2007	Adrian Flanagan	UK	*Barrabas*	1	No
East to west, first single-handed into NSR, cargoed Tiksi to Murmansk					

Fiction

The Burden of Proof – Scott Turow

The Island of the Day Before – Umberto Eco

The House of Blue Mangoes – David Davidar

Absolute Friends – John le Carré

Hold Tight – Harlan Coben

The Lincoln Lawyer – John Connelly

Fierce Invalids Home from Hot Climates – Tom Robbins

No Second Chance – Harlan Coben

Villa Incognito – Tom Robbins

Little Infamies - Panos Karnezis

The Road – Cormac McCarthy

The Shadow of the Wind – Carlos Ruiz Zafón

Sons and Lovers – D H Lawrence

Lord of the Flies – William Golding

The Plot Against America – Philip Roth

Life of Pi – Yann Martel

Shalimar the Clown – Salman Rushdie

The Kite Runner – Khaled Hosseini

The Broker – John Grisham

Jigsaw – Campbell Armstrong

Critical Judgement – Michael Palmer

The Solitary Man – Stephen Leather

The Lasko Tangent – Richard North Patterson

Modern English Short Stories

Salmon Fishing in the Yemen – Paul Torday

Eddie's Bastard – William Kowalski

Jig – Campbell Armstrong

Sight Unseen – Robert Goddard

Traitor's Kiss – Gerald Seymour

Heat – Campbell Armstrong

Fade Away – Harlan Coben
Deadline – Campbell Armstrong
Pandora's Clock – John J Nance
The Client – John Grisham
The Partner – John Grisham

Medusa's Child – John J Nance
The Da Vinci Code – Dan Brown
Mambo – Campbell Armstrong
The Agony and the Ecstasy – Irving
    Stone

Non-Fiction

The World According to Clarkson –
    Jeremy Clarkson
Psycho-Cybernetics – Maxwell
    Maltz MD
Long Way Round – Ewan
    McGregor & Charley Boorman
Six Questions of Socrates –
    Christopher Phillips
Longitude – Dava Sobel
How to Get Rich – Felix Dennis
The Tao of Pooh – Benjamin Hoff
The Hynek UFO Report –
    Dr J Allen Hynek
The God Delusion – Richard
    Dawkins
The Northeast Passage – from the
    Vikings to Nordenskiold – John
    Nurminen Foundation
Between a Rock and a Hard Place –
    Aron Ralston

Breaking the Spell – Religion as a
    Natural Phenomenon – Daniel C
    Dennett
The Tibetan Book of Living and
    Dying – Sogyal Rinpoche
Singlehanded Sailing – Richard
    Henderson
The Illustrated Guide to
    World Religions – Michael D
    Coogan
The Voyager's Handbook – Beth A
    Leonard
Northwest Passage Solo – David
    Scott Cowper
Heavy Weather Sailing – Peter
    Bruce
Complete Sailing Manual – Steve
    Sleight
Socrates Café – Christopher
    Phillips

Biography

Lawrence of Arabia – Jeremy Wilson

Navigation

Reeds Nautical Almanac 2005
Nautical Almanac 2006 –
    Commercial Edition
Rapid Sight Reduction Tables for
    Navigation – volumes 1, 2 & 3

Weather at Sea – David Houghton
The Weather Wizard's Cloud Book –
    Louis D Rubin Sr & Jim Duncan
Instant Weather Forecasting – Alan
    Watts

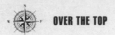

Celestial Navigation – Tom Cunliffe

Admiralty Arctic Pilot – volume 1, 1985

Ocean Passages of the World – 4th edition

The Mariner's Handbook – 7th edition, 1999

Admiralty Bering Sea and Strait Pilot – 5th edition, 1980

Admiralty Arctic Pilot – Volume 3, 7th edition, 2001

Admiralty South American Pilot

Technical

Boatowner's Mechanical and Electrical Manual – Nigel Calder

Marine Diesel Engines – Nigel Calder

The 12-Volt Bible for Boats – Minor Brotherton & Ed Sherman

Marine SSB Operation – J Michael Gale

Reference

The Oxford Companion to Ships and the Sea

Maritime Safety Information Services (Oceans, The Americas and the Far East) – volume 3 (2), 2005/6

Maritime Safety Information Services (Europe, Africa and Asia (Excl the Far East)) – volume 3 (1), 2005/6

Global Maritime Distress and Safety System (GMDSS) – volume 5, 2004/5

SAS Survival Guide – John Wiseman

A Seaman's Guide to the Rules of the Road

Pocket Guide to Knots and Splices – Des Pawson

Games

Brain Teasing Crosswords

The Word Search Book

ACKNOWLEDGEMENTS

Any sailor alone at sea is never truly single-handed. Were it not for the many people – often met as strangers but left as friends – who offered their time, help and encouragement, the voyage would have been so much more difficult if not impossible.

Rather than name those many people here, I hope I have done them credit in the telling of this story.

Bernard de Castro built a truly magnificent boat. I hope that her journey around the world has made him as proud of her as I am.

My thanks to the team at Bloomsbury – Janet Murphy, Liz Multon and Jonathan Eyers.

And of course to Louise – for her to have done what she did, as my ex-wife, says all that needs to be said about the type of person she is. However much I thank you, it will never be enough.

BY THE SAME AUTHOR

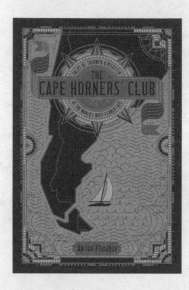

Cape Horn – the most terrifying and lethal place on the world's oceans, and the supreme test of sailors and vessels. It is the oceanic equivalent of the climbers' Everest, and the challenge to some has been irresistible. The roll call of sailors who have managed to round the Horn glitters with the names of sailing legends: Francis Chichester, Robin Knox-Johnston, Bernard Moitessier, Chay Blyth.

In this book, Adrian Flanagan – himself a Cape Horn veteran – recounts the history of the Cape through the stories of those who have succeeded in crossing the most savage stretch of water on the planet.

'A rollicking good read' – Tom Cunliffe

'Breathtaking' – *Sailing Today*

'Beautiful… With Flanagan at the helm it is never less than fascinating' – *The Lady*

Available now in hardback and ebook from Adlard Coles